Studies in Anthropology, No. 7

ETHNOHISTORY IN SOUTHWESTERN ALASKA AND THE SOUTHERN YUKON

MARGARET LANTIS, *Editor*
UNIVERSITY OF KENTUCKY

ROBERT E. ACKERMAN
WASHINGTON STATE UNIVERSITY

CATHARINE McCLELLAN
UNIVERSITY OF WISCONSIN

JOAN B. TOWNSEND
UNIVERSITY OF MANITOBA

JAMES W. VanSTONE
FIELD MUSEUM OF NATURAL HISTORY

STUDIES IN ANTHROPOLOGY, 7

Ethnohistory in Southwestern Alaska and the Southern Yukon

Method and Content

The University Press of Kentucky

Standard Book Number 8131-1215-X
Library of Congress Catalog Card Number 75-111513

COPYRIGHT © 1970 BY THE UNIVERSITY PRESS OF KENTUCKY

A statewide cooperative scholarly publishing agency serving Berea College,
Centre College of Kentucky, Eastern Kentucky University, Kentucky State
College, Morehead State University, Murray State University, University
of Kentucky, University of Louisville, and Western Kentucky University.

Editorial and Sales Offices: Lexington, Kentucky 40506

CONTENTS

ACKNOWLEDGMENTS

I am much indebted to William Y. Adams for his discussion not only of these papers but of the whole field of ethnohistory. I am especially grateful to the Bancroft Library, of the University of California libraries, Berkeley, whose staff thirty years ago was so helpful in locating and making available manuscripts at that time not fully cataloged.

M. L.

Part One

INTRODUCTION:
THE METHODOLOGY OF ETHNOHISTORY

by *Margaret Lantis*

Anthropologists with special competence in the archaeology and ethnology of Alaska and Yukon Territory have not until now had much discussion of ethnohistory, perhaps because so many of them have been too busy practicing it. Oswalt (1963), VanStone (1967), and de Laguna (1960), for example, have published valuable books utilizing various combinations of archaeology, ethnography, and documentary history.[1] Four representatives of the small number in anthropology who are becoming specialists in the ethnohistory of northwestern North America reveal here the methodological problems that they have dealt with in their work and some of the results of this work. They discuss not such details of method as how to authenticate a given document or how to decide between specific conflicting statements in an early traveler's journal and an Eskimo informant's account. Instead, they agreed to tackle, for a symposium at the 1967 annual meeting of the American Society for Ethnohistory[2], basic problems in ethnohistoric work and the hoped-for or the achieved results. They have given a personal account of some of their own programs, so that one has in-process contemplation of the objectives and accomplishments of these writers of Alaska-Yukon Eskimo and Indian history after approximately 1750.

Although all are broadly experienced, one writes chiefly from the standpoint of an archaeologist, one an ethnohistorian, one a social anthropologist, and the fourth an ethnologist and folklorist.

Definitions of Ethnohistory

Terms to be distinguished and kept in mind while reading these papers are *culture history, ethnohistory,* and *ethnogenesis.*

Culture history may be written from any and all available sources, and it may cover the long period before the development of writing or the short period following it. For the very early periods of most cultures, it must be compiled necessarily from archaeological data. For groups still preliterate in modern times, all but their recent history depends usually on archaeological and linguistic evidence and less often on local legends or rare accounts by early literate travelers. Although archaeology, according to Strong (1953:393), "by its very nature is the most objective, long-term, historical tool in the kit of anthropology," nevertheless it has its limitations, as indicated in the papers that follow. The term *culture history* should connote only "the history of a culture," from whatever sources it is compiled. However, especially for a region like northwestern North America, it has until recently implied a reconstruction from archaeology of the early history of a culture and a reconstruction by ethnographic techniques of the late history of the culture.

Ethnogenesis is a subject of strong current Soviet interest. Soviet anthropologists are writing on the origin and early development of such peoples as the Buryat, Koryak, and Kirghiz, using evidence chiefly from linguistics, physical anthropology, and archaeology but also from historical documents where these are available (Michael 1962). The difference between the work of the people addressing themselves to problems of ethnogenesis and the work of culture historians is that the former are studying not culture per se but the ethnic unit: how did any recognizable

[1] See references cited at end of Ackerman paper.

[2] Meeting held at Lexington, Kentucky, sponsored by the Department of Anthropology, University of Kentucky.

"tribe" come to be such? Generally they have been quite eclectic regarding methodology.

Of ethnohistory there are two principal definitions: (1) *Use of written historical materials in preparing an ethnography* (often a reconstruction of a culture as of one past period), the documentary data supplemented if possible by the memory of informants or else the "memory culture" supplemented by historical records (see, for example, Bowers on the Mandan and Hidatsa, 1950, 1965); or *use of historical materials*—in the Old World often including recoveries by classical archaeology—*to show culture change*. Thus the "history" can be either synchronic or diachronic. (2) *Use of a people's oral literature in reconstructing their own history.* There may be subsidiary studies of a group's attention to and use of history or of the forms in which their history is preserved. Ethnohistory in this sense is comparable with ethnobotany and ethnozoology.

In this collection of papers we have examples of ethnohistory in each of its meanings, the first three (by Ackerman, VanStone, and Townsend) in the first category and the last paper (by McClellan) in the second category.

Past Work

Ethnohistory in Europe and in North America until recently has had different emphases. The history of cultures in the period after the introduction of writing has been written by Europeans from documentary materials supplemented chiefly by archaeology. A comparably late culture-history (that is, after the coming of writing) typically has been written by Americans from ethnography, with early travelers' observations included as ethnographic sources, supplemented by archaeology. Giving due attention to all types of sources almost never is achieved because of local limitations in the sources themselves and limitations of the training and interests of the writers of ethnohistory. Very few of us can handle all three with equal competence. But we can strive for better balance in this work. I think that these papers will aid the effort.

The Present Work

Ackerman attempts to solve principally the problems of relating ethnography and archaeology, with documentary sources as a supplement. He and his group have undertaken more meticulous ethnographic fieldwork than one sees on the usual expedition presumably combining these specialities. He has tackled forcefully the problem of how to make ethnography comparable with archaeology. (One should note that his effort required more people than VanStone and others have had on one project.) Ackerman's program may prefigure the American fieldwork of the future. His viewpoint is that of the person who is primarily an archaeologist seeking ethnographic and historical aids. Although some of the benefits of his approach are already evident in the samples of his work given here, a full accounting of its usefulness must await integration of all his data. Ackerman's introductory survey of the relevant literature serves also as a good introduction for the two following papers.

VanStone's and Townsend's papers belong together: for the most part they have used the same historical sources; they have cooperated on some of their archaeology, and their geographic areas are almost contiguous. VanStone, however, has been studying an Eskimo culture-area—as has Ackerman—while Townsend's culture-area is Athabaskan.

Although both Townsend and VanStone have used all three types of sources, the latter's emphasis is clearly on the documentary record. He has already published what he calls "an ethnographic history," *Eskimos of the Nushagak River* (1967). In this book, "Part One: Agents of Change" is largely documentary; "Part Two: Emerging Socioeconomic Patterns" combines all three types of sources. The discussion of settlement patterns, for example, depends heavily on archaeology supplemented by other kinds of data, while the discussion of "Nushagak Today" depends principally on ethnography, fortified by government and other records.

Of the several problems that he has broached, VanStone seems especially concerned about the need for and the difficulty of ascertaining the "aboriginal baseline culture." Anyone working in this field will note sympathetically his struggles with this problem. He has said in a personal communication, "the Eskimos of the Nushagak region could not be studied as an aboriginal people"; why they could not is discussed in his paper. Therefore, "my major problem is the reconstructing of 19th century Eskimo culture. . . . The term 'baseline culture' as I have used it does not have any significance apart from suggesting the ideal point from which to begin a study of culture change."

Townsend relies more on ethnography, perhaps partly because she is the only one for whom there exists an earlier ethnography by a professional anthropologist (Osgood 1937). Moreover, archaeology in her locality is difficult, and not much has been done. It appears that each of these three writers has emphasized so far a different one of the three basic resources (Ackerman: archaeology; Van-Stone: documentary history; Townsend: ethnography) without ignoring the others.

Ackerman is not yet ready to present a full ethnographic history of his locality, while VanStone has already done it. In these papers, each is more interested in method than in content and results. Townsend has done it, too, but she tries to give here a statement of her conclusions from her work; specifically she tries to reconstruct broadly the social and economic persistences and changes that have occurred to the Tanaina Indians, using whatever sources have been available. Thus she shows, at least in broad outline, what can be done.

VanStone mentions that one can get data but that culture pattern is hard to obtain from the kinds of sources that he has had. Probably one should say that pattern is always in the eye of the beholder. As, when looking at a complex painting, one sees much of the composition that the artist consciously incorporated but may not see all of it and at the same time sees forms and relationships that he was not conscious of, so also the patterns as seen by the creators and carriers of the culture, by the early untrained observers (who may not have seen any composition), and by the specialist restoring the picture of the culture are quite unlikely to be congruent.

A trend or a broad culture change—like pattern, both of them interpretations made by the ethnohistorian—seems easier to discern than the patterns in a selected baseline culture. From the nature of history, this is expectable: it is comparative. The outstanding features, at least, of a person, an institution, or a culture in one period are compared with those in another period. Furthermore, readers do not anticipate in a statement of a trend the completeness that they expect in an ethnography that includes detail and pattern as of one period. Yet a statement of directional or patterned change, not merely a list of additions to or losses from a cultural inventory, can be even more tricky than other kinds of interpretation from variable original data, since the past is another world, a world that no one today has experienced or can experience. It is hard enough to understand another people's culture in the present—it is even harder to understand it at various times in the past. Because of the difficulties and hazards, Townsend's and McClellan's accomplishments in the present papers are all the more impressive.

McClellan illustrates the second definition of ethnohistory: a people's own version of history. Her objectives were, first, "to indicate the range of documented events with which the oral testimonies intermesh; second, to suggest how a few findings about the classification, function, style, and content of this group of stories may relate to the particular bodies of literature in which they occur." Besides discerning the traditional form and style—pattern, one might say?—in the new historical tales, her interesting work is a test of the usefulness of oral history, or in her term, "oral testimony." The reader can discover for himself her conclusion following this evaluation of the ethnohistoric sources.

All these frontline soldiers in behalf of ethnohistory sound rather discouraged, yet all have used and are using its techniques effectively. Perhaps they had hoped for too much. Their expressions of faith and hope for it in the future indicate such an attitude. The value of this collection of papers is not its expression of faith but its evidence of scientific care in the use of the techniques, which should be a guide to others.

References

Bowers, Alfred W.
   1950   Mandan Social and Ceremonial Organization. Chicago.
   1965   Hidatsa social and ceremonial organization. Bureau of American Ethnology Bulletin 194. Washington.

Michael, Henry N., ed.
   1962   Studies in Siberian ethnogenesis. Anthropology of the North. Translations from Russian Sources, No. 2. Toronto.

Strong, William D.
   1953   Historical approach in anthropology. *In* Anthropology Today, ed. A. L. Kroeber, pp. 386-97. Chicago.

ARCHAEOETHNOLOGY, ETHNOARCHAEOLOGY, AND THE PROBLEMS OF PAST CULTURAL PATTERNING

by Robert E. Ackerman

In recent years there has been a determined attempt to broaden the scope of American archaeology. Further formulations in typological studies characteristic of earlier work continued, but a significant number of archaeologists in the 1950s and 1960s enjoined by Taylor's admonitions (1948) began to concern themselves with the areas of prehistoric settlement pattern analysis (Chang 1958, 1962, 1968; Cook and Heizer 1965; Ritchie 1961; Trigger 1967; Willey 1953, 1956), processual analysis (Binford 1962, 1965; Binford and Binford 1968; Braidwood 1960; Chang 1967a, 1967b; Rouse 1964; Willey and Phillips 1958), and the ethnology-archaeology relationship (Ascher 1961; Binford 1967; Chang 1967a, 1967b; Thompson 1958). Departures from the direct-historical approach (Steward 1942; Baerreis 1961) were evident in the attempts to reconstruct early prehistoric social and cultural systems (Binford and Binford 1966, 1968; Clark 1952, 1957; Narr 1962; Washburn 1961). More commonly, the analogy frame from ethnology was applied to recent prehistoric-to-historic period archaeology. Terms such as *socio-archaeology* (Gjessing 1963), *social archaeology* (Pilling 1966), *ethnoarchaeology* (Oswalt¹ and VanStone 1967), and even *archaeoethnology* (Riley 1967) are in vogue and we now have contributors to social unit and social integration studies in archaeology (Dozier 1965; Haviland 1966; Longacre 1966). Studies pointing out the uses of detailed data from ethnography or cautioning the unwary archaeologist against unwise use of analogy are given in Ascher 1962, Binford and Binford 1968, Heider 1967, and Matson 1965.

Although these studies point out the need for the increased use of archaeological resources made meaningful by the use of formulations available from other disciplines, particularly ethnology, there are some disturbing notes in this orchestration. The major difficulty appears to be one of proceeding from one set of data to another. In his discussion of cultural processes based upon the study of northern Georgian prehistory, Wauchope demonstrates the lack of correlation between general cultural evolutionary laws and his recovered data (1966:19-38). The difficulty lay in the comparison of basically noncomparable data. Specific evolutionary models were felt to be appropriate to archaeological data, since they "would be subject to empirical testing on the individual cultural level in the light of history" (Wauchope 1966:36). The ethnological data to be used in the archaeological construct thus should be specific to the archaeological context. A generalized ethnographic frame, i.e., hunting and gathering stage, without details specific to the geographic area is of limited use.

The archaeologist immediately is confronted with two problems in his attempt to study past cultural behavior. The first is how to present the information from an archaeological site in a manner that will be meaningful to both archaeologists and nonarchaeologists. The second problem and the more difficult is how to relate the cultural manifestations evident at a site to other cultural and natural systems in time and space. The solution of these problems is central to the discipline as further levels of interpretation and analysis emerge from these formulations.

Taking a rather restricted viewpoint, one that is incumbent upon the archaeologist due to the limitations of his data, the starting point for the beginning at least of a solution to the above problems would appear to be the instigation of comparable research in ethnography and archaeology. Initially, this would limit the scope of the ethnographic investigations to the areas of archaeological possibility. Currently the largest lacuna in archaeology is the lack of comparable data from ethnography. The archaeologist is urged to seek ethnographic correlates for his archaeological recoveries, but generally finds little beyond the passing mention of an object in a partial listing of an ethnographic material array. Perplexed, the archaeologist feels that he should probably do some ethnography on his own, just as he takes soil profiles or pollen samples. The needs of the archaeologist in this area of supporting data are specific, needs that have to be satisfied in regard to his recovery situation. Work in the recovery of information on the paleoenvironment of the site is a cooperative effort of the geomorphologist, the palynologist, the zoologist, and the archaeologist, often together in the same trench. Ethnographic recovery is generally away from the site unless the archaeologist is excavating within the confines of an occupied village. Even when the native population is nearby, the archaeologist must shift his viewpoint, rushing forward in time from his artifacts to the activities of living people. The transition is abrupt and frequently fraught with anxiety. Time spent at the village is time away from the excavations. The result is generally a token attempt at field ethnography. De Laguna's study of the ethnography and archaeology of the northern Tlingit rather pointly illustrates the benefits and the difficulties ensuing from the acceptance of a dual role (1960:1-23).

The solution at first seems to be a simple one—get someone to collect the needed data—but the question of personnel arises. As Chang has observed, "Should the ethnologist observe and record these data so that they might be of some use to an archaeologist? Or should he do so in any event? Or should there perhaps be a branch of archaeology (ethnoarchaeology) to take care of such things? The solutions to these problems are left to anyone who is willing to attempt them" (1967:230). The answer to the first question is that ethnologists are rarely interested in doing a detailed study of material culture and most would respond (and have!) rather negatively to requests for such data. The demands of the field situation preclude a dual role for the archaeologist. The solution thus lies in a third alternative, the creation of a special position on the field research team, that of an archaeologically oriented ethnographer. Interestingly, Freudenthal writing about the lack of ethnographical recovery in the course of Middle Eastern excavations came to a somewhat similar conclusion, "It would be a solution to supply the archaeological expedition with an ethnographer for field research and to finance the matter with archaeological funds. He should have access to the ancient materials, i.e., have a view of the past, on one hand, and on the other, obtain information about the people and problems with which the archaeologist comes in daily contact at the excavations site" (1965:95).

Especially important to this type of study is a third discipline, history, the written outpourings of those who lived in the period of the now excavatable past. The efforts to match the present and past cultural configurations will obviously require our attention to these written records. In this dalliance with time it is reassuring to feel the hands of ancestors reach across the span to link today with the yesterday world.

The initial stage in the establishment of joint ethnographic and archaeological research involves more than the creating on paper of an anthropological subfield—ethnoarchaeology or archaeoethnology. For the archaeologist, the benefits of such a joint effort will have to be clearly visualized, since the direction and funds for the ethnographical research will at this time have to come from the archaeological project. The ethnographer will probably require some rather convincing statements that such an attack will present new avenues into the study of cultural processes in the present as well as into the past. Foreseeably, the ethnologist in this position may become a specialist in his own right in the future.

The development of such a program of research came about in my case through a series of rather fortunate field situations. During the period 1963 to 1965 I had the opportunity to work in the Glacier Bay National Monument region of Southeastern Alaska under the auspices of the National Park Service. The archaelogical investigations were directed toward uncovering information regarding the Tlingit occupation of the monument area as well as attempting to determine the prehistoric base of northern Northwest Coast culture. Fortunately, we were successful on both tasks (Ackerman 1968). Most of the sites discovered were datable to the early to late historic period. These historic sites proved to be very productive and yielded data of a volume and nature hitherto unrealized by one whose prior experience was restricted to prehistoric site archaeology.

Available historic documents, missionary accounts, and the occasional ethnographic report of the late 1800s were valuable assets in our research. Items such as village plans, house construction, house floor plans, photographs of house interiors and exteriors provided us with information that gave our investigations a dimension not often realized in archaeology (Ackerman 1965, 1968). With such supporting data, the possibilities for archaeological interpretation increased and with this, in turn, came the realization that it was necessary to excavate cultural units that were comparable to those given in the historic and ethnographic sources. We modified our testing procedures, based mainly on small sample survey programs and turned to the complete excavation of cultural units such as structures (plank houses, smokehouses, trapping cabins, etc.) and activity areas (outdoor cooking areas, areas around houses, particularly near entrances, between buildings, etc.). This continuous sampling within a unit eliminated some of the sampling errors and provided better behavioral frames from archaeology than those that could be abstracted from the analyses of the materials recovered from unstructured behavioral frames or areas such as midden deposits. Our focus thus shifted from one of object-recovery to a pattern-orientation-of-object-distribution within a cultural frame, i.e., feature analysis. With the tightening up of our archaeological methodology we found that the historical and ethnographical data by comparison were loosely structured. The historical and ethnographical materials were mainly presented in generalized activity categories, although on occasion there were fairly good descriptions of settings such as household interiors (Jones 1914). Even here, there was a consistent lack of attention to detail in the relation of one object to another, the number of objects in an area, the nature of the distribution of objects, etc. It was apparent then that the data from other sources did not begin to be comparable to the highly controlled data resulting from our excavations.

Around our campfires members of the field crew often expressed a desire to travel back through time to the period of the occupation of the abandoned villages, to see the pageant of ceremonial display, and to observe the interplay of the elements of daily living expressed so scantily in the excavations. It occurred to me then that we did not need to be time travelers in the science fiction sense but could look into the past through the study of a living community, focusing on objects, their distribution, their place of use, the types of activities involving objects, and the number and kind of objects associated in a single activity.

Further, although it is a common assumption that people do create objects with an established procedure of manufacture, have fairly well-thought-out concepts regarding an object's final disposition or use, and regard the object as belonging to a particular class of objects, we fail to consider the net effect of possessing these objects. We readily admit the effect of the introduction of firearms or steel axes in a primitive technology, but somehow do not see the continuing effect of these items in the lives of the generations of users from that point forward. Men make objects, work to obtain objects, surround themselves with objects. These mute occupants of time and space thus condition their very way of living. LeBar's study of household goods on Truk (1964), Collier's study of twenty-two Indian households in the San Francisco Bay area (1967:81-104), and to a lesser extent Roberts's study of Navaho households near Ramah, New Mexico (1951), illustrate the use of objects to determine value orientation or the psychological levels of adjustment in culture change. As Collier discovered, "The 'look' of the Indian home shows a significant relation to the way the Indian family is coping with the problems of urban adjustment and living" (1967:93). Even within the fairly stable cultural situation there will be differences in household inventories that will reveal much about the occupants and their ways of relating to the world about them. The object-orientation frame is then a way of investigating some of the dynamics of human behavior, a frame that can be applied to the past as well as the present. As an axiom one can say that the people of today are the cultural inheritors of the past: the study of their object orientations will reveal segments of past cultural patterning. From today's study, then, we can curve the circle of time back upon itself to learn from the present revelation more about the human behavior of the past where our recovery is restricted to the world of material goods. A somewhat similar but more generalized approach is to be seen in the living-community archaeology advocated by Kleindienst and Watson (1956).

An opportunity to blend a modern village study based on an object orientation with an archaeological program came in 1966. That year the National Science Foundation agreed to support a two-year program of ethnological and archaeological research in the Cape Newenham region of Southwestern Alaska. This research project was based upon the data recovered by Larsen (1950) and by a survey team under my direction in 1962 (Ackerman 1963).

In the Cape Newenham region, four bays (Goodnews,

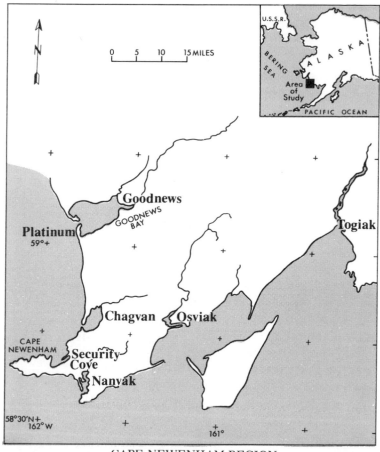

CAPE NEWENHAM REGION

Chagvan, Nanvak, and Osviak) contain traces of an Eskimo occupation that continued unbroken for some 2,000 years. Separated by a time interval of some depth is the Security Cove occupation dating to 4,000-5,000 years ago. Today three of the bays are silent, with house depressions as mute reminders of a life that once filled the area. Only Goodnews Bay is filled with the raucous roar of outboard motors, the sharp bark of a rifle, the mournful wail of a dog, or the titter of small children. Two villages, Platinum and Goodnews Bay, are home for the Eskimos who work in the local mine, fish commercially for the cannery at Togiak some 150 miles away by sea, or live by odd jobs, with a strong dependence on the local resources. Goodnews Bay, the larger of the two villages, is a stable settlement, having evolved from the nearby abandoned village of Mumtrak. Eskimos with memory's gleam in their eyes still talk of life in Mumtrak and other abandoned villages. These "old time" Eskimos in the village of Goodnews Bay were part of the ethnographic resources to be "excavated."

Progress in the life of a people, however, is represented by change. The old village of Mumtrak is now gone, buried under the fill of a landing strip for the small planes that service the modern village. Lights from the old semisubterranean houses still twinkle out on the point for some of the old people, but these memories could not be checked by archaeology. The gap in the record was filled by the historic level at the Chagvan Beach site on the southern shore of Chagvan Bay. As reported by the Tenth Annual Census, the historic village of Tzahavagamute was an active settlement in 1880 (Petrov 1884). Backing up this historic component at the Chagvan Beach site were six prehistoric villages that slowly receded in time to a period around the beginning of the Christian era. For some two thousand years the record is then fairly complete. The Goodnews Bay-Mumtrak ethnographic segment extended about eighty years backward in time. Further pursuance of the continuum led into the realm of archaeology.

The responsibility for the investigation of cultural patterning across a moderate sweep of time was divided along the well-established lines of cultural anthropological research. The ethnographers under the direction of Mrs. Lillian Ackerman were located for both of the field seasons in the Goodnews Bay village. About thirty miles to the south of this village, Richard Ross with his crew established a field camp on the Chagvan Beach site (see Figure 1). The third

Figure 1. Chagvan Beach site on the South Spit of Chagvan Bay. House pits can be seen along the beach ridges with a clustering toward the bay side.

party under my direction worked at the Security Cove site and at sites in Nanvak Bay, Osviak Bay, and the Goodnews River drainage. The archaeological work at the Chagvan Beach site initially formed a comparison model for the ethnographic research. Since the recovery of a piece of information by one of the field crews might affect the course of research of the others, it was important to maintain the lines of communication. Portable two-way radios and a light plane rented locally served this purpose quite well.

The ethnographers assumed the role of recorders of archaeology-in-the-making. The work began with the mapping of the village of Goodnews Bay in 1966. The archaeologists with their surveying instruments quickly laid out a base map which included the major structures of the village. The tar-paper covered frame houses, storehouses, generator sheds, fish drying racks, sweatbaths, the Bureau of Indian Affairs school complex, and the general store were located on the map. For the remainder of that season and part of the next, the ethnographers were busy mapping grave locations, stake-out areas for dogs, children's play areas, refuse dumping areas, adult work areas, boat landings, net locations near the village, and other such details left behind by daily living.

The village is divided into two parts by a small stream. As a source of water, a place to cut fish, a mighty river for the small children, and a fresh water lure to guide the salmon to the nets at its mouth, the stream is vital to the people. The area of the village near the old site of Mumtrak is known as Gixchik ("a glance away," meaning a short distance from old Mumtrak), while that part of the village on the far side of the stream is known as Gixchiknuk ("a glance a little farther away"). The latter section of the village, due to the restricted land area available for housing, is rather crowded and heavily littered with debris. Gixchik, the older section of the village, is more spacious with greater distances between the houses and outbuildings. A large open space in this part of the village turned out to be an old cemetery upon which no self-respecting Eskimo would set a house. One did, though, thereby creating a local scandal. Even at the outset of the project, patterns were apparent that could have immediate implications for archaeology. One variable we did not forsee was the success of two VISTA volunteers (Volunteers in Service to America) who instigated a clean-up campaign in Gixchik in 1967. Some of the details that we hoped to record disappeared in the wake of "improvements." The full glory of Gixchiknuk, however, is on record and may represent the last "unimproved" view of the cluttered living surface of an Eskimo village (Figure 2). For our research, we have detailed ground plans not only of house and other structure

Figure 2. Western section (Gixchiknuk) of Goodnews Bay village.

locations, but also of the artifact and activity area distributions for most of the village.

With the external environment mapped, the ethnographers turned to the detailed inventory analyses and mapping of the interiors of fish drying racks, storage houses, food caches, sweatbaths, and houses. Generally indifferent to the mapping of the village, the Eskimos became reluctant. Permission was granted to inventory the outbuildings, but the inventory of the household interiors was another matter. Vitally important for the interpretation of materials taken from the house pit excavations, this area of study was regarded as too personal by the Eskimos. The ethnographers were able to obtain a complete inventory for one house, and

Figure 3. House interior, Goodnews Bay village.

partial inventories for two others. A technique felt to be within permissible bounds was the photographing of interiors with the occupants of the houses being a conspicuous feature (Figure 3). The individuals were given pictures of themselves in their homes, and, by taking several shots and by careful framing, we had a partial household inventory.

Goodnews Bay village, however, had a diachronic dimension as well as the synchronic one under study. House order construction and order of occupation, together with the village census, were obtained as a possible method of gaining insight into the dynamics of intravillage settlement patterns. Clustering of kindred was perhaps obvious, but several other factors were involved. Families from other villages were found living near an affinal relative or near friends who had married into the village. Pushing back in time, the ethnographers reached into the earlier building period with its pit house structures. Informants drew maps of the house locations, listed the occupants of each dwelling, and made some remarks about village life then. Similar information was given for Mumtrak. Remembered too were the placement of salmon nets, the people who used them, and the kashims (ceremonial houses) where the men stayed. Areas of uncertainty were the number of tools that a man or woman would have and use, where each was kept, and the plethora of details forgotten in daily living. We found that the commonplace world of objects was taken for granted, forming a rather unconscious perceptive field that was difficult to uncover even in an ongoing society. Without the object cues of the past to guide them, our informants were vague in their recollections. The inadequacy of this area of the memory culture is an evident loss to archaeology. A possible way out of this dilemma was considered. If the Eskimos of today pattern many of their daily village activities in a way that is similar to the recent past as the Eskimo informants indicate, then the artifact sets in these activity frames may be interpolated backward, i.e., with a nearly complete artifact set recovered in an excavation, it will be possible to complete the activity frame. Since we are working with detailed orderings, this may not be necessarily so even if it appears at first to be simplistic and obvious.

The study of land utilization and of living space revealed that the area which could be lumped under a home territory concept was larger than that which we first realized. Additionally, both of the villages of Platinum and Goodnews Bay shared the same biome. The Goodnews River, which we considered Goodnews Bay village territory as it lay adjacent to the village, was freely utilized by the Platinum village people. Our informants denied the existence of any claimed hunting or fishing territories. Current use of a particular spot, e.g., a net location, was respected, but failure to use the location during a season would allow others to establish a use claim. It was also found that the villagers would move around rather freely, hunting, fishing, working, or just visiting friends and relatives even though this meant leaving their fixed property in the village for some time. A picture of a former mobile population, not fixed by property or by responsibilities toward governmental agencies as they are today, shifting from one area to another in the environmental realm that supported them, emerged with a clarity that received quick corroboration from informants, historical sources, and our archaeological surveys. The unit of study in the local area was thus the population, not the settlement. Settlements were only places occupied by the shifting population in its yearly round. An important point for archaeology was that few settlements were ever totally abandoned at any one time of the year. New settlements were certainly created and old ones abandoned as the historical and archaeological records show, but in the yearly pattern the settlement was but part of a greater realm. Informants also indicated that, although there were separate resident populations at Goodnews, Chagvan, Nanvak, and Osviak bays, these communities were inter-linked through kinship and other reciprocal bonds. The Eskimos of Goodnews Bay and Chagvan Bay oriented themselves in large part to the resources of Kuskokwim Bay and the mainland interior area, as did the people of the Kuskokwim River. They are thus considered to be a section of the Kuskowagmiut, Eskimos of the lower Kuskokwim River (Petrov 1884). According to Petrov (1884: 135) the people of Nanvak and Osviak Bay were a branch of the Togiagamiut to the east and were known as the Chingigumiut or Cape people. Archaeologically these distinctions are not evident. A general sequential similarity has been noted for the entire area, and to date we have not discovered within the last two-thousand-year span an artifact or artifact-cluster that is specific to a small local area.

While the ethnographers' work was in progress, the archaeologists were busy attempting to establish comparable frames for archaeology. At the Chagvan Beach site with its seven house clusters stretching across the numerous beach strands (Figure 1), the problem was to obtain an adequate sample and to obtain maximal returns for the work expended.

Numerous problems involving the sequential ordering of the house clusters and the temporal ordering of houses within a cluster had to be met and resolved. The resolution of such problems, familiar to archaeologists who excavate large sites with multiple occupations, can be attained only by extensive testing and excavating. Fortunately there was a gradual change in house form from the older section of the site to the more recent. Houses within a cluster tended to be uniform in construction. Where there occurred an invasion of an older cluster by an outlying house from a more modern occupation, it was frequently marked not only by the different house form but also by a different vegetation cover. This was most obvious in the forward part of the site.

Starting with the most recent occupation, a single log cabin constructed in 1935, the archaeologists began the detailed excavation of house units. This particular cabin proved to be a fine test of the ethnoarchaeological approach. One of the members of the excavating team was given the task of reconstructing the cultural pattern of the unit without recourse to ethnographic data. Questions involving the nature and duration of the occupation, the number of occupants, the sex of the occupants, etc., were considered. When the archaeological construct was completed, the available ethnographic data obtained from the builder and first occupant of the cabin was introduced for comparison. This study (Koch 1968) has proved to be a most valuable contribution, since it revealed several serious errors that could be made concerning the nature of archaeological remains and the length of occupation. It also raised the disturbing possibility of inadequate ethnographic reporting. Even when we knew what we required, we failed to obtain the necessary details to answer the questions raised by the excavations. The inadequacy of the ethnographic data may be in part our failure to push the informant into a more detailed recounting, but more to the point was the informant's inability to recall such details. The inadequacy of the memory culture for detailed archaeological constructs again emerges. This should not be surprising, for what American housewife would be able to recall from her childhood the details of her mother's kitchen cabinet drawers or even tell us without peeking the contents of her own?

From this modern occupation, the archaeologists moved from one house cluster to the next, testing and excavating house units. Continuous wall profiles and the locating and mapping of literally every item recovered in the excavations was tedious and time-consuming, yet this work has revealed that the houses often had multiple occupations. There were instances of a house being reoccupied after a period of abandonment as well as several instances of use after the roof structure had fallen into the house pit. The latter type of occupation was probably a temporary camp out of the wind, which forcefully sweeps across the low lying beaches.

We realize that our knowledge of the structure of camp sites was virtually nonexistent. Three recent Eskimo tent camps on the new beach section of the site were photographed and mapped by the archaeologists. The camps were small and of temporary character. No effort had been expanded to alter the area for human comfort. A rather different type of camp was visited while we were conducting an archaeological survey of the Goodnews River valley. At the site of Ekhtagamuk we came upon an earth and sod-covered pole dwelling with an outlying sweatbath and covered cache pit. The construction details of the three units with their plentiful material inventory gave us valuable data for archaeological comparison. The amount of material debris was surprisingly large and, more important, consisted of many items that a Euro-American probably would not leave behind.[1] It would appear that

[1] Items enumerated at one family's unoccupied fish-camp, Goodnews River. It was only temporarily, not permanently abandoned.

white plastic dishpan
outboard carburetor and gas tank
2 D flashlight cells, motor bracket, allspice can
D cell flashlight battery
motor plate
broken wood shaft, 8 cm. diameter
motor parts
paper
cardboard box
magazine, cardboard box
vacuum bottle top, tin can
stick with fishline around it
cardboard box tacked against wall
outboard motor parts: head, gaskets, mounting assembly, piston
7 25-35 REM-UMC rifle cartridges, 6 unfired, 1 fired (a dud), 3 bullets taken from cases
nails (wire drawn), flashlight bulb RS 3.6 V
½ in. plywood board, 35 x 60 cm.; under it a lighter fluid can; a stick with a nail drawn through; a spring as in the base of a flashlight, probably from motor
head of outboard motor—2 cylinders
leather pistol holster
cardboard boxes laid on floor and tacked on entrance posts
canvas-covered folding cot
bowl fragments
lighter fluid can
leather combat boot, right foot
airline travel bag, containing 2 unfired 25-35 REM-UMC rifle cartridges, part of gasoline fuel line, 3 gears of some sort, 1 12-ga. shotgun shell, unfired
2 x 4 plank with cut notch
flattened crimp-cut tobacco can, pocket size
1-lb. can coffee
motor part—fits over cylinder (no. 18), plywood guitar back with name and date (12-15-60), Vienna sausage can, bottle with screw-top lid, peanut butter jar, plastic coated wire
tin can (probably part of sausage can cut in middle), band-aid flip-top can, tobacco box for roll-your-own cigarettes

the patterns of artifact discarding are different from our own. It was rather curious that a search made through the dumps of the Goodnews Bay village did not reveal this pattern, although a somewhat similar distribution of debris could be found around some of the houses. In the village we were not sure whether the items were discarded or represented temporary placements, even though a bit

---

pail, 1-lb. shortening can, automatic shotgun 12 ga. (goes under stove)
milk glass sherd with F in shield on bottom, with world "proof" below
    probably "oven proof")
gill net of 1 in. mesh and screw-top lid for peanut butter jar
D flashlight cell, mixture controls for outboard motor, screw-top jar
2-tin can, Vienna sausage can half, outboard motor parts, sock, 1 pr.
    man's shorts, cardboard box having recipe on back, china bowl
feather pillow, cardboard
gallon jug, glass of bleach, milk-glass saucer, screw-top pickle jar
screw-top pint jar with grease or petroleum jelly
tin can cut in middle (use of key opener)
2 D cell flashlight batteries
1½ lb. can "beef dinner," peanut butter, ½ lb. can Vienna sausage
D cell battery, spark plug, rubber covered clamp for outboard motor
magazines
half of wood net-float
magazines, tide book
billfold, with name, place, and date (8-21-59) written on inside
insect bomb
1 lb. can of coffee
glass jar of instant coffee
soy sauce bottle
plastic garment bag
enamel ware washbasin
22 cal. cartridge, unfired
kitchen knife blade, screw-top cap

On ceiling:

nails in supports
bit of cord stretched between 2 nails
spring-type clothespin clamped on nail
ivory socket-pieces wedged between ridge and rafters

In entry:

plastic top
zipper, button plate
ring
lantern generator
ballpoint pen

Note: Trade names on cans and other items were recorded but are not repeated here. Similarly, personal names were recorded.

random. Another interesting detail for the archaeologist came to light when we were photograping the construction of the roof in the sod hut at Ekhtagamuk. Stuck between the ridge pole and the sod covering was an ivory harpoon socket piece. Upon the collapse of the structure this "heirloom" would give the roof level an older date than the floor zone. A similar mixing of the old and the new was found in the cemeteries on the Osviak River. A woman's grave contained a very nice example of the corrugated pottery lamp local to Southwestern Alaska with a badly rusted tin bucket. A similar item relationship was seen in the inclusion of an ivory seal dart head with a .300 Savage rifle in a man's grave.

Such information is applicable to the recent past, but to the more distant past one must be cautious, yet optimistic. An example comes to mind. A flat, incised pebble depicting three conical tents on a low rise of land was found near two artifacts of the side-notched point complex at the Security Cove site. The site was a summer encampment, located not far from the sea. The summer structure for the area in historic times was a sod and pole structure (Nelson 1899: 248-50), similar to the one from the village of Ekhtagamuq on the Goodnews River. The conical summer tent, said to be of Athabascan origin, was common in Kotzebue Sound (Nelson 1899:259-63). Was the summer conical tent a local precursor of the sod-covered pole structure, a change brought about by the disappearance of caribou from the area, or do the conical tents indicate an Indian occupation of the coast as the artifact inventory also tends to suggest?

New relationships and the associated questions continue to arise from the investigations but it might be worthwhile to pause at this juncture to consider what exactly we have accomplished. Two seasons' worth of archaeological and ethnographical data would seem to warrant some conclusive statement, yet such a statement at this point would be premature. This was in many ways a pilot study in which the investigators tried new approaches, gathered different masses of data, and succeeded and failed in different ways. They learned much, however, in both the investigational and analytic aspects of this piece of research. The simple act of asking different questions or recording different bits of data had their effect. What I should like to present briefly in the remaining section of this paper are not "conclusions" but the "effects" of having used this particular approach in the study of an ethnographic and archaeological area.

Much has been said already about the specific approaches of ethnographers and archaeologists, their kinds of data, and how these have been attained. In this project the archaeologists were the mobile field men who attempted to verify archaeologically an ethnographic statement of site location, settlement pattern, etc., and who supplied ecological data as well as a number of questions on intersite and intrasite patterns. The ethnographers worked basically with their intravillage data and saw the connections to the outside world and the surrounding area through the eyes of their informants. The informational overlay, the result of data exchange between the two groups, was found to be richer in information than would have been the case where either group worked in isolation. The following four items from our research will serve as illustrations: (1) determinants of site location, (2) settlements and the kashgee (kashim), (3) intravillage articulations, (4) house spatial analysis.

Determinants of Site Location

The major sites (villages) in the Cape Newenham area were located just inside the bays on the enclosing spits and near the mouths of the rivers that emptied into these bays. These small embayments are estuary areas and tidal basins where the salt waters of Kuskokwim Bay at high tide intermix with the fresh water flow from the rivers. The large sites are located at sheltered points for boat anchorage and are at the zone of marine and riverine water intermix. Such an area is acknowledged to be one of the richest resource zones in the world (Odum 1963:114). This factor was brought clearly to our attention by the large amount of fish hauled in from the nets of Goodnews Bay village during the summers of 1966 and 1967.

The Goodnews Bay village data also indicated that village size was limited by the number of available net locations in the near vicinity of the village. Uppermost in importance would be a fresh water stream or rivulet which would not only provide water for the inhabitants of the village but would also lure the salmon toward the shore in their search for a fresh water spawning ground. Near the mouth of the small fresh water stream was a prime net location. Nets could be placed on both sides for some distance but this space was limited. Before the advent of motor-powered boats, net locations a mile or more from the village would require a population shift to that location. This might result in a temporary fishing camp or perhaps a new village location if the resource area was capable of supporting more than a family group.

Upriver site locations mapped by our survey teams are today seasonal fishing camps or have been totally abandoned. In the past, several villages were occupied during the winter. Behind these village sites we found on the high overlooking ridges, chipping debris, mute evidence of a hunter waiting for caribou to appear on the trails far below. In the upriver villages caribou meat substituted for the seal meat of the bay villages. The upriver villages were in an edge area situation similar to that of the intertidal zone villages of the bay, for they were backed by the tundra-covered uplands and fronted by the river and shrub-tree-covered valley bottomlands. The convergence of two or more ecotones is evident in most of the site locations.

Settlements and the Kashgee

In this approach to the typology of northern settlements, Chang has utilized ecological considerations and for community structure, the organization of kindred (1962:30, 33). He has also attempted in later writings (1967, 1968) to make such types applicable to archaeology. As Rouse pointed out in his criticism of Chang's approach, the settlement is not always possible to define archaeologically (Rouse 1968:23). Settlements (following Chang's definition [1967: 41-42] and Rouse's interpretation [1968:23]) in the Cape Newenham region are fairly easy to define, since the settlements were physically isolated, were occupied contemporaneously for approximately two thousand years, and each settlement occupied a similar but geographically separate ecological niche. The cultural adaptations evident in the artifact inventories are, unfortunately, similar enough so that one cannot distinguish culturally between communities. Through the use of early census data and the genealogical fragments obtained from informants we have been able to distinguish the communities and name some of their inhabitants. The artifact inventories indicate only that the people belong to the same cultural group, for as Rouse has clearly indicated (1968:26-28), artifacts identify people, not social groups. Our definition of communities came through our ecological, historical, and ethnographical data.

Further problems were encountered in the site-to-settlement relationship. Near the mouth of the Osviak River, I located three sites that were fairly close together, but were separated by open stretches of ground. The first site contained seventeen house pits, the second, four or five, and the third, eight. I equated the first site with the historic village of Osviak, which appeared on the maps for the area. Happily, a former resident of the area drew us a map of the village from memory. In matching his map of the village against my survey map, I found that the historic village of Osviak encompassed my three sites. I had thought of the village in terms of a tight house cluster and was unwilling to include the intervening open spaces within the village area.

Passing on to a further behavioral level of interpretation, the question arose as to the function of a village. What did a population aggregate provide that a couple of neighboring households could not? We wanted some measure that we could use archaeologically. From our archaeological sites came an answer. Every large house cluster had one or more very large pit-houses. The answer was there all the time. The kashgee or men's house was a club house for the men of the village, a workshop, a boys' school, a bathhouse, the equivalent of a New England townhall, and a ceremonial center. As Oswalt notes, "the kashgee was the only place where people cooperated as a cohesive social unit; the kashgee was symbolic of common village interests" (1963:71). The assembly of males acted as a corporate decision-making body that gave a particular structural character to the village life. The kashgee then as a multidimensional institution was the integrating dynamic in the settlement. It is not surprising that the pull of the winter village was as strong as it was.

Our oldest informant indicated that there had to be about five households together to build and maintain a kashgee. The maintenance factor was not just the care of the structure but the satisfying of the needs of the community through the institution. This estimate of a minimal residential aggregate for village organization has some support from historic and archaeological village data. Crow village on the Kuskokwim River, which was occupied in the late 1890s had ninety individuals living in five houses with one kashgee (Oswalt and VanStone 1967). Ten houses and two kashgees were found at the Tikchik village site on a tributary of the Nushagak River although not all the houses or both of the kashgees were continuously occupied (Van-Stone 1968). In sites located by the archaeological survey in the Cape Newenham vicinity, the house-to-kashgee ratio was 5:1, 6:1, and 8:1.

Earlier settlements in the Osviak Bay area contained more of the large structures than we had anticipated. Either there was considerable pressure for building new kashgees every few years or there is here some evidence for the existence of an earlier, larger household unit. At the moment, I favor the latter possibility as these large pit-houses (12-14 meters across) in one village describe a close-ly set curved arc of twelve units. Twelve other such units were found nearby and scattered through the village. It was impossible to speak of a village kashgee there. One, of course, wonders about parallels with the clan or sib houses of South Alaska.

Intravillage Articulations

The plotting of the locations of structures, work areas, places to haul up boats, etc., drew our attention to the small dislocations constantly occurring in a village (cf. Ascher 1968:43-52). During the time between our 1966 and 1967 field seasons, two households had moved to different parts of the village. The detective work of gathering information on house histories and the movement of people could fill a book by itself. Why do people live where they do, store things where they do, or discard things where they do? The last question was fairly simple to answer, i.e., nearby their dwellings—unless a new order is introduced (clean-up campaigns by VISTA workers). The first two parts of the question were more complex. In his discussion of the archaeological site Chang delves into the "microarticulation of the archaeological structure" in terms of social divisions and event analysis (1967:93-94; 102-109). With an occupied settlement we also were able to ask why? in addition to

what? and where? Taking the individual's house location
first, what is the pattern of his adjacency interaction with
others? Considering that the individual is "place-based"
to a considerable degree in his consciousness (Webber 1964:
60-61) one would perhaps expect the house to be a focal
point of radiating patterns of interaction. Pred in his study
Behavior and Location points out: "However, the private-
information field, or spatial arrangement of an individual's
total array of personal contacts, does not only vary from
a theoretically ideal circular shape because of eccentricities
in the local population distribution about the dwelling
which serves as the center of the field, but also has areal
and configurational irregularities that are associated with
the specific person's personality, background, occupation
and social position" (1967:33). We found a considerable
variation in the shape and size of the "yard" areas around
the houses. As a spatial measure of communication and
cooperation we noted the following: (1) a cluster of
three-family households of related kin (father, two sons),
(2) two separate family households of brothers on opposite
sides of the village: wives wished to live near their mothers,
(3) a single male household on the edge of the village: his
aunt had refused him the building space next to her house,
(4) family household isolate on the edge of the village:
sisters of wife regarded her as incompetent and rejected her,
(5) family builds house on the other side of village, to be
nearer relatives and to get son away from next door lover.
The list could go on. We noted also a gradual shift of the
village to the west with a beginning commercialization of
the eastern section (Gixchik) with the school, post office,
store, national guard armory, church, and landing strip.
The answer most frequently given for a household move in
the village was "to be nearer the water." With the almost
complete dependence on washable clothing and the instilled
Christian ethic of cleanliness, the Eskimo women have been
quick to see the benefits of a washing machine. Washday

demands and the increased use of water in the household for bathing have required more daily trips to the water supply. Faced with the onerous task of hauling water, the Eskimo solution has been to move the house.

The mapping of the generator line networks that carry electricity to some of the households in the village provided us with further insights into the social relationships between households. Two cooperative nets were made up of immediate kindred while the third included nonkindred some distance away from the owner's generator shed. The generator nets indicate that the investigator cannot assume the residents of nearby houses necessarily to be partners in a cooperative venture.

House Spatial Analysis

The ethnographers using a modified "living archaeology" approach were immediately beset by the world of objects whose meanings and impacts were specific to a culture other than their own. The cognitive aspect of such a material orientation has been presented explicitly by Ruesch and Kees (1956) and has been mentioned by Collier (1967). One of the problems encountered in this cognitive field of material objects concerned how objects were ordered in an Eskimo household. The patterns should be rather culturally specific but they should also reveal a variable amount of individualized structuring. With this internalization of object orientation there should be cues to the status of household members, their psychological reaction to community pressures, and a rather good insight into personality structure. But how to apply this to archaeology? Taking only the object order and those objects present in a household, we found several areas of relevance.

The size restriction of the family unit structures (winter heating requirements necessitate space and fuel considerations) resulted in compact activity and storage areas. These areas were generally well defined in the one- to two-room structures. An activity area such as a bed was used as a multipurpose area (for sleeping, eating, bathing, work and play) while in contrast the cooking area was limited to a single activity.

Sex-linked spatial control was marked by the storage of items specific to male or female activities. Using a single family household (Figure 4) with father, mother, and three children in a one-room dwelling as an example, we found a fairly well-defined woman's corner and a man's corner. Most of the items on the shelves within these locations were fairly specific to male or female activities, but there were some that appeared to threaten the consistency of the sets. In the woman's corner the storage shelves held, besides food and kitchenware, hair curlers, medicine bottles, screwdriver, rubber patch kit, twine, and a record player and records. In the opposite corner on a set of shelves lay a variety of tools, matches, rifle ammunition, a Sears, Roebuck catalog, a Bible, and letters. If one is not to infer mixing of male-female activity zones, then the woman of the house administers medicine as well as food, patches her boots, ties up things, does repair work on the side with a screwdriver (or pries at things), fixes the children's or her own hair while in the cooking area, uses a hymnal on occasion, and plays music from a record player. The man, on the other hand, is the carpenter and general repairman and also orders goods from a mail-order house, reads the Bible, and writes letters. The correlation between sex-specific behavior and an activity area turned out to be fairly correct. During the summer of our study of this household the man of the house was away working in the cannery at Togiak. His wife was busy at her net, gathering fish for the winter food supply. Her rubber hip boots probably needed a bit of patching now and then, and the twine could have been used in repairing the net. The record player was near the parent's bed and thus could be the special interest of either or both parents. The wife is poorly educated and cannot read. The

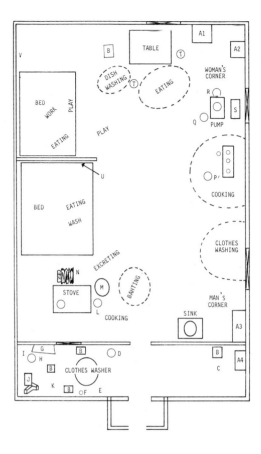

Figure 4. Plan view of the interior of a household, Goodnews Bay village. A1-4, shelves made of Blazo (gasoline) can cases; B, boxes, wooden or cardboard; C, tricycle; D, no. 10 tin can with paintbrush; E, shovel; F, gallon paint can; G, sheet tin; H, chemical drum; I, crosscut saw; J, old Coleman camp stove; K, section of tin air-duct; L, bucket for ashes; M, chamber pot; N, firewood; O, three-burner Coleman camp stove; P, Coleman gasoline lantern hanging from ceiling; Q, metal teapot; R, tin pail; S, bench made from wooden Blazo box; T, boxes of Krustease pancake mix; U, portable radio; V, model 70 Winchester rifle and carpenter level. Not all items are shown here, as suitcases under beds and clothing hanging from ceiling.

husband is literate and wrote letters to his wife from the cannery. She was not skilled in the use of money so that he purchased most of the major items for the family. With the husband away the wife had to care for the children when they were ill (medicines) and also was responsible for their Sunday church observances (hymnals). There is nothing to preclude the woman's use of the man's tools during his absence.

Our fair degree of success at correlating objects in activity areas to the behavior of the household members should be balanced against the large amount of information that we had on this family.

The use by one sex of the other's equipment is not un-common and constitutes, particularly for the archaeologist, a difficult problem in social unit identification. What is the proof of a man's or woman's presence? Men frequently camp out by themselves for a day or two in the fall. They carry with them women's gear (cooking utensils, food). In this situation men are using women's equipment and it is difficult if not impossible at times to determine 'from the camp debris or the items left at a permanent camp whether a woman was present. Diagnostic female items in a modern camp would be an uluak (woman's knife, rarely left behind), clothing, sewing equipment, and items from the Euro-American culture that are markedly feminine (hair curlers, cosmetics, jewelry). In early historic to prehistoric sites there would be fewer clues, due to the smaller recoverable inventory. Women do not so often invade the man's object world, but the house study in the Goodnews Bay village indicates that it does occur and perhaps more than we realize. In the archaeological setting the definition of sexes by tool forms and activity areas is important to the determination of the type of social group using the structural unit. A large household dwelling probably can be distinguished from a kashgee by the presence of women's implements.

Facilities for the storing of clothing reflect the continuing mobile character of the Eskimo household. Clothing was stored in suitcases and boxes. Bureaus were noted in a few households, but these have not been widely accepted. The relatively small amount of household goods in some dwellings contrasts with the more substantial inventories of others. More and more families are adding to their dwellings oil-burning stoves, gasoline-powered washing machines, electric generators, and water pumps.

The study of the use of household space in the setting of a modern village where the patterns of the past still color strongly the life ways of today quickened our interest in the evidence for space utilization in early historic to prehistoric houses. Using the house interiors in the Goodnews Bay village as guides to activity area zones, we were able to discern in a sixteenth-century pit house on Chagvan Bay, specific male and female use-areas on either side of the house with a common area on the back bench. One tender touch was the finding of man's and woman's knife handles lying side by side under the bark and mat coverings of the sleeping platform.

The success of such a research venture is obviously tied to the existence of a native population in an area with sufficient occupational time depth and density to provide archaeological contrasts or comparisons to the ethnographic frame. The region of the Kuskokwim-Bristol Bay area of Southwestern Alaska is one of many such areas available for study. A considerable body of ethnographic literature exists for the area (see especially Edmonds 1966; Lantis 1946; Nelson 1899; Oswalt 1963a, 1963b; and VanStone 1967), although there is little of the quantifiable ethnographic data available in these publications. Archaeological research has been largely of the survey type (Ackerman 1964; Larsen 1950; Le Febre 1956; Oswalt 1952; VanStone 1957). A departure from this tradition can be seen in the study by Oswalt and VanStone (1967) of Crow village, a historic site on the Kuskokwim River. Employing ethnographical, historical, and archaeological materials, the authors attempted to reconstruct the culture of the site. While not as successful as they had hoped, the investigators have presented in the interpretations of their findings an excellent summation of the difficulties and shortcomings of this type of research (Oswalt and VanStone 1967:101-105). A recent archaeological study of a nineteenth-century river village in the Nushagak region has been completed by VanStone (1968) and serves as a followup of the earlier work on the Kuskokwim River area.

Conclusion

This has been a brief statement of the research efforts of the Cape Newenham archaeological and ethnological expedition with an attempt to call attention particularly to the constant interplay between the ethnological and archaeological units. With such close cooperation and communication we hope that new avenues of research have been opened. It is apparent that we have different kinds of material and that it will be possible to view the data in somewhat more sophisticated ways than was formerly possible. It is hoped that some insight into the world of objects in their behavioral frames will be possible through attempts to generate concepts of artifact space, establish activity spheres, study the stability of complexes from one time unit to the next. The approach is not a substitute for typological or seriational studies in archaeology but is an addition to these studies.

Regarding the methodological approach advanced here, we feel at this writing that the ethnographic studies oriented to the recovery possibilities of archaeology have resulted in the acquisition of a body of data that archaeologists in the Eskimo area and perhaps also in other areas can utilize immediately. Furthermore, with this body of comparable ethnographic data available, the discoveries made by the archaeologists can have more meaning to ethnographers. The study of traditions, stability, and change, we hope, has been given a new dimension.

References

Ackerman, R. E.
1964   Prehistory in the Kuskokwim-Bristol Bay Region, south-western Alaska. Report of Investigations No. 26. Laboratory of Anthropology, Washington State University.
1965   Archeological survey, Glacier Bay National Monument, southeastern Alaska, pt. II. Report of Investigations No. 36. Laboratory of Anthropology, Washington State University.
1968   The Archeology of the Glacier Bay Region, Southeastern Alaska. Report of Investigations No. 44. Laboratory of Anthropology, Washington State University.

Ascher, R.
1961   Analogy in archaeologival interpretation. Southwestern Journal of Anthropology 17:317-25.
1962   Ethnology for archaeology: A case from the Seri Indians. Ethnology 1:360-69.
1968   Time's arrow and the archaeology of a contemporary community. In Settlement Archeology, ed. K. C. Chang, pp. 43-52. Palo Alto, Calif.

Baerreis, D. A.
1961   The ethnohistoric approach and archeology. Ethnohistory 8:49-77.

Binford, L. R.
1962   Archeology as anthropology. American Antiquity 28:217-25.
1965   Archaeological systematics and the study of cultural process. American Antiquity 31:203-10.
1967   Smudge pits and hide smoking: the use of analogy in archeological reasoning. American Antiquity 32:1-12.

Binford, L. R., and Binford, S. R.
1966   A preliminary analysis of functional variability in the Mousterian of Levallois Facies. American Anthropologist 68 (2, pt. 2):238-95.
1968   (eds.) New Perspectives in Archeology. Chicago.

Braidwood, R. J.
1960   Levels in prehistory: a model for the consideration of the evidence. In The Evolution of Man, pp. 143-51 (Evolution after Darwin, ed. S. Tax, Vol. 2). Chicago.

Chang, K.
1958   A study of the neolithic social grouping: examples from the new world. American Anthropologist 60:298-334.

1962   Settlement and community patterns in some circumpolar societies. Arctic Anthropology 1:28-41.
1967a   Major aspects of the interrelationship of archeology and ethnology. Current Anthropology 8:227-43.
1967b   Rethinking Archaeology. New York.
1968   (ed.) Settlement Archeology. Palo Alto, Calif.

Clark, G.
1952   Prehistoric Europe: The Economic Basis. London.
1957   Starr Carr. Cambridge, Eng.

Collier, J. Jr.
1967   Visual anthropology: photography as a research method. In Studies in Anthropological Method. New York.

Cook, S. F., and Heizer, R. F.
1965   The quantitative approach to the relation between population and settlement size. Reports of the University of California Archeology Survey No. 64, Berkeley, Calif.

de Laguna, F.
1960   The story of a Tlingit community. Bureau of American Ethnology, Bulletin 172.

Dozier, E. P.
1965   Southwestern social units and archeology. American Antiquity 31:38-47.

Edmonds, H. M. W.
1966   The Eskimo of St. Michael and vicinity as related by H. M. W. Edmonds, ed. D. J. Ray. Anthropological Papers of the University of Alaska 13, pt. 2.

Freudenthal, P.
1966   Archaeology and ethnographic field research. (Fourth Conference of Nordic Anthropologists). Ethnos, supplement to vol. 31, pp. 89-91.

Gjessing, G.
1963   Socio-archaeology. Folk 5:103-12.

Haviland, W. A.
1966   Social integration and the classic Maya. American Antiquity 31:625-31.

Heider, K. G.
1967   Archaeological assumptions and ethnographic facts: a cautionary tale from New Guinea. Southwestern Journal of Anthropology 23:52-64.

Jones, L. F.
1914   A Study of the Thlingets of Alaska. New York.

Kleindienst, M. R., and Watson, P. J.
  1956   Action archeology. the archeological inventory of a
          living community. Anthropology Tomorrow 5:75-78.
          Chicago.

Koch, W. B.
  1968   An inventory analysis of a late historic Eskimo house in
          southwestern Alaska, and insights into the sources of
          error in archeological interpretation. Master's Thesis,
          Washington State University.

Lantis, M.
  1946   The social culture of the Nunivak Eskimo. Transactions
          of the American Philosophical Society 35, pt. 3.

Larsen, H.
  1950   Archeological investigations in southwestern Alaska.
          American Antiquity 15:177-86.

LeBar, F. M.
  1964   A household survey of economic goods on Romonum
          Island, Turk. In Explorations in Cultural Anthropology,
          ed. Ward H. Goodenough, pp. 335-49. New York.

Le Febre, C. C.
  1956   A contribution to the archaeology of the Upper Kus-
          kokwim. American Antiquity 21:268-74.

Longacre, W. A.
  1966   Changing patterns of social integration: a prehistoric
          example from the American Southwest. American
          Anthropologist 68:94-102.

Matson, F. R., ed.
  1965   Ceramics and man. Viking Fund Publications in An-
          thropology No. 41.

Narr, K. J.
  1962   Approaches to the social life of earliest man. Anthropos
          57:604-20.

Nelson, E. W.
  1899   The Eskimo about Bering Strait. 18th Annual Report,
          Bureau of American Ethnology, pt. 2.

Odum, E. P.
  1963   Ecology. Modern Biology Series. New York.

Oswalt, W. H.
  1952   The archeology of Hooper Bay Village, Alaska. An-
          thropological Papers of the University of Alaska 1:47-91.
  1963a   Mission of change in Alaska: Eskimos and Moravians on

the Kuskokwim. The Huntington Library, San Marino, Calif.

1963b   Napaskiak: An Alaskan Eskimo Community. Tucson, Ariz.

Oswalt, W. H., and VanStone, J. W.
1967   The ethnoarcheology of Crow Village, Alaska. Bureau of American Ethnology, Bulletin 199.

Pilling, A. R.
1966   Life at Porter Site 8, Midland County, Michigan. Michigan Archeologist 12:235-48.

Pred, A.
1967   Behavior and location. Lund Studies in Geography (Series B. Human Geography No. 27). Royal University of Lund, Sweden (C.W.K. Gleerup, Lund, publisher).

Riley, C. L.
1967   Comment on Kwang-Chi Chang's article "Major Aspects of the Interrelationship of Archeology and Ethnology," Current Anthropology 8:239.

Ritchie, W. A.
1961   Iroquois Archeology and settlement patterns. In Symposium on Cherokee and Iroquois Culture, ed. W. N. Fenton and J. Gulick, Bureau of American Ethnology, Bulletin 180, pp. 27-38.

Roberts, J. M.
1951   Three Navajo households: a comparative study of small group culture. Papers of the Peabody Museum of American Archeology and Ethnology, 40 (3), Harvard University.

Rouse, I.
1964   Archeological approach to cultural evolution. In Explorations in Cultural Anthropology, ed. W. Goodenough, pp. 455-68. New York.

1968   Prehistory, Typology, and the Study of Society. In Settlement Archeology, ed. K. C. Chang, pp. 10-30. Palo Alto, Calif.

Ruesch, J., and Kees, W.
1956   Nonverbal Communication: Notes on the Visual Perception of Human Relations. Berkeley and Los Angeles.

Steward, J.
1942   The direct historical approach in archeology. American Antiquity 7:337-43.

Taylor, W. W.
1948   A study of archeology. American Anthropological Association, Memoir No. 69.

Thompson, R.
1958   Modern Yucatecan Maya pottery: a study of the nature of the archeological inference. Society for American Archaeology, Memoir 15.

Trigger, B.
1967   Settlement archaeology—its goals and promise. American Antiquity 32:149-60.

VanStone, J. W.
1957   An archeological reconnaissance of Nunivak Island, Alaska. Anthropological Papers of the University of Alaska 5:97-111.
1967   Eskimos of the Nushagak River: an ethnographic history. University of Washington Publications in Anthropology No. 15, Seattle.
1968   Tikchik Village: a nineteenth century riverine community in southwestern Alaska. Fieldiana: Anthropology, 56 (3), Field Museum of Natural History. Chicago.

Washburn, S. L., ed.
1961   Social life of early man. Viking Fund Publications in Anthropology No. 31.

Webber, M. M.
1964   Culture, territoriality, and the elastic mile. Papers of the Regional Science Association 13:59-69. University of Pennsylvania, Philadelphia.

Willey, G. R.
1953   Phehistoric settlement patterns in the Viru Valley, Peru. Bureau of American Ethnology, Bulletin 155.
1956   Prehistoric settlement patterns in the new world. Viking Fund Publications in Anthropology No. 23.

Willey, G. R., and Phillips, P.
1958   Method and Theory in American Archaeology. Chicago.

ETHNOHISTORICAL RESEARCH
IN SOUTHWESTERN ALASKA:
A METHODOLOGICAL PERSPECTIVE

by James W. VanStone

The purpose of this paper is to describe and evaluate a research methodology which I have utilized for the study of nineteenth-century culture change in the Nushagak River region of southwestern Alaska. Specifically, the project, which is still in progress, consists of a systematic attempt to analyze the diverse aspects of Russian and early American influence on the Eskimos of this area through an application of several research methods. These methods will be discussed along with the broad aims of the project, its achievements to date, and anticipated studies in the future. On the evaluative level, advantages and limitations of the research methodology will be considered along with a brief comparative reference to a similar project in an area contiguous to the Nushagak River region. An attempt will also be made to suggest other areas where similar research might be carried out by historically oriented students of Alaskan Eskimo culture change.

By way of introduction, and as a background against which to view the data presented in this paper, it is perhaps worth noting briefly some recent trends in the development of American Eskimo studies. Archaeological research in Alaska has grown tremendously during the past twenty years, but Alaskan prehistorians have been preoccupied almost exclusively with the earliest cultures in their area. This is understandable when it is remembered that the western arctic is certain to be the region which will provide the most data concerning man's entry into the New World. With a fascinating problem such as this confronting them, it is indeed not surprising that archaeologists have avoided sites belonging to the late prehistoric and historic periods. This emphasis, however, has also meant that many chronological and developmental problems in the area are not yet clearly understood. But it is only fair to note a slow and steadily increasing trend in the other direction. In southeast Alaska (de Laguna 1960; Ackerman 1968), along Prince William Sound (de Laguna 1956, 1964), the Gulf of Alaska (Ackerman 1965), the lower Copper River (VanStone 1955), the middle Kuskokwim River (Oswalt and VanStone 1967), and in the Lake Clark area (VanStone and Townsend 1970), excavations have been made in historic sites.

Turning to a consideration of recent ethnographic studies, we can note that students of Alaskan Eskimo culture have long been aware that the precontact way of life in their area has never been so well documented ethnographically as that of central Canada and Greenland. This has been due largely to the fact that the Eskimo cultures of the eastern arctic remained relatively uninfluenced by external forces right up until the period of modern ethnographic fieldwork in the 1920s. Most of the Alaskan Eskimo groups, on the other hand, had already undergone profound changes by the end of the nineteenth century (Hughes 1965:27-28). Some Alaskan ethnographers, notably Rainey (1947), Lantis (1946), Giddings (1961), and Spencer (1959), were remarkably successful in reconstructing precontact culture, but in recent years the work of anthropologists has focused on modern communities and problems of culture change. To a greater or lesser degree, these studies fail to present a detailed historical perspective (see particularly Hughes 1960; Oswalt 1963b; VanStone 1962). Frequently, the community under discussion seems to exist in a kind of temporal vacuum and it is impossible for the reader to see it as the contemporary end-point in a long process of cultural change, the most significant aspects of which, perhaps, took place in the nineteenth century. This approach to the study of communities may have arisen from the aforemcntioned feeling on the part of northern specialists that the reconstruction of ethnography is no longer profitable or even possible. One suspects, however, that current "fashions" in the study of cultural anthropology may be equally responsible for the neglect of traditional ethnography in Alaska as elsewhere.

Be that as it may, the current interest in modern Eskimo communities and culture change has focused the attention of some specialists, myself included, on the historical process of change. Since present-day Eskimo culture represents the current end-point of change, it has been realized that this culture, studied at the present time, is meaningful to the student of culture per se—its form, its dynamics—only in terms of what can be learned about the earlier periods of its continuum. With this in mind, some ethnographers are beginning to realize that a wealth of historical materials exists for the early period of contact between Eskimos and Europeans in Alaska. At the same time, some students are using the techniques of archaeology not only as a key to an understanding of the remote past but also as an extension of ethnography and history, an important research method for reconstructing the impact of an alien way of life on the culture of the nineteenth-century Eskimos.

My own interests along these lines developed as a result of experience in contemporary Eskimo and Indian communities and the growing realization that the nineteenth century was the decisive period as far as understanding culture change was concerned. Therefore I decided to follow the lead set by Frederica de Laguna in her comprehensive cultural-historical studies of the Tlingit Indians in southeastern Alaska (1956; 1960; 1964) and combine the research methods of history, ethnography, and archaeology for the study of culture change.

In searching for an area in which to begin a long-range research program, my attention focused on southwestern

Alaska for a variety of reasons. To begin with, it is an area that has been generally neglected by anthropologists in spite of the fact that out of a total population of approximately 29,000 Eskimos in all of Alaska, nearly 25,000 of them live in the region between the Yukon and Kuskokwim rivers. This is an area where contact between Eskimos and Europeans took place earlier than in regions farther to the north, and there were a greater number and variety of agents of contact. Most important of all, perhaps, was the opportunity afforded by research in southwestern Alaska to utilize the vast amount of historical source materials in the Russian language that have previously been little used by either historians or anthropologists.

Another attraction of the southwestern Alaska area centered around a research program similar to the one I envisaged but already in progress in the central and lower Kuskokwim River region since 1954 when Wendell Oswalt of the University of California, Los Angeles, began work in that area. In a ten-year period, his studies have included extensive archaeological survey and the plotting of overall shifts of ethnic groups through the historic period, ethnographic research with Kuskokwim River informants, the study of published and unpublished ethnographic and historical source materials, and the investigation of a contemporary Eskimo community (see Oswalt 1962, 1963a, 1963b, 1964). In 1963 his attention turned to archaeological excavation in a nineteenth-century site (Oswalt and Van-Stone 1967).

Because of the many problems that Oswalt's research raised which could be applied to southwestern Alaska as a whole, I decided to begin my studies in an area encompassing the drainage of the Nushagak River, a major river system immediately to the south of the Kuskokwim. Here it would be possible to carry out a program of research that would not only be meaningful in itself, but also an extension of the work being done by Oswalt and thus form part of a major attack on the process of cultural change throughout that vast area between the Yukon River and Bristol Bay. Therefore, his work and my own should be considered closely related because of our common interest in nineteenth-century culture change and our utilization of many of the same research materials.

Historical Sources for the Nushagak River Region

The Nushagak River region is a particularly suitable area for the study of nineteenth-century culture change. The area was penetrated by the Russians early in that century, and the mouth of the river was the site of Aleksandrovski Redoubt, the first Russian trading post north of the Alaska Peninsula, constructed in 1818 (see map). A mission of the Russian Orthodox Church was established at the post in 1842 and the Moravian Church entered the mission field in the area in 1886. The fur trade was well developed throughout the period of contact, and miners, the commercial fishing industry in Bristol Bay, the reindeer herding program, health and education services have all at various times been instrumental in bringing about change in the culture of the population of the region. Of particular importance in this regard has been the commercial salmon fishing industry which began in the ninth decade of the last century and has, since that time, been the major economic factor influencing the lives of the Eskimos of the Nushagak River and Nushagak Bay.

As might be expected, all these agents of contact have provided a rich store of published and archival information on the Eskimos of the region, information that covers most of the nineteenth and early twentieth centuries. Foremost among these are two large collections of archival materials, both of which are of vital importance to anyone undertaking ethnohistorical research concerning Russian America. These are the Alaska Russian Church Archives, deposited in the

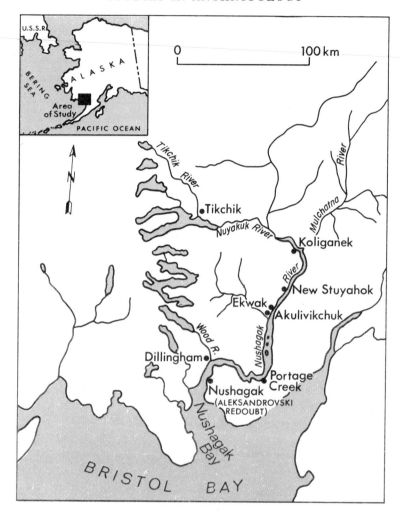

NUSHAGAK REGION

Manuscript Division of the Library of Congress, and the Records of the Russian-American Company in the National Archives. The church records, which represent the complete archive of the Ecclesiastical Consistory of the Russian Orthodox Church in Alaska, are preserved in 1,062 box-portfolios. The material was placed in the Library of Congress in two installments, the first in 1928 and the second in 1940. A partial index and selected translations are included in "Documents Relative to the History of Alaska," a set of fifteen typewritten volumes, copies of which are located in the University of Alaska Library and the Library of Congress. These volumes, the first four of which contain most of the Russian era materials, were compiled as part of the Alaska History Research Project (1936-1938) of the University of Alaska. Since there is no general index to the collection, however, this valuable source has been used only sporadically by historians and ethnohistorians with Alaskan interests. One important section of the collection, the vital statistics for all the Orthodox churches in Alaska, has been microfilmed and is thus more readily available to students. For the area under the jurisdiction of the church at Aleksandrovski, the vital statistics provide a virtually complete record of births, baptisms, deaths, and various other rites of the Orthodox Church from 1842 to 1931. This information is extremely valuable for settlement pattern and population studies and can be used in many other ways as well.

The Records of the Russian-American Company between 1802 and 1867, written in Russian longhand, were transferred to the United States government in accordance with the treaty of cession. The entire collection is on microfilm and has been used to some extent by historians, particularly economic historians concerned with Russian political and economic policies in the nineteenth century. With the assistance of Mr. Winston Sarafian, a graduate student in the Department of History at the University of California, Los Angeles, I have been going through the Records systematically. At the present time, all data dealing with the Kuskokwim and Nushagak river peoples has been extracted and translated. Without becoming involved in a detailed discussion of these sources, it is sufficient to note here that the church archives and the company records have proved invaluable for reconstructing the activities of the two most important Russian institutions in the Nushagak River region and determining their relationship to the aboriginal population.

The Alaska Commercial Company emerged as successor to the Russian-American Company shortly after the purchase of Alaska by the United States in 1867. Unfortunately, however, merchandise inventories and other archival materials dealing with the fur trade in the Nushagak River region during the early American period have not turned up in any of the archival depositories where records of the Alaska Commercial Company are known to exist. It seems fairly certain that these records were destroyed in the San Francisco earthquake and fire of 1906.

A third archival source, the Archives of the Moravian Church in Bethlehem, Pennsylvania, has been consulted but its usefulness is limited, since the Moravians maintained their mission at the mouth of the Nushagak River for a period of only twenty years. The Moravian Archives do, however, contain much valuable data on the related Kuskokwim River region, including the diaries, letters, and papers of John H. Kilbuck, pioneer Moravian missionary on the Kuskokwim.

Notable among published historical sources providing ethnographic data and dealing with culture change in the Nushagak River region are the works of such outstanding authors, scholars, and explorers as I. Veniaminov (Barsukov 1886–1888; 1897–1901), F. P. Wrangell (1839a; 1839b), L. A. Zagoskin (1967), V. N. Berkh (1823), H. J. Holmberg (1856–1863), V. S. Khromchenko (1824), M. D. Tebenkov (1852), P. A. Tikhmenev (1939–1940), W. H. Dall (1870; 1875; 1877), H. W. Elliott (1875; 1886), J. T. Hamilton (1890; 1906), S. Jackson (1886), and A. Hrdlička (1944). Certain official published reports of United States government agencies, notably the bulletins of the Fish Commission, reports of the Commissioner of Fisheries, census reports, bulletins of the Geological Survey, annual reports of the Commissioner of Education, and annual reports of the Governor of Alaska are valuable for tracing the development of Eskimo participation in the commercial fishing industry in Bristol Bay and the activities of other agents of contact during the early American period. Equally important for information on the activities of the Moravian missionaries are the annual *Proceedings of the Society of the United Brethren for Propagating the Gospel among the Heathen,* published by the Moravian Church at Bethlehem, Pennsylvania.

In 1963 I began a detailed study of these and other published and unpublished source materials and prepared an annotated ethnohistorical bibliography on the region (VanStone 1968a) for my own use and the use of others who might become interested in the area. It should be emphasized that in addition to their value for the study of early phases of contact between Eskimos and Europeans, these materials provide a firm foundation from which to consider contemporary Nushagak Eskimo culture.

I have treated the data of the historical source materials always as ethnography rather than as history. My emphasis has not been on the details of discoveries and explorations, although these obviously cannot be ignored, but on the nature of the contact situation. I have been concerned primarily with the attitudes and values of the explorers, traders, and missionaries, since it was these individuals with whom the Eskimos of the Nushagak River region came in the closest and most prolonged contact.

Serious drawbacks, of course, arise from the inadequacies of the historical source materials. Apart from the obvious, and understandable, failure of early observers in the Nushagak River region to record ethnographic data in a manner sufficiently detailed and sophisticated to satisfy the present-day anthropologically trained investigator, it must be noted that the diaries and journals of some of the most important of the earlier explorers are either missing completely or available only in abbreviated form. One thinks immediately of the journal of I. F. Vasiliev, the first Russian to penetrate the upper Nushagak and cross over into the Kuskokwim drainage. His journal, although apparently seen and used by Wrangell and Zagoskin, has never been published and is probably lost. Similarly, the journal of A. Glazunov, the first Russian to explore the Yukon, is available only in a very brief summary (see VanStone 1959). Since Glazunov also traveled on the Kuskokwim and its tributaries, his journal would presumably provide much valuable data on areas peripheral to the Nushagak.

The Records of the Russian-American Company are somewhat disappointing in that they apparently do not contain detailed reports of the various officials who were in charge at Aleksandrovski Redoubt and, for some unexplained reason, maps and other supplementary materials included with communications from the post to company headquarters in Sitka are missing. In the absence of such ideal sources, I anticipate a more thorough analysis of known documents in the future, particularly those in the Alaska Russian Church Archives.

Archaeological and Ethnographic Field Research

Turning now to a consideration of the ethnographic and archaeological dimensions of the Nushagak research project, we come to the actual field research.

The Archaeology

As background, it should be mentioned that my first intensive introduction to historical archaeology in Alaska occurred in the summer of 1963 when I assisted Wendell Oswalt in the excavation of Tulukaghogamiut (Crow Village) on the central Kuskokwim River (Oswalt and

VanStone 1967). This settlement was occupied between about 1840 and 1906, thus embracing both the Russian and early American eras. The major difficulty in interpreting this excavation was that, contrary to our expectations, Russian trade goods and general Russian influence could not be separated stratigraphically from the remains of the early American period. We were able, nevertheless, for the first time to judge the impact of early Euro-American influence, within the sphere of material culture, on the middle Kuskokwim River Eskimos.

With that experience behind me, during the summer of 1964 I conducted an archaeological survey along the Nushagak River and three of its major tributaries, the Wood, Nuyakuk, and lower Mulchatna rivers, locating forty-five sites belonging to the period of historic contact and mapping many of them. During the survey, familiarity with historical source materials for the area was extremely useful, for I already knew the names and locations of many sites. The names of others, together with some population estimates and much ethnographic information, were obtained from informants at the present-day villages of Koliganek, Ekwak, New Stuyahok, Portage Creek, and various locations on Nushagak Bay. Additional ethnographic data and information on nineteenth-century settlements were obtained from informants at Koliganek, Ekwak, and Dillingham after the completion of archaeological excavations during the summers of 1965, 1966, and 1967. The material from historic sources and much of the survey and ethnographic data mentioned above form the basis of a monograph on the ethnohistory of the Nushagak River region (VanStone 1967). Next to come is a detailed report on nineteenth- and early twentieth-century settlement patterns throughout the river system. Information for this study has been obtained on a total of sixty-four sites in the area.

The archaeological survey revealed, among other things, two population centers during the period of historic contact:

an upper and a middle river center. Nushagak Bay, of course, constituted a third and somewhat more populous center. I decided, therefore, to begin intensive excavations in 1965 with one of the upriver sites, the abandoned village of Tikchik near the mouth of the Tikchik River, then continue later with the excavation of one middle river settlement and at least one on Nushagak Bay. Tikchik, a large and important interior settlement, was occupied at least as early as 1829 when it was visited by Vasiliev and was abandoned at the time of the influenza epidemic of 1899–1900. The inhabitants of Tikchik appear to have maintained frequent contact with Aleksandrovski Redoubt and there is evidence that an Orthodox priest was paying infrequent visits to the village as early as 1850. A total of ten houses and two kashgees (ceremonial houses) were excavated and more than 2,000 artifacts recovered (VanStone 1968b). In 1967, archaeological work was continued with the excavation of Akulivikchuk, a nineteenth-century settlement in the middle river area just below the modern village of Ekwak. Here seven houses and a kashgee were excavated and approximately 1,000 artifacts recovered. Akulivikchuk appears to have been abandoned some time between 1880 and 1890 (VanStone, n.d.). In 1969, the archaeological phase of the project was completed with test excavations at Nushagak (Aleksandrovski Redoubt).

Although the materials from these excavations are still in the process of being described and analyzed, certain conclusions are apparent. At each site I was impressed with the adaptability of Eskimo material culture when faced with exotic raw materials as well as finished products of Russian, and later American, import. At the same time, especially impressive was the persistence of traditional Eskimo material culture, particularly in the sphere of subsistence activities, in the face of a pronounced stimulus toward change from the outside. This persistence not only characterized the Russian era but carried over into the early American period during which there was a marked increase in the number and variety of trade goods offered to the people.

As with the historical data, definite drawbacks occur with reference to the archaeological dimension of my studies. The Tikchik, Akulivikchuk, and Nushagak excavations, like those at Crow Village, were characterized by lack of stratigraphic separation between the Russian and American periods. A partial solution to this problem may have been provided by excavations carried out at Kolmakovski Redoubt, a trading center on the middle Kuskokwim River, by Wendell Oswalt during the summers of 1966 and 1967. At Kolmakovski, for the first time such a stratigraphic separation was possible. When the large collection of artifacts from this important site has been studied, we should have new insights into the nature and variety of Russian trade goods to supplement the information in historical sources. It would also be useful to locate, if possible, sites that were occupied solely by Russians or sites occupied by Eskimos during the Russian period only. This appears to be the only certain way in which Russian influences can be assessed accurately apart from American influences, since there will be apparently few sites covering both periods in which a stratigraphic distinction between the two is clear. The total time period, less than a hundred years, is apparently too short for the occurrence of meaningful stratigraphy except under unusual circumstances.

The Ethnography

Much of the ethnographic information collected in Nushagak River villages between 1964 and 1967 consists of settlement pattern data and details concerning the seasonal round of subsistence activities in the early twentieth century. In treating these materials, I have not followed the course of traditional ethnography. American anthropologists have usually considered ethnography, in a narrow sense, to be the descriptive study or natural history of an aboriginal people at essentially one point in time. The Eskimos of the Nushagak River region, however, could not have been studied as aboriginal people except by the earliest Russian travelers. Eskimo culture in the area soon was modified by Russian contacts, and in some localities these changes were rapidly incorporated into the old way of life. Thus my studies have not been strictly ethnographic as the term is usually defined. Rather, I am inclined to consider my work as historical ethnography, the descriptive analysis of a culture as it changes through time. The historical dimension is definitely the key to the analysis. The term *acculturation* expresses the same basic idea as *historical ethnography* but has a more contemporary connotation. The latter term seems preferable because it stresses primary interest in the temporal aspects of culture change with the emphasis on cross-disciplinary research.

In viewing the changes that occurred as the result of contact throughout southwestern Alaska, attention is immediately focused on the trading and mission centers. In the Bering Sea area there were the redoubts of Aleksandrovski at the mouth of the Nushagak River (later called Nushagak by Anglo-Americans), Mikhailovski north of the mouth of the Yukon River, and Kolmakovski on the middle Kuskokwin River, as well as the Orthodox Church center at Russian Mission on the lower Yukon. These settlements, which might be termed contact communities, were located either in small Eskimo villages or on previously unoccupied sites near aboriginal settlements. These outposts were supplied under conditions which necessitated hazardous sea voyages or long trips with portages along inland rivers and streams. The trading center inventories appear always to have been limited in variety and abundance. Each post was manned by a few individuals representing the Russian-American Company, the Orthodox Church, or both, and resident Eskimos aided in maintaining the establishments.

The traders and mission officials were often of a mixed racial and cultural heritage. They were educated by the Russians and thus reasonably familiar with both Russian and Eskimo ways. From these centers, particularly the redoubts, trade goods and food products flowed to the adjacent settlements, primarily in exchange for furs. The spheres of influence of these isolated posts represented zones of contact intensity between the Russians and Eskimos.

With the sale of Alaska to the United States, this overall pattern did not change a great deal. The American firm, the Alaska Commercial Company, that acquired the holdings of the Russian-American Company continued to maintain posts in the three trading centers. There are indications, however, that after 1880 the inventory of goods traded to the Eskimos throughout southwestern Alaska increased considerably. The Russian Orthodox Church, after expressing initial concern about the continued presence of its clergymen, eventually decided to operate much as before. In fact, it is probably safe to say that not until the advent of commercial salmon fishing in Bristol Bay in the 1880s did the Eskimos of the Nushagak River region begin to experience contact situations radically different from those they had been accustomed to during the Russian period.

Use of the Data

Through the use of historic source materials and the ethnographic and archaeological approaches just outlined, I have attempted to establish as far as possible the near-aboriginal baseline culture of the Nushagak Eskimos in the early nineteenth century as well as the subcultural systems introduced by the Russians and, after 1867, by the Americans. In each instance I have been concerned not only with specific traits such as bows, sleds, and fish spears, or tea, trade beads, and iron tools, but with the patterns into which these and other items fitted. These objectives seem simple and straightforward enough, but they are proving difficult to achieve.

With reference to the ethnographic dimension of the research, it is most important to note that the type of fieldwork carried out in the past is not possible today. A picture of the aboriginal culture or the early period of contact with Europeans may not be adequately reconstructed through work with informants alone. Even in a comparatively isolated area such as the one under discussion, where aboriginal lifeways have persisted for a long period of time compared with other areas of North America, few informants are to be found who recall even the period when the impact of an alien culture was relatively restricted. The best that can be hoped for is that historically minded individuals will preserve information obtained from older relatives and that they will be able and interested enough to pass the information along at secondhand or thirdhand to the ethnographer. Hence the need for the primary sources: the archaeological and documentary records.

Before leaving the subject of ethnography, something should be said concerning ethnographic collections in museums from the Nushagak River region. Although a number of American and European museums have small collections from the area, the largest and best documented is in the United States National Museum in Washington, D. C. This collection, consisting of approximately 400 specimens, was made by C. L. McKay and J. W. Johnson, United States Army Signal Service observers at Nushagak in the early 1880s. I have found these materials extremely useful not only because many interesting items of aboriginal material culture are represented but also because the collection reflects changing technology of the late nineteenth century. Data on the McKay and Johnson collections is being incorporated into a report on archaeological excavations at Nushagak.

Conclusions and Suggestions

It will be apparent from the previous discussion that in spite of the utilization of a varied methodology for the study of nineteenth-century culture change in the Nushagak River region, my accomplishments to date have been very modest. I am convinced, however, that given the material and recognition of the fact that such a project is essentially a salvage operation, the methodology is sound. Furthermore, I also feel strongly that if the complexities of changing Alaskan Eskimo culture today are to be fully understood, it is necessary to construct as much of a baseline of aboriginal culture as possible in any area and then deal chronologically and progressively with the changes as they occurred in the earlier periods of historic contact. Because of the inadequacies of any one approach to this problem, I believe that desirable results can be achieved only through a combined use of history, ethnography, and archaeology.

It seems likely that the research combination described in this paper could be extended to other areas in southwestern Alaska. Excavations at early historic sites along the lower Yukon River, for example, particularly in the vicinity of the mouth of the Innoko River, would broaden our perspective considerably. Settlement patterns for this area were carefully documented by Zagoskin (1967:231-42) in 1842–1844, and Frederica de Laguna conducted an archaeological survey there in 1935 (de Laguna 1947:74-76). The proximity of the important Russian post at Nulato is also a significant factor.

Farther to the north, similar studies might profitably be carried out on Seward Peninsula. This region was heavily populated during the nineteenth century and much of the basic settlement pattern research has already been done by Dorothy Jean Ray (1964). The archaeological dimension is the one that is especially needed now.

In conclusion, I emphasize that the research methods on

which my Nushagak studies have been and will continue to be based are basic to more sophisticated anthropological studies and interpretations in the area. Given the virtual impossibility of reconstructing a complete aboriginal baseline against which to measure Nushagak Eskimo culture today, the next best thing is to provide a record of the early cultural acquisitions and losses and perhaps from these—incomplete as the record is—to delineate patterns and processes that help to make the present understandable. Despite the difficulties, I firmly believe that the time is rapidly approaching when it will be possible, by use of historical, ethnographic, and archaeological data, to make broad generalizations about the impact of Euro-Americans on Eskimos during the nineteenth and early twentieth centuries.

References

Ackerman, R. E.
1965   Archeological survey, Glacier Bay National Monument, southeastern Alaska, pt. 2. Report of Investigations No. 36. Laboratory of Anthropology, Washington State University.
1968   The archeology of the Glacier Bay region, southeastern Alaska. Report of Investigations No. 44. Laboratory of Anthropology, Washington State University.

Barsukov, I., ed.
1886–1888   Tvoreniya Innokentiya, Mitropolita Moskovskago. 3 vols. in 2. Moscow.
1897–1901   Pisma Innokentiya, Mitropolita Moskovskago i Kolomenskago 1828–1878. 3 vols. St. Petersburg.

Berkh, V. N.
1823   Puteshestvie uchenika morekhodstva Andreya Ustiyugova, i sluzhiteley Rossiiskoy Amerikanskoy Kompanii Fedora Kolmakova i Petra Korsanovskago v 1819 godu. Severnyi Arkhiv, pt. 4.

Dall, W. H.
1870   Alaska and Its Resources. Boston.
1875   Abstract of population of the native tribes of Alaska. *In* Annual Report of the Commissioner of Indian Affairs to

the Secretary of the Interior for the Year 1875. Washington.

1877   On the distribution and nomenclature of the native tribes of Alaska and the adjacent territory. *In* Tribes of the extreme northwest. Contributions to North American Ethnology 1. Washington.

de Laguna, F.
1947   The prehistory of northern North America as seen from the Yukon. Society for American Archaeology, Memoir 3.
1956   Chugach prehistory: the archaeology of Prince William Sound, Alaska. University of Washington Publications in Anthropology 13.
1960   The story of a Tlingit community: a problem in the relationship between archeological, ethnological, and historical methods. Bureau of American Ethnology, Bulletin 172. Washington.

de Laguna, F., et al.
1964   Archeology of the Yakutat Bay area, Alaska. Bureau of American Ethnology, Bulletin 192. Washington.

Elliott, H. W.
1875   A report upon the condition of affairs in the territory of Alaska. Washington.
1886   Our Arctic Province: Alaska and the Seal Islands. New York.

Giddings, J. L.
1961   Kobuk River people. University of Alaska, Studies of Northern Peoples No. 1. College.

Hamilton, J. T.
1890   The Beginnings of the Moravian Mission in Alaska. Bethlehem, Pa.
1906   Report of the Official Visit of Bishop J. Taylor Hamilton to the Mission in Southern California and Alaska, 1906. Bethlehem, Pa.

Holmberg, H. J.
1856–1863   Ethnographische Skizzen über die Völker des Russischen Amerika. 2 vols. Helsingfors.

Hrdlička, A.
1944   Alaska Diary. Lancaster, Pa.

Hughes, C. C.
1960   An Eskimo Village in the Modern World. Ithaca, N. Y.

1965   Under four flags: recent culture change among the Eskimos. Current Anthropology 6 (1):3-69.

Jackson, S.
1886   Report on Education in Alaska. Washington.

Khromchenko, V. S.
1824   Otryvki iz zhurnala plavaniya g Khromchenki, v 1822 godu. Severnyi Arkhiv, pts. 10, 11.

Lantis, M.
1946   The social culture of the Nunivak Eskimo. Transactions of the American Philosophical Society 35 (3). Philadelphia.

Oswalt, W. H.
1962   Historical populations in western Alaska and migration theory. Anthropological Papers of the University of Alaska 11 (1):1-14.
1963a   Mission of change in Alaska. Eskimos and Moravians on the Kuskokwim. San Marino, Calif.
1963b   Napaskiak: An Alaskan Eskimo Community. Tucson, Ariz.
1964   Traditional storyknife tales of Yuk girls. Proceedings of the American Philosophical Society 108 (4):310-36.

Oswalt, W. H., and VanStone, J. W.
1967   The ethnoarcheology of Crow Village, Alaska. Bureau of American Ethnology, Bulletin 199. Washington.

Rainey, F. G.
1947   The whalehunters of Tigara. Anthropological Papers of the American Museum of Natural History 41 (2):231-83.

Ray, D. J.
1964   Nineteenth century settlement and subsistence patterns in Bering Strait. Arctic Anthropology 2 (2):61-69.

Spencer, R. F.
1959   The north Alaskan Eskimo: a study in ecology and society. Bureau of American Ethnology, Bulletin 171. Washington.

Tebenkov, M. D.
1852   Atlas severozapadnykh beregov Ameriki ot Beringova proliva do mysa Korrientes i ostrovov Aleutiskh c prisovokupleniem nekotorykh mest Severovostochnago berega Azii. Gidroograficheskiya zamechaniya k atlasu severozapadnykh beregov Ameriki, ostrovov Aleutskikh i nekotorykh drugikh mest Severnago Tikhogo okeana. St. Petersburg.

Tikhmenev, P. A.
1939–1940 The historical review of the formation of the Russian-American Company and its activity up to the present time. 2 pts. St. Petersburg. (Translated by Dimitri Krenov, Works Progress Administration, Seattle, Wash.)

VanStone, J. W., and Townsend, J. B.
1970 Kijik: an historic Tanaina Indian settlement. Fieldiana: Anthropology, 59.

VanStone, J. W.
1955 Exploring the Copper River country. Pacific Northwest Quarterly, 26 (4):115-23.
1959 Russian exploration in interior Alaska: an extract from the journal of Andrei Glazunov. Pacific Northwest Quarterly, 50 (2):37-47.
1962 Point Hope: An Eskimo Village in Transition. Seattle, Wash.
1967 Eskimos of the Nushagak River: An Ethnographic History. Seattle, Wash.
1968a An annotated ethnohistorical bibliography of the Nushagak River region, Alaska. Fieldiana: Anthropology, 54 (2).
1968b Tikchik village: a nineteenth-century riverine community in southwestern Alaska. Fieldiana: Anthropology, 56 (3).
n.d. Akulivikchuk: a nineteenth-century Eskimo village on the Nushagak River, Alaska. Fieldiana: Anthropology. (In press.)

Wrangell, F. P.
1839a Obitateli severo-zapadnikh beregov Ameriki. Syn Otechestva 7:51-82.
1839b Statistische und ethnographische Nachrichten über die Russischen Besitzungen an der Nordwestküste von Amerika. In Beiträge zur Kenntniss des Russischen Reiches und der angrenzenden Lander Asiens, Bd. 1. St. Petersburg.

Zagoskin, L. A.
1967 Lieutenant Zagoskin's travels in Russian America, 1842–1844. The first ethnographic and geographic investigations in the Yukon and Kuskokwim valleys of Alaska, ed. Henry N. Michael. Arctic Institute of North America, Anthropology of the North, Translations from Russian Sources, No. 7. Toronto.

TANAINA ETHNOHISTORY:
AN EXAMPLE OF A METHOD
FOR THE STUDY OF CULTURE CHANGE

by Joan B. Townsend

One of the more significant trends in anthropology in recent years is an increased attempt to understand the processes of culture change.[1] Quite valid alternative methods of going about this have been suggested by numerous researchers, but I agree with Herskovits (1958), Steward (1942), and others who consider time depth essential to comprehend the dynamics of culture change. In my opinion, one of the more effective ways to work toward such an understanding is to analyze one culture in detail in order to determine in what ways it has changed and, if possible, what were some of the factors motivating a change in one direction rather than in some alternative direction. It seems most reasonable to utilize methods which will provide data from the longest timespan possible for the culture considered. Significant features in the process of change then may be perceived which might be overlooked in a study concerned with a very short time period.

Ethnohistory, as it is generally understood and as it is defined by Herskovits (1958:473), is the fusing of historical documentation with ethnographic materials of the same period to provide a more complete picture of a culture. Ethnohistory, then, becomes one of the mechanisms for realizing this first and all-important goal of establishing the basic data and making the analysis of it, upon which more general work may be later initiated. It is not, however, the only method used in such a study of change. A direct historical approach to both archaeology and ethnography can be incorporated with ethnohistory to give a cultural sequence its greatest range. To give a culture as great a timespan as possible would involve ideally a linking of archaeology, accounts by explorers, traders, missionaries, and other early observers, ethnographic information concerning the more recent past from elderly informants, as well as observation and ethnographic study of the modern population. Only after several cultures have been documented in this way, can we begin to compare results of the analysis of evidence and derive some generalities permitting us to continue our investigations of culture change at a higher level of abstraction.

The objective of this paper is to demonstrate a method of establishing data from archaeology, ethnohistory, and ethnography and interpreting them. The concern of this paper is with the most tangible level of study of culture change: the documentation of persistence and change within a specific culture. On the basis of this information, I will suggest some of the possible causal factors in the dynamics of that culture.

The Culture Studied

The Tanaina Indians, the Athabaskan group to be used in this study, are distributed along the Susitna River, at Tyonek, on the Kenai Peninsula, and in the Iliamna Lake region, all in Southwestern Alaska, north, east, and west of Cook Inlet (see map). In this paper, I am specifically interested in the Tanaina who occupy the Iliamna region.

Iliamna Lake is approximately ninety miles long and forty miles wide. Today, the Tanaina occupy the forested areas of the mountainous northeastern shore of Iliamna. Their village is Pedro Bay. Tanaina are also found at Nondalton, a village on Sixmile Lake, between Lake Clark

[1] I would like to express my appreciation to Dr. William J. Mayer-Oakes for his assistance in the preparation of this manuscript. His suggestions, criticisms, and editorial comments have been invaluable.

MODERN TANAINA BOUNDARIES

and Iliamna Lake. In 1900 they maintained two other villages: Kijik on Lake Clark and Old Iliamna at the eastern tip of Iliamna Lake. These have been abandoned in the last forty years in favor of Nondalton and Pedro Bay.

The fauna of the area is rich. Big game animals, birds, and fish are plentiful. One of the largest salmon runs in the world enters Bristol Bay each summer and many of these fish find their way up the Kvichak River into Iliamna Lake and the small streams tributary to it. Since the salmon is a plentiful and reliable source of food, the Tanaina have based their subsistence on it. Because of the abundance of food, the Tanaina have been able to maintain a relatively stable and sedentary way of life and maintain villages of some

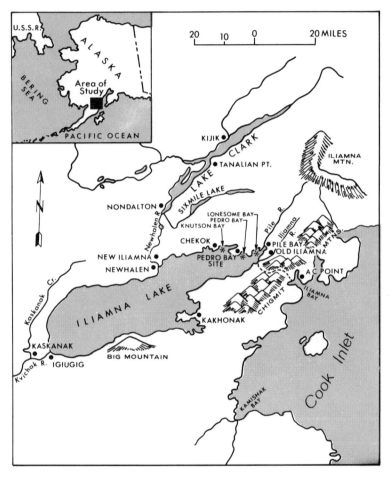

LAKE ILIAMNA AND LAKE CLARK REGION

time depth. They can be classified in the scheme of cultural stages proposed by Beardsley et al. (1956) as "semipermanent sedentary."

In a study of Tanaina culture change, general information is needed concerning their location at early contact and precontact times, the size of their populations, and their relationships with the Europeans who began to enter the

Cook Inlet area of southwestern Alaska in the late 1700s in quest of furs. Together with this general historical context, facts are needed which deal with a more specific study of the Tanaina culture itself. In this respect, I am particularly interested in the kind of social organization as well as the kind of economy the Tanaina had as far back in time as it can projected. Further, I am interested in the changes in these aspects of culture that have occurred through the timespan considered.[2] The social organization and the subsistence and trade aspects of the economy are seen as highly integrated major aspects of the culture. The Russian fur trade most obviously and directly affected the economy of the Tanaina. Because of the interrelationships of the economy with the social organization, one cannot be considered without reference to the other. I think that in these two areas of the culture, the more significant aspects of change can be discerned. Presumably, general information regarding the population, its movements and its relationships with Europeans also will have a direct relationship to the changes or persistences which may be discovered in the culture itself. Conversely, the culture of the Tanaina would be reflected in their relationships with and reactions to the Europeans.

Sources of Data

Ethnohistory

The Russian fur traders began to enter southwestern Alaska toward the end of the 1700s, establish fur trading stations, and enter into trade with the Indians and Eskimos of the area. Other Europeans, including Davydov, Lisiansky, Cook, Vancouver, Portlock, Dixon, and Meares, occasionally entered the Cook Inlet area with ships on missions of

---

[2] Total timespan would be about 250 years: from just before Russian contact to the present, that is, approximately 1710 to 1960. My major attention necessarily was focused on the period of documented change, which would be about 150 years.

exploration and trade. These latter recorded their observations of native peoples in journals which were later published as books of the voyages (see Part 2, Lantis: The Sources). The Russians stationed in Alaska, however, confined their writings usually to diaries and correspondence between the Alaskan outposts and the fur trading companies' headquarters in Siberia. After 1799, the Russian-American Company was formed and documents pertaining to that company's relationships with the Alaskans occur. In 1794 Russian priests began to enter the Cook Inlet area, and they continued to be active throughout the nineteenth century.

The Alaska Russian Church Archives are now located in the Library of Congress of the United States. The Archives contain vital statistics from the various Russian missions that existed in the nineteenth century. They provide lists of births, confirmations, marriages, and deaths of people within the mission's sphere. These records are the only fairly accurate source of population data for the Iliamna area during most of the nineteenth century, so far as I am aware. "Documents Relative to the History of Alaska" was an attempt to establish an index to these materials and translate some of the more pertinent sections. The manuscript contains a collection of translations of materials from the Russian Orthodox Church files, private letters and papers, and other materials. Within this collection the priests' journals have been found to be particularly significant. Priests were required to travel to all the villages of their parish as often as possible. In southwestern Alaska, trips were supposed to be made every year or two. Their travel journals were then sent to the bishop at Sitka for appraisal of their works. Descriptions in the journals provide additional information concerning the native populations.

There are various summaries which include translations of Russian documents and take into consideration the history of southwestern Alaska. Among the more significant are

Tikhmenev's *Historical Review of the Formation of the Russian-American Company and Its Activity up to the Present Time* (1861–1863) and Bancroft's *History of Alaska 1730–1885* (1886). The Bancroft Library in Berkeley, California, retains some English translations of Russian materials in their Pacific Manuscripts which Bancroft used in writing his history. Andreyev has published papers concerning the Russian activities in the Pacific and North America in the late eighteenth and early nineteenth centuries. An English translation of Andreyev is available. Ivan Petroff not only contributed to Bancroft's *History of Alaska* but also compiled the *Report on the Population, Industries and Resources of Alaska* for the U.S. Census of 1880 (1884). Porter was responsible for the Alaskan census report for 1890 (1893). Both these census studies incorporate information on native populations of Alaska in the latter half of the nineteenth century. Works concerning the middle part of the nineteenth century include Richardson's *Arctic Searching Expedition* (1851) and Vrangel's *Statistische und ethnographische Nachrichten über die Russieschen Besitzungen an der Nordwestküste von Amerika* (1839).

Ethnography

Cornelius Osgood visited several Tanaina communities in 1931 and spent one or two weeks in the Iliamna area. His *Ethnography of the Tanaina* (1937) provides the first anthropological study of them. He attempted to reconstruct the culture of the Tanaina in the ethnographic present primarily through interviews with elderly informants. Some current demographic, health, and other information is available in government reports such as the Base Line Studies of the Arctic Health Research Center. My work presented in *Ethnohistory and Culture Change of the Iliamna Tanaina* (1965) includes current information of a wider range as well as culture historical data. There are numerous other minor sources for information which will contribute to a historically oriented study of the Tanaina, and the reader is referred to Townsend (1965) for a fuller bibliography.

Archaeology

Unfortunately, very little archaeology has been done in the Iliamna Tanaina area (Townsend and Townsend 1961; VanStone and Townsend, 1970). The paucity of the work is partly explained by the difficulties for archaeology in this region which is in the boreal forest. Sites are virtually impossible to locate unless the archaeologist is taken to them by local people who have come across the semisubterranean houses of former villages during their hunting and trapping activities. Preservation in such sites is very poor, and even bone decays rapidly. Another major problem is one of interpretation. The Tanaina of Iliamna live in very close contact with the Aglegmiut Eskimo of the western portion of Iliamna Lake. In the past, the two populations fought, kept each other as slaves, and occasionally intermarried. Consequently, considerable cultural borrowing occurred, and it is often difficult to decide whether an archaeological site of precontact or early contact times is Eskimo or a site of Tanaina Indians who have adopted some of the material culture of the neighboring Eskimos. It also is difficult to date the late prehistoric and protohistoric material. The late Pedro Bay component may be dated, with reservations, at about 1750.[3]

Integration of Types of Data

The historical study of Tanaina culture requires using what little archaeological material is available, from all time periods, and gleaning significant and pertinent data from the Russian and other sources of the eighteenth and nineteenth centuries. Osgood's ethnographic material may

[3] The dating depends on whether one wants to interpret the few trade beads as the result of long-range, intertribal trade or of Russian movements into the Southwest Alaskan area.

be assumed to reflect a period after 1850, since he was relying on the recollections of informants who were old in 1931. Finally, my own data from informants include myths and legends that provide details of material and social culture which may reflect aboriginal patterns, recollections of elderly informants referring to a period between the late 1800s and early 1900s, and my own observations of the culture as it exists today (as of 1962).

The following brief description of Tanaina culture change and persistence using the combined resources of ethnohistory, archaeology, and ethnography is presented only as an example. It is necessarily sketchy because of the space limitations of this paper. It is not intended to provide a detailed analysis; this will be the basis of a forthcoming book.

General Tanaina Historical Data

It seems quite certain that the Tanaina occupied the region surrounding Cook Inlet in precontact times. Archaeological work has not proceeded far enough, however, to determine with any degree of certainty just how long they have been there. I would suggest that they moved into the area at least a hundred years prior to the coming of the Russians in the last quarter of the eighteenth century. This date is simply an estimation based on the indications including those given below and cannot and should not be used as though it were supported by facts from extensive archaeological excavation and carbon-14 dates. The descriptions of the people encountered by the early Europeans, both Russian and English, after about 1784 indicate not only that the people in Cook Inlet were Tanaina, but they were quite well established in the area in sizable numbers.

Location at Time of European Contact

According to Bancroft (1886:144), when Glottov reached Kodiak in 1762 to trade with the Koniags, a boy told him that they often traded with the "Aglegnutes of Aliaska Peninsula and with the Tnaianas of the Kenai Peninsula" [*sic*]. This is the earliest reference to the Tanaina, and it indicates that they had already established themselves in the Cook Inlet region before European contact.

Captain James Cook visited southwestern Alaska in 1778. At Prince William Sound he met and described Eskimos. Later he entered Cook Inlet and met other native peoples. These he also described and contrasted with the Eskimos of Prince William Sound. The individuals and the material culture he reported strongly resemble some later descriptions of Tanaina, including some of Osgood's ethnographic-present descriptions. In December 1785 Shelikov, the head of one of the fur trading companies, wrote that during the previous year the Russians had taken four hundred child hostages as a pledge of friendship by the Indians and Eskimos (Andreyev 1952:34).

Portlock and Dixon sailed into Cook Inlet to trade in July 1786. The description of the people with whom they traded closely parallels descriptions of Tanaina recorded by Osgood from information provided by his informants.

An English translation of a diary, alleged to be that of Father Juvenal, is available in the Bancroft Library and has been published in the *Kroeber Anthropological Society Papers* (1952). If we can assume that this diary is authentic, then we have additional evidence that the Tanaina were established in Cook Inlet and the Iliamna region at the time of European contact. Juvenal, one of the first Russian missionaries to Alaska, at first was stationed at Kodiak among the Koniag Eskimo. He was later sent to the Kenai Peninsula and then across Cook Inlet into the interior in the region of Iliamna Lake and Lake Clark in 1796. Juvenal's description of the Kenai and Iliamna people contrasts with his description of the Koniags. There is no doubt that he is describing Tanaina Indians.

Negative evidence can also be marshaled to establish that the Tanaina were in the Cook Inlet-Iliamna region before the Russians arrived. We have no remarks stating that there was a movement of an Indian population into an area which was populated by another (Eskimo) group. If such a population movement had occurred, we can be certain that skirmishes and probably more severe battles would have been fought. Surely these would not have missed the attention of the Russians who were located in the midst of the Kenai population after 1786.

Nature of First Contact with Europeans

At the time of Russian contact, the Tanaina had a reputation among the native populations of being powerful and certainly a group to be reckoned with. Tanaina legends continually refer to battles between their villages and with the Eskimo. Slaves were often taken and whole villages were occasionally annihilated. From the stories, it would appear that the hostilities between Indians and Eskimos continued through the Russian contact period. There had been battles also between the native peoples, particularly the Tanaina, Chugach, and Koniag Eskimos, and the Russians in attempts to expel the latter. The Koniag "chief" of Shuyak Island, just north of Afognak Island, in 1786 went so far as to enlist the aid of his enemies, the Chugach and Tanaina. He was able to organize a war party of a thousand men but, because of intertribal enmity, the party broke up before it was fully organized (Bancroft 1886:228). Dixon (1789:60) observed in 1786 that the Russians who were camped on the Kenai Peninsula did not seem to be on particularly friendly terms with the Tanaina. They never went to sleep without their arms loaded and ready by their sides. The Russians had been instructed to establish a fort on the Kenai Peninsula only if reinforcements of men from Russia arrived (Bancroft 1886:229-30, *n.* 15).

After the aborted attempt by the Koniags of Shuyak Island to wipe out the Russians, the latter counterattacked. By the end of the season, they reported success along the coast of Cook Inlet "after severe chastisement of the hostile

Kenaitsy" (Petroff 1884:99). In 1786, after violent battles the Russians did succeed in establishing a trading post among the Tanaina of Cook Inlet. Between 1788 and 1789, the Tanaina again attempted to kill the Russians who settled among them (Andreyev 1952:107), but subsequently accepted them. When Juvenal planned his trip into the Iliamna Lake region seven years later, he was repeatedly warned about the "very bad" Iliamna Tanaina (Juvenal 1952:47). Some limited trade was conducted between the Russians and the Iliamna Lake people, mainly using the Kenai Tanaina as middlemen. Russians had attempted repeatedly, after 1785, to establish a post among the most powerful Tanaina, those of Iliamna. On at least one occasion a post was established, but it was destroyed in 1799 by the Indians, according to both Bancroft (1886:392) and Davydov (1812:134) and the Indian legends (Townsend 1965:54, 318-19). It was not until after 1818 that they were finally successful in establishing a permanent post there.

Portlock and Dixon came into Cook Inlet to trade in the summer of 1786, presumably not long after the unsuccessful Shuyak Island Koniag battle and the Russian reprisals on the Koniags and the Tanaina. Dixon reported a number of recently deserted huts, especially in the Graham Harbor area (Portlock 1789:107). The present-day Tanaina of Nondalton and Pedro Bay recall that their grandparents came from the Mulchatna River and Stony River regions which are inland, north of Iliamna Lake. However, they say that their ancestors actually were from the Cook Inlet area. They merely moved into the interior to escape the contacts with and subjugation by the Russians. It is possible that Dixon's observation of deserted huts is associated with the movement of the Tanaina into the interior to escape the Russians which was described by my informants.

Population
Population information is minimal for the Tanaina during the nineteenth century. By using vital statistics of the

Alaska Russian Church Archives after 1849, Tikhmenev's numbers (1861–1863), and the census reports of Petroff (1884) and Porter (1893), we can estimate the size of the Tanaina population. For the latter half of the nineteenth century the population probably was about 1,000.[4] It must be recalled that this is an estimate after the severe smallpox epidemic of 1836 which decimated the native populations (Bancroft 1886:561). Consequently, the population at the end of the eighteenth century and the first half of the nineteenth century could easily have reached 3,000. (For a fuller account of the method of deriving the population figures from assorted census sources, see Townsend 1965: 85-99.)

Osgood's work (1937) and my research indicate that during the mid-nineteenth century the Tanaina had classes and a concept of wealth related to prestige. For a social organization comprising classes and wealth concepts to develop to the degree that it did among the Tanaina after they began to be involved in the fur trade, a relatively large population would be requisite. We would hardly expect a development such as the Tanaina prestige system to occur among small mobile bands.

Historical Conclusions

In summary, legends and historical documents indicate that the Tanaina Indians were in Cook Inlet and the Iliamna area in sizable numbers at the time of Russian contact. Further, it seems quite certain that they were a powerful group, able to hold their own among other powerful native peoples and against the Russians. While population movements of the Tanaina into the interior after Russian contact seem to have originated from the Cook Inlet area, research indicates that the original Iliamna population did not make moves farther inland. After 1786, some of the Cook Inlet

[4] The population appears to have remained fairly stable. Although enumeration of the mobile Tanaina is inexact, total population probably is slightly less than 1,000.

population moved into the interior as far as the Mulchatna
and Stony rivers. Toward the latter half of the nineteenth
century, according to informants, the people began to drift
back down toward the coast. The village of Kijik was
established on Lake Clark by 1840 and was abandoned in
favor of Nondalton, about fifteen miles nearer to Iliamna
and Cook Inlet, by 1910.

Tanaina Social Organization and Economic Data

The main source of the following material is my study
Ethnohistory and Culture Change of the Iliamna Tanaina
(1965). To avoid repetition, it is not cited after each topic.
Some other sources are cited in reference to specific comments even though they are to be found within my 1965
study. This procedure has been followed here not only to
provide additional support to my discussion but also to make
it simpler for the reader to locate the original source of a
statement.

The aboriginal and historic social organization and
economy of the Tanaina are more difficult to ascertain than
the general history. For this information we must rely on
comments from European observers in the early period as
well as the ethnographic data and folk tales. Data from all
these sources have been ordered chronologically, taking into
consideration the period in which the Europeans observed
the people. It was assumed that both Osgood's information
and my historical information obtained from informants did
not reflect the aboriginal period, but rather the time after
the Russian fur trade began to affect the culture of the
people. This would have occurred after the middle of the
nineteenth century and would have been about the time
Osgood's and my informants' parents and grandparents were
living. Folk tales, particularly those which incorporated the
trickster and had no reference to Europeans, were usually
considered aboriginal.

Aboriginal Period

Social Organization. In aboriginal times it is probable that the Tanaina society was composed of at least eleven matrilineal sibs divided into two moieties. One function of a moiety was at the time of a death. The members of one moiety prepared the body and did other necessary jobs for the opposing moiety. In payment, the bereaved moiety members gave a potlatch for the assisting moiety. Richardson (1851:406), who described the sibs and moieties in the first half of the nineteenth century, also remarked that a child belonged to the "race" (sib) of the mother. It is very doubtful that a sib organization of the magnitude described could have developed only during the first fifty years of Russian contact. Portlock (1789:113), at the time of very early contact, noted that the Indians wore red and black face paint. Osgood (1937:53) identified red and black face paint as sib markings. Further, matrilineal sibs are known from other Na-déné peoples of southern Alaska including the Tanaina Athapaskans and the Tlingit.

Residence patterns are particularly unclear from aboriginal times. Folk tales from my informants suggest that residence was matrilocal or possibly bilocal. Matrilocality appears to have been more of a tendency than a hard-and-fast rule. Davydov (1812:148), who observed the Tanaina before much change from Russian influence could have occurred, stated that a boy went to a girl's home and presented her parents with a gift. He then slept with the girl. If the girl wanted to stay with her parents, she and her husband would build an addition to the girl's parents' house and assist them. According to the folk tales, houses tended to be large extended-family semisubterranean dwellings, and archaeological excavations substantiate the house type (Townsend and Townsend 1961).

It is possible that a loose class system may have existed at this time. Portlock (1789:113) recorded that the adornment of the Indians seemed always in proportion to their individual wealth. They seemed to have persons of authority who directed the trade, and some of the other people appeared to be in some degree of subordination.

Economy. The underlying subsistence base on which the society was founded was, in aboriginal times, salmon. Early traders commented on the abundance of this food (Dixon 1789:63). Trade was conducted by the Tanaina with neighboring Koniag and the Copper River people for such items as copper arrowheads, cedar arrow shafts, and animal skins. At no time did the Tanaina rely on trade for essentials. Their subsistence base, salmon, was readily available at home. Trade was for luxury goods only: those items which were not necessary for survival although they might permit added enjoyment, ease, or pleasure in life.

Fur Trade Period

Social Organization. Matrilineal sibs continued to function through the nineteenth century. Osgood (1937) provides considerable information on them, and my informants recalled some aspects of them. Until 1850, inheritance still tended to be matrilineal (Richardson 1851:406), but in the final half of the nineteenth century, apparently a shift began. Osgood (1937:141, 143) had conflicting evidence. Some informants maintained that inheritance was from parent to child. However, subtle evidence suggested that property was owned by the matrilineal sibs. Evidences from other sources (Learnard 1900:667) suggests that by the end of the nineteenth century some property began to be passed from father to son.

Another indication of social organization in a state of change was the uncle-nephew relationship. The uncle still assisted in the training of the boy, but it no longer had to be the mother's brother; an uncle from either the father's or mother's side of the family could be in charge (Osgood 1937:143-44; Sheldon 1908:272).

In the last half of the nineteenth century, the residence patterns and the way of obtaining a wife were also shifting. About 1850, bride-service was performed for a year. Then it was said that a boy could return "home" with his bride (Richardson 1851:406-407). It is not certain whether "home" referred to patrilocal or neolocal residence. A girl took along a dowry. It remained her property, however, and she took it back with her if she were later divorced. Osgood's informants (1937:163-65), reflecting back to the latter half of the nineteenth century, indicated that both bride-service and bride-price occurred. A boy had to accumulate property and experience before he could acquire a wife, and he might be as old as thirty before this was possible. A potlatch became necessary in order to validate the marriage. A poor man also had to do a bride-service from one to five years. However, if a rich man wanted a girl, he merely paid a large bride-price and took the girl. Iliamna informants indicate that a girl was "tried out" by the boy's parents before they made the investment in her. She lived in their house for a year so that they could see whether she was accomplished at cooking and sewing and was industrious before the final decision was made.

Polygyny, although it was permitted earlier, became a status symbol for a wealthy man (Osgood 1937:164). Wives were becoming so expensive that only a rich man could afford more than one.

Potlatches began to be given not only at a death, but also to honor a living person and to legitimize a marriage. A rich man might give one in order to help a poor man. It became one of the main mechanisms for establishment and display of status through wealth (Osgood 1937:133-35, 149-60; Abbot Nicholas DRHA 2:54).

Osgood, using data of the ethnographic present (1937: 55-62), described semisubterranean houses similar to those of the aboriginal period. Toward the last quarter of the nineteenth century, houses began to be constructed above ground of logs, but generally they remained extended-family dwellings (Petroff 1884:26; VanStone and Townsend, 1970: 29-45). Presumably the inhabitants could be composed of the wealthy family and the poorer relatives and slaves.

Any wealthy man was considered a chief at Iliamna. Among his wealth was counted the poor relatives and slaves who worked for him as well as his material goods.

The Russian Orthodox Church missionaries did not become active in the Iliamna area until after 1840. It is doubtful, however, whether their influence began to be felt very strongly until the last third of the nineteenth century.

Economy. Salmon, supplemented by game animals, continued to be the basis of subsistence throughout the Fur Trade Period. Intertribal trade in skins, copper, and other goods also persisted throughout the Fur Trade Period and until the beginning of the twentieth century.

The Russians were able to establish a trading station at Iliamna after 1818. This would suggest the beginning of more intense economic involvement of the Iliamna Tanaina with the fur trade after this date. The men of the society were the ones who usually participated most directly in the fur trade, although their related women enjoyed some of the wealth which accrued.

With the sale of Alaska to the United States in 1867, the assets of the Russian-American Company found their way ultimately into the hands of the Alaska Commercial Company. The latter based its relationships with the Indians and Eskimos on the policies of the earlier company, providing supplies for trappers on credit in time of trouble in exchange for exclusive rights to the furs taken by the Indians. During the 1870s, rivalry between the Alaska Commercial Company and a competitor, the Western Fur and Trading Company, perpetuated the prosperous situation of the fur trade and prices paid for fur soared higher than ever. Many Indians and Eskimos were allowed to become indebted to the companies during this period. When the Western Fur and Trading Company went out of business in 1883, the prices of furs immediately dropped, and the economic shock was severe (Porter 1893:247-51; Abercrombie 1900:400; Shalamov DRHA 2:186; Brotnovsky DRHA 2:73, 82; Learnard 1900:667). Credit was no longer extended and attempts were made by the company to collect debts. Independent traders in the area eased the economic hardship somewhat. Miners had begun to filter into the Iliamna area in search of copper and gold. These people also presumably bolstered the staggering economy to some degree (Martin and Katz 1912:20-21). Further, in the 1880s salmon canneries began to operate in southwestern Alaska and the Iliamna Tanaina were participating in the commercial fishing industry by 1915.

Modern Period: After 1900

Social Organization. Sibs have become progressively less important. They may still function occasionally at a death, and marriage tends to respect sib exogamy. Potlatches have lost their great prestige significance although some of my informants report that a form of potlatch is occasionally held in more conservative villages. A potlatch no longer seems to be the mechanism for establishing status or validating a marriage. A wife is obtained in ways similar to those of Western civilization. Boys and girls attend parties, dances, and recreational games together, both in their resident village and in neighboring villages. Other opportunities to meet prospective spouses present themselves while the boys and girls are away at boarding school after completion of their grade-school work in the village. A boy is expected to be able to support his wife, and because of this as well as the demands of schooling, marriages are seldom transacted before about the age of twenty-one. Residence has become neolocal although the couple may live in the village of one or both sets of parents. House structures began to be single family dwellings after 1900 and remain such today.

All Tanaina are nominally Russian Orthodox although there is no resident priest in the Iliamna area villages. Fundamentalist missionaries have begun to come into the area in the last forty years and some Tanaina have converted to their faith.

Economy. Subsistence remains primarily salmon and game animals although the diet now is supplemented in varying degrees with processed foods. Canned vegetables, flour, tea, coffee, noodles, rice, powdered milk, and other products are popular additions.

Commercial fishing in Bristol Bay during the summers has come to play a larger and larger role in the economy of the Tanaina in recent years. For enterprising individuals among the Tanaina, commercial fishing offers opportunities similar to those formerly offered by the fur trade. In Bristol Bay, a Tanaina arranges to fish for a cannery. If he proves to be productive, he is encouraged by the company in much the same way as the earlier Tanaina was encouraged by the fur trading companies. If a man decides he would like to own his own powerboat and ultimately to fish independently, he approaches his company and asks for its assistance. The company will help him in obtaining a boat costing some $14,000. He is required to fish exclusively for this cannery until the mortgage on the boat is paid through his profits from fishing. His nets and other equipment are also purchased through the company. If a man wishes, the company will withhold part of his wages from fishing and purchase his winter's supply of food for him. The fisherman may also be permitted to borrow from the cannery against his next year's wages.

Money received from fishing assists in buying necessities in the form of additional foods and readymade clothing. Beyond this, the money goes for luxury goods which act, again, as status symbols. A very affluent family may have several skiffs, four or five outboard motors in varying states of repair, an airplane, and several appliances. Poorer relatives of the affluent often depend on the wealthy to assist them when times become difficult during the winter. While this is not a stated concept, it seems to be latent and expected behavior.

Summary

In aboriginal times the Tanaina were able to sustain a sizable population in a semisedentary condition because of a rich environment. Their subsistence then as now was based on the large salmon runs which enter Bristol Bay and find their way into Iliamna Lake each year. Trade networks were established with other tribes for luxury goods. Upon this base, a social organization existeded which included matrilineal sibs and moieties. There was some tendecy toward a class system and the potlatch was already established. Individual initiative seems always to have been a significant facet of Tanaina culture. Residence tended toward matrilocality although it seems to have been of little real consequence whether the couple maintained their residence patrilocally or matrilocally. They did, however, join the household of one of the sets of parents. House structures, reflecting the residence patterns, were extended-family dwellings.

When the Russians arrived in Alaska, they were soon able to defeat the more accessible Kenai Tanaina and initiate trading with them. However, some Tanaina refused to be subject to Russian control and moved inland from Cook Inlet, beyond Iliamna into the Mulchatna and Stony River region. The Iliamna Tanaina destroyed a trading station which the Russians had attempted to establish among them and consequently had no reason to move farther inland.

After 1818 the Russians were successful in establishing

a trading post at Iliamna, and the Tanaina of the region began to trap for furs and enter into more extensive trade with them. Perhaps the lure of wealth to be obtained in fur trading was one factor in reversing the population movement inland and bringing the other Tanaina from the interior back nearer the coast, to Lake Clark and Iliamna.

Throughout the entire fur trading period, the Tanaina continued their trading enterprises with other tribes in southern Alaska. The fur trade seems merely an extension of the previously established trading pattern and provided simply another method of obtaining luxury goods for symbols of wealth to increase individual prestige.

Luxury goods supplied by the Russians, however, were desired, and they became more and more significant in the social system. The new wealth seems to have been incorporated into a compatible social system which was already in existence.

By permitting the Tanaina to obtain on credit luxury goods as well as trapping equipment, the Russian trader was able to acquire an entourage of the best hunters who were obligated to work for him because of their indebtedness. Thus, the Iliamna Tanaina continued to become more and more involved in the fur trade in order to enhance their status in their own society and because they were indebted to the trader. Dentalium shells, beads, and various European-made items were acquired through this fur trade and became symbols of wealth. Beads were displayed on elaborate clothing of the wealthy. Soon a more clearly defined class system began to emerge. Probably because fur trapping was primarily man's work, the economic importance of men over women in the society became more significant. A slow but definite shift away from matrilineality and matrilocality can be discerned. A man's wealth became significant in obtaining a wife, and although polygyny presumably was permitted earlier, this also became an important symbol of status. A wealthy man could now pay for his wife outright and consequently was not obligated to her family for assistance in residence. The weak matrilocal residence pattern and somewhat bilocal tendency of aboriginal times perhaps became crystallized, after movable wealth became more significant, in a more formal bride-service or bride-price.

The movable wealth primarily in the hands of men possibly tended to undercut the matrilineally based inheritance system and thus the sib organization. Toward the end of the nineteenth century, then, some goods were retained and handed down within the nuclear family.

At Iliamna, there was no single chief. Any rich man, *kushká*, became synonymous with a "chief." Poorer relatives gravitated around him and worked for him. The extended-family residence pattern was thus maintained. Eskimo slaves were owned and considered a part of a man's wealth. It is interesting that the word for both "commoner" and "slave," according to one informant, is the same.

The potlatch continued to be developed as the main mechanism for the establishment and display of status through wealth. During the competition between the Alaska Commercial Company and the Western Fur and Trading Company soon after the purchase of Alaska in 1867, the value of furs reached an all-time high. There are indications that this coincides with the greatest elaboration of the potlach system and its related wealth and status complex.

When the Western Fur and Trading Company went out of business, the fur prices dropped back to normal. Alaska Commercial Company traders ceased to extend credit and attempted to collect some of the debts already incurred. With the severe deflation of the economy, evidently the social structure which was built upon it also faltered. Without the wealth to be displayed, the potlatches rapidly began to lose their importance as a main mechanism for the establishment of a high-status position. Toward the end of the nineteenth century, the matrilineal sibs, which were already being undermined during the prosperous economic period, continued to drop in importance. With the loss of wealth, the "chief" was no longer able to maintain a large household of poorer relatives and slaves. Residence began to be neolocal and the house structure reflected this in single-family dwellings. The Christian church was, by 1900, well established among the Tanaina. The church had long preached against polygyny and this harassment, together with the depressed economy, undermined another wealth symbol of the old social structure.

The intertribal trade continued to be conducted until about 1900, but by that time the items traded were presumably beginning to lose their appeal. This form of trade died out soon after the turn of the present century. Miners and small traders prevented the Iliamna Tanaina from becoming completely destitute after the crisis in the economy. This seems to have had a stabilizing effect on the social organization as well as the economy, preventing immediate chaos and perhaps social disorganization from which the Tanaina might not have recovered.

In recent years, the Tanaina of Iliamna have been drawn more and more into the commercial fishing industry of Bristol Bay. Like the fur trade, this also stresses individual initiative and holds out the possibility of large rewards for the successful man. In many ways the commercial fishing parallels the old fur trading complex. By borrowing from the cannery in time of need, by relying on the cannery to purchase the winter's supply of food, by arranging for the cannery to back him in the purchase of a large boat, the fisherman can easily become dependent upon the cannery in much the same way as the trapper became dependent upon the fur trading company. Today, the successful and affluent fisherman spends his extra money on luxury goods for display of wealth in a way quite similar to that of the rich man of the late 1800s. Similarly he assists his poorer relatives in the village.

Conclusions

Changes

The social organization has thus changed considerably although not precipitately. Inheritance has shifted gradually from matrilineal to patrilineal. In residence pattern, there has been a four-stage shift from:

1. a matrilocal or bilocal residence in aboriginal times
2. to initial matrilocal residence due to bride-service in the middle 1800s
3. to patrilocal residence by the latter part of the 1800s
4. to neolocal residence after 1900.

In accordance with shifts in residence patterns, house types have changed from extended-family dwellings to nuclear-family structures. Potlatches have virtually ceased to be held and sibs (clans) rarely function.

These shifts are seen in the context of the increasing intensity of the fur trade during the latter half of the 1800s. As more wealth entered the economy in the form of luxury goods derived from some men's success in the fur trade, the social organization began to be elaborated in those areas in which status could be expressed. Basic elements of social organization tended to shift in response to the increasing concentration of prestige and wealth in the hands of a few families. Wealth began to be transmitted within the nuclear family rather than along the original matrilineal sib lines. When two trading and fur-buying companies were competing, the resultant rise in fur prices brought the prestige aspects of the social organization to its highest peak of development. The loss of the greatest bulk of the fur trade at the end of the nineteenth century removed the ready access to large quantities of wealth symbols, seriously weakening the social elaborations based upon them.

Persistences

In spite of the apparent major shift in the social organization and some aspects of the economy, persistences can be discerned in the most basic parts of the culture. An analysis of some of the economic persistences has been developed and presented in two papers, "The Persistence of a Trade Tradition among the Tanaina" and "Tanaina Athapaskan Cultural Traditions . . . Persistence through Change"; the latter presents a revision and development of the concept of Tanaina persistences. In these papers, the concept of tradition as it is known in archaeology was used to analyze persistences. Following Haury et al. (1956:43), "tradition" was used to mean a socially transmitted cultural form which persists in time. In contrast to other terms such as pattern or complex, the concept of tradition possesses most clearly the essential factor for the study of change: time, as well as space. Haury et al. (1956) presented models of traditions within which culture—change data could be organized and interpreted. Of the five different forms of persistence and change within the concept of tradition, three are the most useful for my study. These are the *Direct Tradition* which persists essentially unchanging and the *Elaborating Tradition* which increases in complexity as a result of the addition of traits that are integrated into a single line of development. The *Reducing Tradition* is one which becomes increasingly simplified because of the loss of traits and less complex organization. The two concepts that do not seem to be applicable to those segments of Tanaina culture considered here are *Converging Tradition* and *Diverging Tradition.*

The economic aspects of Tanaina culture lend themselves most readily to an analysis of persistence utilizing the concept of tradition. The subsistence has remained stable and basically the same for the major portion of the diet since aboriginal times. Subsistence, then, would form one very significant Direct Tradition. A tradition of trade was also defined, although it is more difficult to discern immediately than the subsistence tradition. However, I see an Elaborating Tradition of trade persisting from aboriginal times until the present. First, it was expressed in luxury goods of copper and other items in aboriginal times. Next, in the fur trade period it was expressed by beads, dentalium shells, and European-manufactured wealth symbols. Finally, products of commercial fishing are now exchanged for cash with which to buy such status symbols as outboard motors as a conspicuous display of wealth.

In regard to the social organization also, the archaeological, ethnohistorical, and ethnographic sources provide the pertinent data to establish persistence of a tradition over a long period of time. Lacking a better term now, perhaps I can refer to this, for the time being, as an Individual Prestige Tradition. An incipient class system and the importance of individual initiative during aboriginal times were suggested. The occurrence of a simple form of potlatch at that time lends support to this suggested aboriginal pattern. Upon this base and with the introduction of a considerable amount of wealth, a more elaborate system of prestige was structured which was directly related to the individual's initiative and ability for success in the fur trade. It was the rich man's obligation as well as a way to acquire more prestige to assist the poorer people. In recent years, the fur trade has been replaced by commercial fishing. This enterprise also rewards individual initiative. A man obtains money with which he acquires symbols of wealth enhancing his prestige within his village. His prestige is also cemented through his aid to the poorer villagers in their times of need. In terms of tradition, the development has been essentially threefold. Presumably it was, in aboriginal times, a Direct Tradition. During the Fur Trade Period, it became an Elaborating Tradition, and in modern times it has been somewhat simplified and can be considered a Reducing Tradition.

It is suggested that it is the persistence of such basic underlying traditions of the culture from aboriginal times to the present which has contributed to making it possible for the Tanaina to experience less social disorganization than that noted among some of the other Indian groups. Their culture has changed, but it has not been altered so radically that it cannot continue to function.

Another conclusion has also been drawn from study of the data obtained by fusing the archaeological, ethnohistoric, and ethnographic materials. It appears that Tanaina culture has continued to develop by an inner dynamic of its own almost as much as in response to the forces of contact with Western civilization. There seems to have been a kind of cultural preadaptation of the Tanaina which made it possible for them to adjust with relative success to Western civilization. The interest in and the means of manifesting status and individual worth were present in aboriginal times in Tanaina culture. It is fortuitous that this happened to parallel a tradition in Western civilization. Because of this parallel development, intensified through the fur trade, it was relatively simple for the Tanaina to adjust their traditions in some of the outer aspects without destroying themselves. It gives an appearance of acculturation which is somewhat misleading. The Tanaina traditions have moved under their own dynamic into a pattern similar to that of Western civilization rather than being discarded and replaced fully with traditions from the white man's culture or none at all. When the orientation of the traditions happens to be similar to the orientations of Western civilization, persistence through change might be looked for.

There are, of course, other factors which have made it possible for the Tanaina to adjust to Western civilization with a minimum of disorganization. I doubt that the results of culture contact are ever simple or to be explained by reference to a single factor. It is, however, of great aid in understanding the processes and results of culture contact to attempt to pinpoint some of the factors which have operated to bring about the observed result. Ethnohistory when combined with archaeology and ethnography seems to provide some insight which could not have been obtained by simply observing the culture as it exists at the present time.

Future Study

The study of a single culture is merely a first step in an attempt to understand the processes of culture change in general. Other cultures could be studied in a way similar to that outlined for the Tanaina. When such analyses are available for other cultures not only in Alaska but anywhere else in the world where material from archaeology, ethnohistory and ethnography is available, we can begin to compare the results. It is to be hoped that some generalities concerning processes of persistence as well as change might be attained.

References

Abercrombie, W. R.
   1900   Supplementary expedition into the Copper River Valley, Alaska. *In* Compilation of Narratives of Exploration in Alaska, pp. 383-408. Washington.

Alaska History Research Project
   Ms   Documents Relative to the History of Alaska (DRHA).
   1936–1938 12 vols. Division of Documents, Library of Congress. Washington.

Alaska Russian Church Archives
   Ms   Vital Statistics; Kenai Mission; Nushagak Mission (in Russian). United States Library of Congress.

Andreyev, A. I.
   1952   Russian Discoveries in the Pacific and North America in the Eighteenth and Nineteenth Centuries. English translation by Carl Ginsburg. Published for the American Council of Learned Societies. Ann Arbor, Mich.

Bancroft, Hubert Howe
   1886   History of Alaska 1730–1885, San Francisco.

Base Line Studies
   Ms   Arctic Health Research Center, Public Health Service,

1960   Department of Health, Education and Welfare. Mimeo-
            graph. Anchorage.

Beardsley, Richard K., et al.
    1956   Functional and evolutionary implications of community
            patterning. Seminars in Archaeology, 1955. Memoirs
            of the Society for American Archaeology 11:130-57.
            Salt Lake City, Utah.

Bortnovsky, John
    Ms   Travel journal of Priest John Bortnovsky of Kenai, 1896.
            Documents Relative to the History of Alaska 2:68-83.

Davydov, Gavril I.
    1812   Two Voyages to America. Vol. 2, St. Petersburg, Naval
            Printing Office. English translation of portions of the
            book. *In* Pacific Manuscripts 7 (3). Bancroft Library,
            Berkeley, Calif.

Dixon, George
    1789   A Voyage Round the World Performed in 1785, 1786,
            1787, and 1788 in the King George and Queen Charlotte.
            London.

Haury, Emil, et al.
    1956   An archaeological approach to the study of cultural
            stability. *In* Seminars in Archaeology, 1955, ed. Robert
            Waucope. Memoirs of the Society for American Archae-
            ology 11:31-57. Salt Lake City, Utah.

Herskovits, Melville J.
    1958   Cultural Anthropology. New York

Juvenal, Rev. Ieromonakh
    1952   A daily journal kept by the Rev. Father Juvenal, one
            of the earliest missionaries to Alaska, 1796. Kroeber
            Anthropological Society Papers 6:31-59. Berkeley, Calif.

Learnard, H. G.
    1900   A trip from Portage Bay to Turnagain Arm and up the
            Sushitna. *In* Compilation of Narratives of Exploration in
            Alaska, pp. 648-77. Washington.

Martin, G. C., and Katz, F. J.
    1912   A geologic reconnaissance of the Iliamna Region, Alaska.
            United States Geological Survey, Bulletin 485. Washing-
            ton.

Nicholas, Abbot
    Ms   Travel journal of Abbot Nicholas of Kenai, 1858–1860.
            Documents Relative to the History of Alaska 2:54-59.

Osgood, Cornelius
   1937   The ethnography of the Tanaina. Yale University Pub-
             lications in Anthropology No. 16, New Haven, Conn.

Petroff, Ivan
   1884   Report on the population, industries, and resources of
             Alaska. *In* Tenth Census. Washington.

Porter, Robert P.
   1893   Report on the population and resources of Alaska at the
             Eleventh Census: 1890. Department of the Interior,
             Census Office. House of Representatives, Misc. Docu-
             ment No. 340, pt. 7. 52d Cong. 1st sess. Washington.

Portlock, Nathaniel
   1789   A Voyage of Discovery Round the World but most
             particularly to the Northwest Coast of America per-
             formed in 1785, 1786, 1787, 1788 in the King George
             and Queen Charlotte by Captains Portlock and Dixon.
             London.

Richardson, Sir John
   1851   Arctic Searching Expedition. London.

Shalamov, Priest Tikhon
   Ms   Travel journal of Priest Tikhon Shalamov, Kodiak, 1895.
             Documents Relative to the History of Alaska 2:84-88.

Sheldon, Charles
   1908   The Cook Inlet Aborigines, Appendix C. *In* To the Top
             of the Continent, by Frederick A. Cook, pp. 269-77.
             London.

Steward, Julian H.
   1942   The direct historical approach to archaeology. American
             Antiquity 7 (4):337-43.

Tikhmenev, Peter Aleksandrovich
1861–1863   The Historical Review of the Formation of the Russian-
             American Company and its Activities up to the Present
             Time. St. Petersburg, Edward Vermar. English trans-
             lation by Demitri Krenov, 1939. Works Progress Admin-
             istration, Seattle. Microfilm at the University of Alaska.

Townsend, Joan B.
   1965   Ethnohistory and culture change of the Iliamna Tanaina.
             Ph.D. Dissertation, University of California, Los Angeles.
             Microfilm available through University Microfilms, Ann
             Arbor, Mich.

1966a   Persistence of a trade tradition among the Tanaina. Paper presented to the Northwest Anthropological Association, Banff, Canada.
1966b   Tanaina Athapaskan cultural traditions . . . persistence through change. Paper presented to the 37th International Congress of Americanists, Buenos Aires and Mar del Plata.

Townsend, Joan B., and Townsend, Sam-Joe
1961   Archaeological investigations at Pedro Bay, Alaska. Anthropological Papers of the University of Alaska, 10 (1):25-58. College, Alaska.

VanStone, James W., and Townsend, Joan B.
1970   Kijik: An historic Tanaina Indian settlement. Fieldiana: Anthropology 59, Field Museum of Natural History. Chicago.

Wrangell, Ferdinand Petrovich, Baron
1839   Statistische und ethnographische Nachrichten über die Russieschen Besitzungen an der Nordwestküste von Amerika, ed. K. E. von Baer. St. Petersburg.

INDIAN STORIES
ABOUT THE FIRST WHITES
IN NORTHWESTERN AMERICA

by Catharine McClellan

Many Indians and Eskimos of northwestern North America have preserved oral traditions about their first meetings with white men, beginning with the Russians who sailed along southern Alaska in the mid-eighteenth century and continuing with various explorers, traders, whalers, missionaries, and other adventurers. Since the earliest contacts took place along the coast, almost all the coastal stories have been handed down through two or more generations. In the interior, however, some of the oldest living people themselves encountered the first whites. Thus an old Eskimo woman at the head of the Kobuk River explained to me quite simply that she had been there for Lieutenant Stoney of the United States Navy when he came in 1884, while her sister was there for the "other man"—presumably Stoney's rival, Lieutenant Cantwell of the United States Revenue Marine (Sherwood 1965:119-32). In Yukon Territory I have known at least a dozen Indians who were children when the first whites came through their country in the last decades of the nineteenth century.

As a preliminary step in the study of the oral literature of several northwestern Indian groups, I have recently considered some of these stories about the first or early whites. They make an intriguing set of data which has, I believe, real ethnohistoric value. The dozens of actual testimonies (using the word in Vansina's sense of "the sum of statements made by any one informant concerning a single series of events" relating to the same referent [1965: 22]) will be published elsewhere.[1] In this paper I can draw on only a few examples. All the stories, however, appear to add interesting details about historic persons or events, and it is this new information which takes us to the heart of our problem: how best to assess the ethnohistoric value of the testimonies.

Probably most of us subscribe to the creed that effective ethnohistoric analysis requires the special skills and knowledge of the historiographer, the ethnographer, and, under favorable circumstances, of the archaeologist. A number of scholars have written excellent programmatic papers suggesting desirable methodologies in each of these fields and ways to interrelate them (Sturtevant 1966; Hudson 1966; Fenton 1966). I should like, ideally, to comment on almost all of their recommendations, but the present paper has much more modest aims. Its first purpose is simply to indicate the range of documented events with which the oral testimonies intermesh. As a specific illustration I cite some of the traditions relating to Robert Campbell, mentioning some obvious ways in which careful historical or ethnographic research might help us to evaluate the

[1] The National Museums of Canada have a typed report, "Through Native Eyes" (cited as McClellan, n.d. a.) which includes English texts for fifteen stories about early whites told by Northern and Southern Tutchone, Tagish and Inland Tlingit informants. Other stories from these groups are in typed field notes for 1948, 1949, 1950-1951, 1962-1963 (in part), 1965, and 1966, also on file in the National Museums. It is hoped that all of the oral literature will form a second volume to accompany My Old People Say, a general ethnography of the peoples in question, to be published by the National Museums of Canada (cited here as McClellan, n.d. b.).

Northern Tlingit stories collected by Frederica de Laguna and myself and her other associates at Angoon and Yakutat, Alaska, are in de Laguna 1960, or will appear in her Under Mount Saint Elias, in press for the Smithsonian Institution (cited as de Laguna, n.d.). Atna stories are in de Laguna and McClellan field notes, 1954, 1958, and 1960.

The Governor and Committee of the Hudson's Bay Company have allowed the use and publication of the material from their archives in relation to Campbell.

Generous support for the fieldwork noted above has been provided by the following institutions: The American Academy of Arts and Sciences, American Association of University Women, American Philosophical Society, National Museums of Canada, National Science Foundation, University of Washington, and University of Wisconsin.

historiographic truth of these stories, but showing that such methods have their limits.

My second purpose is to suggest how a few findings about the classification, function, style, and content of this group of stories may relate to the particular bodies of literature in which they occur, for I believe that full understanding of the tales depends on a thorough knowledge of their total literary contexts.

I cannot stress too strongly that my study represents an initial step toward comprehending these totalities—not a completed analysis of them. I trust, therefore, that they will be received in the proper heuristic spirit in which they are offered.

The Intermeshing of Native Testimonies with Documented History

The oral testimonies under consideration come from a series of contiguous Indian groups: the northern coastal Tlingit and Athabascan Atna of the Copper River, Alaska; the Northern and Southern Tutchone Athabascans and the Tlingit-speaking Tagish and Inland Tlingit of Yukon Territory and northern British Columbia (see map).[2]

Stories from these various groups refer explicitly to such documented events as the eighteenth- and nineteenth-century activities of de La Perouse and of the Russians in Lituya and Yakutat bays, in Lynn Canal and at Sitka (Coastal Tlingit and Southern Tutchone); of the Hudson's Bay Company on the Taku River in 1840 (Coastal and Inland Tlingit and Southern Tutchone); Serebrenikov's ill-fated expedition up the Copper River in 1848 (Atna); Robert Campbell's establishment of Fort Selkirk on the Yukon River in that same year and its destruction by the Chilkat

[2] For a brief characterization of each of these groups and my reasons for not referring to them as "tribes," see McClellan 1961; 1964:6-11; n.d. b:2-108; de Laguna 1960:200-206; Denniston, n.d.

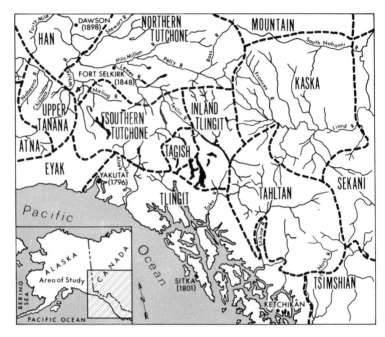

ATHABASCANS OF THE CANADA-ALASKA BORDER REGION

Tlingit in 1852 (Northern and Southern Tutchone); Lieutenant Allen's exploring trip up the Copper River in 1881
(Atna); the *Leslie's Illustrated Newspaper* expedition through
southern Yukon and down the Alsek River in 1890–1891
(Southern Tutchone);[3] Glave's and Dalton's subsequent
return to the White River area in the following spring
(Southern Tutchone); the origins of the great Klondike Gold
Rush of 1898 (Coastal and Inland Tlingit, Tagish, Southern
and Northern Tutchone); and finally the drive of reindeer
from Haines, Alaska through Yukon Territory in 1898–1899
sponsored by the U. S. Government (Southern Tutchone).

[3] Living Southern Tutchone have recognized almost all the Indians
pictured in the *Newspaper* articles. One little boy whom Glave sketched is
now an old man living at Champagne, Yukon Territory (McClellan, n.d.
a:75-78).

Each of these events involved the first appearance of whites in a particular area, and for each occasion we have at least two and sometimes a dozen or more native testimonies, although collecting them was never the main focus of field investigations.

In addition, the Indians tell of early encounters with whites whose presence the history books acknowledge but whose names and specific actions rarely appear in their pages—such men as independent traders, prospectors, members of geological survey parties, and the like. If documents about them exist, they are often difficult to track down and are usually in the form of journals, letters, or account books. Also one cannot always be sure that these individuals are actually the persons referred to in the native traditions.

Since in this short paper I cannot hope to deal with all the ways in which the stories of so many groups intermesh with such a broad range of historic happenings, I shall limit my initial discussion to a specific historical figure: intrepid Robert Campbell of the Hudson's Bay Company.

The documentation about this Scotsman is quite scanty as compared, for example, with that for the Russians on the coast. He himself published only a few pages during his lifetime, telling about his discovery of the upper Yukon River, and until recently only the Canadian geologist, Dawson, had written about some of his other astonishing exploits. Many of Campbell's original papers were stolen, burned, or sunk in northern waters during the course of his adventurous life, but we do have some of his letters and his account books for various Hudson's Bay Company posts, including Fort Selkirk, a summary journal of his life from 1808 to 1853, and a more detailed supplemental journal covering the eventful years from 1850 to 1853 (Burpee 1967 [1945]; Campbell 1837–1838; 1839–1840; 1842–1843; 1843–1844a; 1843–1844b; 1847–1851; 1851–1852; 1958 [1803–1853]; 1967 [1883]; Dawson 1889:14b-16b, 83b-84b, 136b-41b; Kirk and Parnell 1942; McBride 1962a, b; McClellan 1950:178-85;

n.d. a:50-74; n.d. b:1117-32; field notes, 1962–1963, 1965, 1966; Parnell 1942 a, b).

Campbell's services to the Company included driving a herd of sheep from Kentucky to Fort Gary in 1833, daring explorations on the upper Liard and Stikine River drainages where he first met some aggressive Tlingit traders from the coast, a winter of starvation at Dease Lake where he was befriended by a remarkable Nahany "Chieftainess," and finally the discovery of the route down the Pelly River to the Yukon (Kirk and Parnell 1942; Parnell 1942 a, b; Campbell 1958:27-65). The grandparents and parents of my Northern and Southern Tutchone informants met him first during his exploration of the Pelly in 1843. Five years later he established Fort Selkirk at the conjunction of the Pelly and the Yukon rivers.

The new post immediately aroused the ire of the Chilkat Tlingit who for some decades had made arduous annual trips from the coast in order to exchange Russian and American trade goods for the land furs trapped by the local Northern Tutchone and their neighbors. The demand for such furs had greatly increased after the virtual extermination of the sea otter on the coast at the beginning of the century, and the Chilkat middlemen had jealously guarded all coastal routes to the interior (McClellan 1950; n.d. b:1117-36).

Campbell wrote in his journals about the hostility of the Chilkat during their summer visits to Fort Selkirk, and he could not really have been surprised by their final attack on the post in 1852. He vividly described its destruction as well as his temporary retreat down the river with some of his men and their Indian wives and children and his reluctant decision to abandon the post, partly because the local Indians would not help him to follow the Chilkat. He also recorded his subsequent 2,000 mile journey to ask Company permission to rebuild Fort Selkirk. No wonder

J. J. Waddy, who had married Campbell's granddaughter, wrote beside the entry for Fort Gary, January 1853: "Robert Campbell started here, ran on snowshoes to St. Paul, Minn. My God what a man!" (Campbell 1958:146).

Campbell's request was denied, and although he continued to serve the Company well in other parts of Canada, in the end it evidently dismissed him for failing to follow instructions to the letter (McClellan, n.d. a:53-54).

So far as I know, Campbell and his associates were the only whites in the upper Yukon between 1843 and about 1880, and since the documentation of his activities is so limited, the native traditions relating to him are of special interest. Three Southern and two Northern Tutchone have told me about him, all but one of them repeating their stories after intervals of a year or more. McBride (1962b) has published a sixth native account. There is remarkably little variation in the stories told by a given individual, but much variability in the versions given by the different informants (McClellan, n.d. a:50-74). All mention the destruction of Fort Selkirk, but each has its own emphasis, and each tells something unique about Campbell. All the stories thus appear to flesh out Campbell's own version of what happened at the Fort. But are all of the accounts historically "true"?

On some points the oral testimonies obviously corroborate Campbell's own record. Thus Campbell wrote about two "Gens de Bois" (or Northern Tutchone), "Thlin-ikik-thling" and "Hanan," whom he took to be father and son. He described them (1958:68, 82) as "tall, stalwart good-looking men" who "often visited with their bands and were more than pleased at our coming among them with articles of civilized usage for barter." The two are easily recognizable as łingIt tłEn (Tlingit:man, big) and k'anan who also figure prominently in native accounts about Fort Selkirk, and whose illustrious names are held today by various of

their descendants in southern Yukon, even though informants disagree as to whether the two were father and son
or uncle and nephew.[4]

Prior to Campbell's arrival, łingIt tłEn seems to have
been the chief middleman between the Chilkat traders and
the local Northern Tutchone. This "banker" or "lawyer," as
the present-day Indians sometimes refer to him, collected
from his followers most of the furs upon which the Chilkat
counted. Normally he and his band also put up with the
unfair trade and rude behavior of their coastal visitors, since
this was the only way they could get coveted trade goods.
However, according to one Southern Tutchone, just before
Campbell's arrival, the Chilkat had so insulted łingIt tłEn,
that he had deliberately broken off trade and started a
blood feud with them. For several years the Selkirk Indians
simply melted into the bush whenever the Chilkat arrived.
Finally the Chilkat became so desperate for furs that they
made peace with the despised Tutchone on the latter's
own terms.

If this story is correct, the threat of Campbell's competition so soon after the renewal of inter-native trade must
have made the Chilkat doubly edgy. On the other hand,
one reason which the Tutchone gave for their ancestors'
refusal to hunt down the Chilkat who destroyed the Fort
was that they could not afford to break again with those
who had so recently demonstrated their eagerness to maintain trade relationships and who, though so unpleasant,
remained the surest source of white men's goods. Campbell
was, after all, a newcomer, and for reasons beyond his
control, he had been short of goods throughout his stay.
In his journals he complained bitterly of his dearth of trade
goods, but he did not mention the intricacies of the inter-

---

[4] Since the Northern Tutchone have matrilineal reckoning, the confusion
is curious. I have not been able to solve the problem on the basis of my
current genealogies.

native trade system described by my informants (1958:84, 87-88, 93).

Campbell's silence on this latter point is not particularly surprising, for even though he may have known about it, there was little reason to write it. More puzzling are some other aspects of Indian testimonies about Campbell which do not appear in the written record. Thus one Southern Tutchone endowed him with a wife—presumably Indian— and with children. When his wife begged him not to risk his life in pursuit of the Chilkat, Campbell told her that he had shamanistic powers to turn away bullets shot at him. A Northern Tutchone Indian also credited him with this power (McBride 1962b:44). Yet Campbell himself acknowledged only his marriage to a Scottish woman in 1859, and while he twice wrote that the Indians believed him to be a shaman, he mentioned the belief in different contexts —first in relation to his healing of a Pelly River Indian whom he was supposed to have crippled through his powers, and again when he resuscitated a half-drowned Indian child whose parents ever after called the boy "Campbell" (1958: 81-82, 94, 95).

My own informants mentioned neither event; nevertheless, several of them also bear Campbell's name. Thus, one Northern Tutchone explained how Campbell had bestowed his name on the speaker's "grandfather," chief łingIt tłEn, in gratitude for the furs which the chief had traded him. More colorful is the account of a second Northern Tutchone who averred that her "grandfather," k'anan, rescued Campbell from a boat in which the Chilkat had set him adrift, bound hand and foot, just after they had wrecked his post. Following the rescue: "Campbell asked my grandpa, 'Have you any kind of name? Well, I am going to give you my name. Your name is "Robert Campbell" from now on.'"

Another Indian reported that Campbell gave his name

to his father "in return for kindly treatment" after the fiasco at Fort Selkirk (McBride 1962b:44).[5]

Not a word of any of this is in Campbell's papers, except that he gratefully acknowledges the food and shelter he received from the Indians. Again we must ask which of the incidents are historically "true."

In one sense, of course, their validity counts little, for at best they would only be minor footnotes in the history of northwest fur trading. Yet it is the details which ultimately create the larger picture; hence we must assess the evidence by all available means. We can, for evample, carefully compare Campbell's papers with contemporary documents of a similar kind. We can search the archives for further records written by or about Campbell, or we can analyze the internal evidence in the material we already have.

It is at least possible that Campbell really had a native "wife" and children, for we know from other sources that white traders frequently did live with local women and father half-breed children. Samuel Hearne railed eloquently against these callous men who so often abandoned their native families when they left the country (1796:127-28). However, although Campbell mentioned a number of the wives and children of his Indian and white companions at Fort Selkirk, he made no obvious references to any native woman particularly attached to him. He was, of course, far too astute to put unnecessary evidence into official records. In 1834 Sir George Simpson, governor of the Hudson's Bay Company, had admonished him: "Now Campbell, don't you get married, we want you for active service" (1958:27). Even though Simpson was probably

[5] This story was told to Mrs. Katherine Cowaret, an Anglican missionary, by Chief Johnathan Campbell of Fort Selkirk in June 1956 at Fort Selkirk. I have just begun my own field inquiries about Campbell, and my fullest data are from the Southern rather than the Northern Tutchone. The Southern Tutchone refer to him as "Mani," "Manly," or "Scabby" (McClellan n.d. a:59-66).

thinking of a white wife, perhaps this was reason enough for his employee's discretion about mentioning any Indian "wife" he may have had. He did write of his concern for the "women" during the attack on the Fort, and of how they made moccasins for him and his men afterward. Again, however, he seems to have meant only the wives of his men and of local Indians, and he was always concerned about those of whom he was in charge (1958:135-38).

The journals clearly show that he understood the Indians and had a lasting affection for some of them, such as his "2 inseparables," the Liard Indians, Lapie and Kitza (1958: 65, 67). Several times he commented on the honest and pleasant natures of the Northern Tutchone (1958:81, 95), and when the Indians at Pelly Banks took to cannibalism, he did not blame so much as pity them (1958:90). He declared the "greatest attraction" of his exploration of the Yukon River to be the Indians he met, and their illness in the spring of 1851 greatly distressed him (1958:96, 109). Yet all of this still does not tell us whether he had an Indian wife. Although I am inclined to think that if he had, he would have been proud of her and have mentioned her by name, the matter remains open to question.

Did the Chilkat set him adrift in a boat? His journal says he left Fort Selkirk by water, but under his own volition (1958:35). Would he be likely to lie? As I read them, his journals reveal him as a leader of men, courageous and compassionate and with a sense of humor. He had a touching faith in God, but was not above being impressed by the predictions of a native shaman or the omen-like appearance of a magpie not long before the Chilkat attack (1958:51, 66, 126). Although a man of action, he wrote that the smattering of astronomy which he picked up from General Sir J. H. Lefroy was a "sublime study which afforded me many delightful hours afterwards" (1958:74). But Campbell was also proud (1958:31-35, 40-43, 45-46), and he was, for instance, "painfully humiliated" not to be able to make a "suitable return" to the Nahany Chieftainess whom he thought had saved his life at Dease Lake (1958: 48-49). Perhaps he simply preferred not to mention being tied up in a boat. Or is this a fabrication on the part of my informant, or some kind of confusion about another of Campbell's men? Once more, sheer checking of the documents cannot provide an absolute answer.

Ethnographic evidence does not help us much either. Although it is true the Indians like to assume names which commemorate important events in their lives, that they feel that a man should be married, and that their own shamans claim power to deflect bullets, I do not think that any of this sufficiently explains the variety or gauges the truth of the stories about Campbell.

Actually, a more effective ethnographic method of getting at their historic truth might be to examine them primarily as samples of Tutchone oral literature. I say this even though these particular stories have so far yielded little to this approach. Like Campbell's own documents, they are mostly unique testimonies. However, other informants may provide new versions of some incidents, and further analysis may reveal characteristic literary patterns which color these Tutchone stories about Campbell. Once these are detected, the ethnohistorian can properly allow for them in assessing the historical truth of the stories, and he will also have learned other important cultural truths.

The best that I can offer now is the suggestion that the variety in the accounts about Campbell means that Tutchone narrators do not value standardization in literary content. This is a rather vulnerable conclusion; nevertheless in the following sections I shall explore it and other ideas about the oral literatures of the Tutchone and their neighbors. I will first discuss how the Indians classify their stories about the whites, and then comment on some aspects of their functions, style, and content.

The Classification of Indian Stories about the First Whites

We are all familiar with attempts to generalize about categories of oral literature. Bascom, for example, has suggested that two major kinds of prose narrative are myths, which focus on the activities of nonhuman beings in an earlier or other world, and legends, which tell of recent human exploits in a world like that of today. Both kinds of narrative are thought to be true, unlike the third category: folktales, which are pure fiction deliberately devised for entertainment (Bascom 1965; cf. Dorson 1963: 107-08; Fischer 1963:236-37; Thompson 1958). Bascom does not claim that these categories are universal, simply that they are very common. Furthermore, whether one adopts this scheme or any other, there is always the major question of whether the analytical framework of a western scholar actually coincides with categories recognized by those who have created a given oral literature.

As it happens, all the Tlingit and Athabascans being considered[6] distinguish two main classes of story which seem to correspond fairly well with Bascom's "myth" and "legend." The first class is designated by native terms which are often translated as "long ago stories" or occasionally as "fairy stories."[7] The chief actors are usually animal-named beings with superhuman powers, who nevertheless look and behave much of the time like human beings and who only rarely assume animal guise.[8] However, they also participate

[6] Although I base my arguments about the Athabascans largely on Tutchone and Tagish data, I believe that the statements about classification hold for the Atna as well. However, I exclude the Atna from the next section, since I have not had sufficient time to consider their stories. The Tagish are in a somewhat anomalous position in that they prefer to use Tlingit rather than their original Athabascan dialect (McClellan n.d. b:54-55).

[7] Thus Tlingit tłaqᵘ (recorded by de Laguna as tłagu); Southern Tutchone k'udiⁿ kUndUR and Atna yEnida' 'kułnIk all designate a "long ago" story.

[8] For interesting comments on the nature of these animal-named beings elsewhere on the coast, see Boas 1935:180; Jacobs 1959:6-7.

in events which have nonhuman qualities and which help to explain the ordering of the world today. Examples in this category are the familiar Raven stories of the coast (told as Crow stories in the interior) or the Smart Man cycle of the interior.

The second class of prose narratives is designated by terms which the Indians usually render in English as "histories" or "true stories," although "long ago stories" are, of course, thought to be equally true.[9] These tales tell what has happened to the narrator himself, to his contemporaries, or to his immediate ancestors—for example, about a shaman's acquisition of power or the feuding between the Inland Tlingit and the Tahltan. It is in this category that the Indians usually put their stories about the first whites, if they classify such a story at all. In a general way all such stories tell of the ordinary world of today or the not-too-distant past.

Yet these categories are loose ones at best, and neither our own characterization of their nature nor that of the Indians should lull us into thinking that the scheme is absolutely rigorous. Thus, they may explain that "long ago stories" are distinguished from "histories" chiefly by chronological criteria—because they happened in "myth-time"—but myth-time and mythlike events can nevertheless form important parts of "histories." In fact, both the Tlingit and the Athabascans have what appears to be a high tolerance for discontinuity in time, in the sense that it is possible for myth-time to exist simultaneously with either the present or the recent past. This is because the quality of myth-time appears to count as much as, if not more than, its temporal position. For example, while they vary greatly in detail, most Tagish and Inland Tlingit stories about the 1898 Gold Rush tell how the white prospector and his Tagish brother-in-law, Skookum Jim, found gold. But they

[9] Thus Tlingit sqełnik (recorded by de Laguna as chełnik), Southern Tutchone kUndUR, and Atna kułnIk all may be translated as "story" or "history."

also explain how Jim met with Wealth Woman, a figure from a "long ago story" and describe Jim's visit to the house of the Master of the Frogs where these creatures appeared and acted as humans. Jim's visit lasted for four months, although it seemed to him that only four days had passed (McClellan 1963).

The motifs of Wealth Woman and visits to the home of an animal species are both widespread in the oral literature of northwestern Indians (McClellan 1963:124). Although they usually appear in unequivocal "long ago stories," we know that a given motif from one category of literature among one people may well occur in a different category among their neighbors. We also know that it can appear in more than one category of story told by a single group, as is the case here. The question really is how much the flavor of the motif appears to change as it shifts its literary setting. I believe that the mythlike quality of Wealth Woman and the Frog prince remain constant both in Tagish "long ago stories" and in Tagish "history." In any case, it does not take a very sharp ethnohistorian to realize that neither a woman who defecates golden balls nor a Frog prince are historical figures in our sense of the word, and he soon becomes aware that myth-time events are not temporally stable phenomena, no matter what the literary classification may imply.

Even "long ago stories" often seem to lack our idea of true temporal sequence. While many narrators of the Raven cycle tell of certain key events in much the same order, the ordering is really one of logic: after the earth is made, Raven gets water, then he gets daylight, and so on. However, not every storyteller follows this arrangement, and all narrators insert other stories between the crucial cosmological happenings. They evidently do this in order to provide a kind of comic relief, and each raconteur decides for himself on the artistic order which suits him best (cf. Boas 1916:582, *n.* 1; de Laguna n.d. : pt. 17:1-23).

Perhaps it is not surprising that the Indians themselves

are sometimes unsure as to how to classify their stories. For example, the Tlingit apparently run into this problem with their sib traditions, just because some of them incorporate so much mythlike action, yet relate to persons who are presumed to be relatively recent sib ancestors. Different narrators may classify the same story in different ways (cf. de Laguna n.d. : pt. 4:4-5). While their decisions certainly involve more than temporal considerations, the point for us is that the ethnohistorian must not expect the Indians to handle time in the same way that historians do.[10]

None of the Indians, however, should ever face the dilemma of the western historiographer in deciding what is fact and what is fiction in their oral literature. In theory, at least, no deliberately fictitious stories are ever told. So far as I know, Bascom's category of "folktale" does not exist in any of the groups. Like all their other stories, therefore, those about the first whites are "true."

Function, Style, and Content in Native Stories about the First Whites

Although the Indians name only two major categories of literature, within each—or crosscutting both—is a series of stories differing in their functions, styles, and content. Throughout the area, some "long ago stories" instruct, while others focus on sheer entertainment. Often the same story does both. We may cite again the Raven cycle in which solemn cosmological instruction alternates with ludicrous events inserted to make people laugh as well as to provide moral guidance on such evils as excessive pride, gluttony, and the like. Other stories unfold great adventures, but at the same time subtly instruct on how to handle the social and psychological stresses of society.

---

[10] I believe that much the same order of "discontinuity" characterizes the Indians' ideas about space, and that unlike our own historians, they rarely stress the areal relatedness of a series of events. My supporting arguments are too complex to marshal here, and whatever the criteria for exclusive domains of the native literatures may be, spatial dimensions are not critical.

A prime function of many "true stories" about the first whites is to inform about important happenings to the living Indians or to their ancestors. However, the Northern and Southern Tutchone, the Tagish and the Inland Tlingit (all interior Indians) have one set of them in which the overt intent is clearly to amuse. These stories elaborate a kind of numskull motif, with the Indians casting themselves as dupes. By contrast, the Coastal Tlingit seldom develop the comic aspects of their stories about the first whites. There thus appears to be a real difference in the functions of at least some of the contact stories as told in the interior and as told on the coast, and this must ultimately be taken into account in any comparison of the total oral literatures of the various groups.

Inspection of contact stories has also suggested another broad difference between the oral literatures of the Coastal Tlingit and of the interior Indians. This has to do with the overall styles of narration. I have the impression that the inland Indians not only vary the content and arrangements of their stories much more freely than do coastal storytellers, but they also seem to have a marked interest and skill in developing what might be called psychological drama. These qualities are not paralleled in the coastal stories known to me. For example, in the Tutchone story in which Campbell explains his power to turn away bullets, the primary point developed is that he does this in order to reassure his wife who pleads with him not to follow the Chilkat and leave her a widow with helpless children. This reminds me of the way in which each interior narrator who told the popular story about the Girl Who Married the Bear elaborated the psychological stresses within the story which interested him most, thus managing to give a personal and exciting touch to what is, after all, a widespread motif in the American Northwest (Boas 1916:836-37; McClellan n.d. c.).

By contrast, none of the Coastal Tlingit contact stories or their versions of the Girl Who Married the Bear (Krause

1956:185-86; Swanton 1909:126, 252) show much attempt
to develop the psychological motivations of the characters,
although both the narrators and the audiences may have
been well aware of them. My guess is that the whole body
of Coastal Tlingit literature may prove to be more standardized in style and content than any of the interior bodies
of literature. If so, the formalization probably correlates
with the generally more structured mode of coastal life with
its good communications, frequent social gatherings, constant reference to oral traditions in the presence of large
audiences, and with its general preoccupation with social
"correctness" in all matters.

Confirmation of these sweeping generalizations can only
come from further and detailed study of the literatures in
question. In the meantime I offer some further possible
evidence from the content of a set of Tlingit testimonies
about the arrival of the first sailing ships.

One such testimony is by a Coastal Tlingit from Juneau,
named Edgar Sidney, who as an adult married into the
interior "in foolishness." His story purports to tell about
the Russians' appearance at Sitka. We learn that when the
Russian sailboat first arrived, all the native women ran
back into the bush because they thought it was "Crow's
boat." From their hiding places, they looked at the ship
through "fieldglasses" made from the hollow stems of a
bush.

"At first they don't say it's Crow's boat. But when they
saw the sailors—lots—go up the cross-pieces tying up the
sails, then they say it's Crow's boat, yeł yak" (Tlingit: raven,
canoe), because so many are up the mast."

The story goes on to tell how the Russians and Tlingit
gradually made friends and began to trade. The Tlingit
first painted their faces and danced on the beach for the
Russians. The two groups tried to talk to each other, but
the Tlingit thought the Russians were speaking gibberish.
When the Tlingit finally visited the ship, one of the older

men who knew he would soon die anyway, took the risk of copying some of the more bizarre actions of his hosts. Thus, in order to prepare for dining, he washed his face, combed his hair, and looked into a mirror, which so surprised him that he hit it. (One of the Russian sailors had earlier left a mirror on the beach, and the young girl who found it had been charging a slave in payment for the privilege of looking into it.)

Next the Russians gave the Tlingit rice and brown sugar which the Indians at first refused to eat, believing that the rice was worms. Later his compatriots followed the old man in drinking whiskey, which he found to be good, but "not for the women, though!"

A second testimony, by an Inland Tlingit named Jimmy Scotty,[11] is supposed to describe the arrival of James Douglas ("Mr. Daught") with the first Hudson's Bay Company trading ship on the lower Taku River near Juneau. Jimmy told how the Tlingit saw something coming up the river which seemed like a "big animal." However, when the frightened Indians looked through the hollow stems of dry rhubarb plants, they finally saw that it was a big boat with lots of people moving about on the decks. Douglas invited the Indians aboard, and with difficulty persuaded them to eat rice and molasses, for the two groups could not understand each other.

Now some of you already begin to recall Emmons's publication of a Tlingit version of the arrival of La Perouse in Lituya Bay in 1786. According to that account, when the two ships came into the bay, "The people did not know what they were, but believed them to be great black birds with far reaching white wings, and as their bird creator, Yehlh, often assumed the form of a raven, they thought

[11] Although Jimmy was an Inland Tlingit, I include this story as "coastal." Jimmy himself was always careful to indicate which stories belonged to the "inside" and which to the "coast." He evidently did this in terms of who told him the story in the first place, but I wish I had explored his criteria more thoroughly. He had coastal relatives.

that in this guise he had returned to earth. So in their fright they fled to the bush and hid. Finding after a while that no harm came to them, they crept to the shore and, gathering leaves of skunk cabbage, they rolled them into rude telescopes and looked through them, for to see Yehlh with naked eyes, was to be turned to stone" (Emmons 1911: 247). Not only that, but when the sailors climbed the rigging, the Tlingit "saw but the great birds folding their wings and flocks of small black messengers rising from their bodies flying about. These latter they believed to be crows" (Emmons 1911:247).

Then an old man "who thought most of his life was far behind him" undertook to visit the ships. He was almost blind, and when rice was set before him, he believed it to be worms and refused to eat it, although he did arrange the beginnings of a profitable fur trade.

Another native account of the meeting of La Perouse and the Tlingit, recorded sometime before 1927, closely parallels that recorded by Emmons. The boat is thought to be Raven with white wings; the Tlingit look at it through hollow kelp stems; a wise old man offers to approach the ship first, because he will soon die, and he rejects the rice served to him because he thinks it is maggots. He also refuses pilot-bread, which he believes to be a "product of human skulls," and red liquor, which he declares to be human blood. Some other details, especially about a metal bell acquired by the old man are not in the Emmons version. The narrator of the story, Henry Phillips, said the bell had been in his family eight generations. I do not know to what Tlingit group Mr. Phillips belonged. "An identical story" is said to have been recorded in the journal of V. V. Stafief, of Kodiak, Alaska, and to have been transcribed by Rev. A. P. Kashevaroff (Anon. 1927:151-53).

Finally, a Tlingit who told of the wrecking of an early ship near Yakutaga also explained how the Indians took some things, but threw away all the stores of rice, because it looked like worms.

I need hardly point out the content patterning which emerges from these stories—the initial belief that the ship is Raven (Crow) or some "big animal," that the men in the rigging are crows; the use of protective eye tubes; the conviction that rice is worms; the unintelligibility of the strangers' language; the brave leadership of an old man soon to die; the beginnings of trade. But having detected the patterning, how are we to explain it?

We cannot rule out the possibility that like situations have resulted in like reactions, hence in like stories. Since the Tlingit all share a belief in Raven, perhaps it was only natural for them to conclude that the ships were this bird or some other "big animal," particularly since sails are not unlike wings. The Eskimos of northern Alaska also thought that the first ships which they saw were boats with "large wings" (Nelson 1967:757, 762).[12] We know from ethnography that the Tlingit believe that the safe way to view *any* supernatural manifestation is through an eye tube. Rice *does* look like blow-fly larvae or "worms," and this might be reason enough to reject it. (But did all early sailing ships carry rice? Historical records might answer this question.)[13] The Tlingit certainly could not understand Russian, English, or French. The theme in which the very old take risks in order to lead their people occurs in a number of Tlingit sib traditions and is fully compatible with what we know of their ethnography (McClellan n.d. a:984-92). Interestingly enough, it also turns up in a Haida account of the arrival of the first trading ship (Swanton 1905:105).

In short, we might possibly attribute some, or all, of these similarities in content to independent invention. However, the alternate explanation is diffusion, and this, I think, fits in better with the drive to standardization which perhaps characterizes Coastal Tlingit literature. It is undoubtedly

---

[12] This may, of course, have been merely a linguistic accommodation.
[13] The Northern Tutchone reported that the Tlingit also rejected the rice which they plundered at Fort Selkirk (McBride 1962b:45).

significant that the last links in the chains of testimonies cited—Edgar, Jimmy, and Emmons's informant, Cowee—all grew up in or had close ties with the Sitka-Juneau area. Furthermore, because the whites arrived so long ago, there would have been ample time for the diffusion of details to take place and for them to become well incorporated into stories about what were basically quite separate historic occasions.

No group of stories about the first whites from any of the interior literatures shows nearly as much patterning in exact content as does the set of coastal stories just summarized. While I think this is partly a literary phenomenon, another reason may be that there never was as much similarity in the contact situations in the hinterland as there was on the coast. A succession of large ships arriving one after another, each eager to trade, and each enticing the Indians with much the same trinkets, food, and drink, contrasts markedly with Robert Campbell's first appearance on the Pelly in a crude boat, accompanied by three Indians and three "engaged Hudson's Bay Men," or with the small *Leslie's Illustrated Weekly* expedition, also with its Indian guides and interpreters, or with a handful of tired prospectors. Such arrivals were neither very impressive nor very standardized. The shorter amount of time which has elapsed since the first appearance of the whites may also help to explain the lesser degree of patterning in these stories as compared with those from the coast.

Furthermore, in spite of their variety in specific content, many of the stories about first whites in the interior do reveal recurring sets of interests. These may be summarized as: 1) a marked attention to the personal appearance of the newcomers (expressed in such appellations as "Big Noses" applied to Glave and Dalton or "Big Indians" for the Norwegian and Lappish reindeer herders), 2) a distinct curiosity about new foods (the Tutchone would eat rice), and 3) an equal curiosity about new technology. (Campbell remarked on how eagerly the Tutchone watched him build a house [1958:81].)

In broadest terms these quite understandable interests all relate to what might be called a "new situation." However, what is striking is that the interior Indians so often structured the new situation for the laughs, making themselves the butts of the joke.

Thus a Southern Tutchone explained that when Glave and Dalton arrived with their fearsome horses, all the people wrapped themselves in button blankets and sat in a row staring with eyes as big as the Russian pearl buttons on their blankets. When Dalton offered them silver dollars in payment for food, they threw the money on the ground. What a joke! Another Southern Tutchone told how his grandmother rushed to take the dry meat off her racks, because she thought the "big dogs," as horses were called, would eat it. How hilarious, implied the storyteller! The father of another Southern Tutchone made his wife put on her new white man's shoes and walk through the camp, although she could hardly stand up. How silly! A man burned his hands because he refused to believe that there could really be a fire in the black box called a "stove." How amusing! A little boy wondered what kind of animal chewed down the first tree he ever saw cut with a white man's saw. How stupid! Yet another Southern Tutchone chuckled at the way the first muzzle loader in his band blew up in his face.

Similarly, a Tagish elaborated on how two young men spent all day boiling up some beans they had stolen from an early prospector, since they did not know that they had taken coffee beans. An Inland Tlingit laughed about how his father-in-law packed fifty pounds of flour over his trapping grounds for an entire season, because he forgot to ask the white fur trader what to do with it. Another told how the swelling of some dried peaches brought by the first white man in the area so impressed her grandmother that she used them for years as a specially powerful shamanistic poultice.

At first I thought these stories in which the natives laugh at themselves might be a rather recent phenomenon developed on the part of a minority group trying to ingratiate itself with the whites.[14] However, the fact that white men or white men's goods are involved may really be incidental. Now I wonder whether the stories may represent a genre of humor which is old in the oral literature of both the interior and the coast, but which may have received new impetus in the interior with the arrival of the whites.

As noted, the underlying plot in all the stories is that one is likely to do something laughable when confronted by a totally new situation. The stories about the arrival of the first ships and the Coastal Tlingit reaction to them incorporate something of the self-deriding theme in the incidents about the rice and the mirror. So does a story about the tcucanedi sib who turned away the Athabascans who might have made them rich.[15] But the closest parallel I know to the interior stories just summarized is actually Edgar Sidney's account of what befell him when he first married into the interior. He thought that lakes were salt water, so he spent inordinate amounts of time trying to find fresh water streams where he might drink. He was convinced that a cow moose was some kind of mule until he saw her short tail. He was overcome with nausea when he ate his first rabbits, because he supposed them to be puppies. He threw six mink skins into the snow, assuming them to have no value, and so on. Edgar several times regaled me with his early days as a dupe. Possibly this is one of the standard forms for individual reminiscences, as

[14] Sometimes the narrator himself is the dupe; sometimes it is a relative; at other times it is an unnamed person in the group. I detected no particular subgroup being involved, nor could I see any correlation with the joking patterns as discussed in Luomala's interesting paper on numskulls (1966).

[15] Even today a Tlingit may say of a stupid person: "He sent the Athapascans away," or "The Brush People (tcukanedi) sent the Athapascans away from the other side" (Swanton 1909:160, 334).

compared with the almost sacred character of Tlingit sib history.

Note, however, that Edgar never revealed his ineptitude so that those who were around him became aware of it at the time. In this his story differs from the interior tales in which the Indians demonstrate their foolishness at once. Indeed few of the coastal stories seem to capitalize much on Tlingit stupidity arising from situations when new *people* are involved. Even the tales about the first ships stress the bravery of the old leaders. Another whole set of Coastal Tlingit stories—about the defeat of the Russians at Yakutat and at Sitka—definitely caters to the superiority complex of the Tlingit. In real life the self-sufficient Tlingit like to act as though they excel all other people—a stance which again reflects their highly structured society as well as their impressive aboriginal technology.

One can always pique the curiosity of a Southern Tutchone or Tagish by telling him about other inhabitants of the world. Not so the Tlingit, who are often rather indifferent to foreigners or who, if they incorporate foreign elements into their ceremonials, do so in order to show their sophistication or to commemorate a specific incident in sib history. The Northern Tlingit made a great point of impressing their interior trading partners with how inferior they really were and had dominated them for years. Indeed, a favorite Chilkat dance cruelly mimed the starving Tutchone wandering about in the boreal forest. The inland Indians resented the Tlingit attitude, and they habitually complained that both the Tlingit and the white traders always cheated them. But whether this is why they chose to make themselves the numskulls of the contact stories is hard to say. We know that literature does not always reflect "real" life; rather it often seeks to transform it. One might expect the Tutchone to look elsewhere for their drolls, but so far as I know, they do not.[16] Of all the interior

[16] Luomala (1966:171, 191) cites a Gilbert Island sib that tells numskull anecdotes about itself as comic relief to its sib traditions.

contact stories that I know, only the one about the rescue of Campbell from the boat appears to make anything like a hero out of a Northern Tutchone.

Conclusion

In the first part of this paper I indicated that a number of northwestern American Indian groups have stories about the first whites which are well worth the attention of the ethnohistorian. Using some of the testimonies about Robert Campbell as an example, I then tried to show that winnowing out the concrete historical facts within these traditions is not always easy, even if one uses both historiographic and ethnographic methods.

The second half of the paper concentrates on one particular ethnographic approach. Convinced that these stories can be fully understood only in relation to the total bodies of literature in which they appear, I suggest some lines of future inquiry derived from literary analysis of the stories themselves. Thus, although all the Indians seem to classify these stories in much the same way, the Coastal Tlingit appear to value standardization and formality in the content of their tales about the first whites, while the interior groups delight in free variation. While the Coastal Tlingit tend to portray themselves in a somewhat heroic manner, the interior peoples have developed a comic genre of contact literature in which they themselves play the dupes. If these differences are so, I do not know whether they are due to conscious literary constructs or to artless mirrorings of reality, but surely the ethnohistorian must keep both possibilities in mind. I have offered only a handful of illustrations to bolster my highly selective observations. The next step is to see whether any of them will hold up under a systematic review of other stories about the first whites and, even more, to see whether they seem to fit in with our conclusions about the entire bodies of literature to which they belong.

There is a long road ahead. I am all too aware that this paper has been on a very superficial level. For instance, I have ignored obvious problems of sampling and weighting both within and between groups. Although I have quite full data on the various informants who told most of the stories referred to in this paper and know when he or she first learned the tales, I have not explored what happens when a particular story moves from one person to his contemporaries or from one generation to the next. Yet history can tell us quite firmly the chronological starting points of many of these stories about the first whites, so that such tales provide especially good opportunities for learning about change in the transmission of oral literature (cf. Lowie 1942; Bartlett 1965 [1920]).

Finally, I have eschewed the deeper psychological and structural levels beloved by Dundes, Levi-Strauss, and others because I believe that before we can move effectively into the more covert and subtle realms of an oral literature, we must first become thoroughly familiar with all the overt aspects of its content and style, as well as with its general cultural context. On these matters we have made but the barest start. It may prove possible to link the Klondike Gold Rush story to the mythopoeic male or to reduce the tales about the first ships to some kind of dualism between land and sea (cf. Dundes 1962; Levi-Strauss 1967; Leach 1967), but such findings will not help us to solve certain immediate problems of ethnohistory even though they may reveal ultimate truths about the creators of the literature.

In the end, of course, the more methods of analysis that we use, the better will be our evaluation of these stories, for both history and ethnography. Conversely, the better we analyze the stories, the greater will be their value in helping us to build up a full cultural context for the peoples who have told them.

References

Anonymous
1927   How the white men came to Lituya and what happened to Yeahlth-kan who visited them, the Tlingit tradition of La Perouse' visit. Alaska Magazine 1 (3):151-53, March.

Bartlett, F. C.
1965 (1920)   Some experiments in the reproduction of folk stories. Folklore 31:30-47, 1920. 1920, pp. 30-47. Reprinted with introduction *in* The Study of Folklore, ed. A. Dundes, pp. 243-58. Englewood Cliffs, N. J.

Bascom, W.
1965   The forms of folklore: prose narratives. Journal of American Folklore 78 (307):3-20.

Boas, F.
1916   Tsimshian mythology. Bureau of American Ethnology, 31st Annual Report, 1909–1910. Washington.
1935   Kwakiutl culture as reflected in mythology. Memoirs of the American Folk-Lore Society 28. New York.

Burpee, L. J.
1967 (1945)   Campbell of the Yukon. Canadian Geographical Journal 30 (1945):200-201. Reprinted *in* Alaska and Its History, ed. M. B. Sherwood. Seattle, Wash.

Campbell, Robert
1837–1838   Hudson's Bay Company B 85 a 8. Journal for New Fort Halkett (McClellan's attribution of authorship).
1839–1840   H.B.C. B 85 a 9. Journal for New Fort Halkett (McClellan's attribution of authorship).
1842–1843   H.B.C. B 73 a. Frances Lake Journal.
1843–1844a   H.B.C. B 73 a. Frances Lake Journal.
1843–1844b   H.B.C. B 73 d. Accounts, Frances Lake.
1844–1845   H.B.C. B 73 a. Frances Lake Journal (McClellan's attribution of authorship).
1847–1851   H.B.C. B 196 z. Outfit 1950. Fort Selkirk.
1851–1852   H.B.C. B 196 d. Accounts. Fort Selkirk.
1958 (1808–1951) (1851–1853)   Two journals of Robert Campbell, Chief Factor, Hudson's Bay Company, ed. John W. Todd, Jr. Seattle, Wash.
1967 (1883)   The discovery and exploration of the Pelly (Yukon) River. Royal readers: fifth book of reading lessons. Toronto, 1853. Reprinted *in* North 14:9-15, 1967.

Dawson, G.
1887   Report on the exploration in the Yukon district, N.W.T.

and adjacent northern portion of British Columbia. Geological and Natural Survey of Canada, Annual Report, N.S. 3. (1), Report B. Montreal.

Denniston, G.
n d.   The place of the upper Pelly River Indians in the network of Northern Athabaskan groups. Mimeographed copy on file, University of Wisconsin; National Museums of Canada, pp. 31. Ottawa.

Dorson, R. M.
1963   Current folklore theories. Current Anthropology 4:93-112.

Dundes, Alan
1962   Earth-diver: creation of the mythopoeic male. American Anthropologist 64:1032-51.

Emmons, G. T.
1911   Native account of the meeting between La Perouse and the Tlingit. American Anthropologist 13:294-98.

Fenton, W. N.
1966   Fieldwork, museum studies, and ethnohistorical research. Ethnohistory 13:71-85.

Fischer, J. L.
1963   The sociopsychological analysis of folktales. Current Anthropology 4:235-95.

Hearne, S.
1796   Journey from Prince of Wales Fort in Hudson's Bay to the Northern Ocean. Dublin.

Hudson, C.
1966   Folk history and ethnohistory. Ethnohistory 13:52-70.

Jacobs, M.
1959   The Content and Style of an Oral Literature. Chicago.

Kirk, J. P., and Parnell, C.
1942   Campbell of the Yukon. Part 3. The Beaver. Outfit 273: 23-27, December. Winnipeg, Canada.

Krause, Aurel
1956 (1885) The Tlingit Indians, trans. Erna Gunther. American Ethnological Society. Seattle, Wash.

de Laguna, F.
1960   The story of a Tlingit community. Bureau of American Ethnology, Bulletin 172. Washington.
n.d.   Under Mount Saint Elias. To be published by the Smithsonian Institution. Washington.

Leach, E.
1967   Brain-twister. The New York Review of Books, Oct. 12. 11 (6):6-10.

Levi-Strauss, C.
1967   The story of Asdiwal, trans. N. Mann. *In* The Structural Study of Myth and Totemism, ed. E. Leach. Association of Social Anthropologists, Monograph 5:1-47. Tavistock Publications. London.

Lowie, R. H.
1942   Some cases of repeated reproduction. Studies in Plains Indian Folklore. University of California Publications in American Archaeology and Ethnology 40:19-22. Berkeley and Los Angeles.

Luomala, K.
1966   Numskull clans and tales: their structure and function in Oceanic asymmetrical joking relationships. Journal of American Folklore, 79 (311):157-94.

McBride, W. D.
1962a   Robert Campbell, trail-blazer of the Yukon. Alaska Sportsman 28 (7):20-21, 42-43.
1962b   Robert Campbell, trail-blazer of the Yukon. Alaska Sportsman 28 (8):12-13, 43-45.

McClellan, C.
1950   Culture change and native trade in southern Yukon Territory. Ph.D. Dissertation. Microfilm. University of California. Berkeley.
1961   Avoidance between siblings of the same sex in northwestern North America. Southwestern Journal of Anthropology 17:103-23.
1963   Wealth woman and frogs among the Tagish Indians. Anthropos 58:121-28.
1964   Culture contacts in the early historic period in northwestern North America. Arctic Anthropology 2:3-15.
n.d. a.   Through native eyes: Indian accounts of events in the history of the American Northwest. Typed report on file, National Museums of Canada, pp. 73. Ottawa.
n.d. b.   My old people say: an ethnographic survey of southern Yukon Territory. To be published by the National Museums of Canada, pp. 1363. Ottawa.
n.d. c.   The girl who married the bear. To be published by the National Museums of Canada, pp. 117. Ottawa.

Nelson, J. H.
1967   The last voyage of HMS Investigator, 1850–1853, and

the discovery of the North West Passage. The Polar Record 13 (87):753-68.

Parnell, C.
1942a   Campbell on the Yukon, Part 1. The Beaver. Outfit 273: 4-6, June. Winnipeg, Canada.
1942b   Campbell on the Yukon, Part 2. The Beaver. Outfit 273: 16-18, September. Winnipeg, Canada.

Sherwood, M. B.
1965   Exploration of Alaska, 1865–1900. Yale Western American Series 7. New Haven, Conn.

Sturtevant, W. C.
1966   Anthropology, history and ethnohistory. Ethnohistory 13: 1-51.

Swanton, J. R.
1905   Contributions to the ethnology of the Haida. Jesup North Pacific Expedition, Memoir American Museum of Natural History 5 (1). New York and Leiden.
1909   Tlingit myths and texts. Bureau of American Ethnology, Bulletin 39. Washington.

Thompson, Stith
1958   Myths and folktales. In Myth: A Symposium, ed. T. A. Sebeok. Biographical and Special Series, American Folklore Society, 5:104-10. Bloomington, Ind.

Vansina, Jan
1965   Oral Tradition: A Study in Historical Methodology. Trans. H. M. Wright. Chicago.

EDITOR'S COMMENT

The four examinations of cultural anthropologists' problems and methods in writing history provide excellent guidance to beginning fieldworkers, and not only the young but many elders in the discipline might profit from these accounts of the authors' work. The papers' usefulness is not limited, either, to Alaskan specialists.

They can be viewed as case studies. We have been told how a body of fieldwork developed (by VanStone), how fieldwork by cooperating subdisciplines was done (Ackerman), how evidence was interpreted to show tradition in nonmaterial culture rather than the material segment of culture to which archaeologists apply the concept of "tradition" (Townsend), and how ethnohistoric evidence was interpreted to show a cultural style, in this case a style of local oral history (McClellan).

I cannot resist taking these papers as the text for a little sermon. One point of the exhortation, made especially by VanStone, concerns the value of studying records before one goes into the locality. So many people dash out "into the field," then look up the historical records after returning from the field. Proposals for research should allow time for preliminary archival search.

Another lesson is that even those who are interested only in present institutions and processes should know the history of the people being studied. Assumptions often are made regarding the types of changes and especially the rate of change today as if these were very different from the past, without evidence of the past. The assumptions may be right but also they may be very wrong. That is, one may think that a change is new when it is really a new phase in an old process. Or one may take as a fundamental and long-enduring characteristic of a people what is actually recent.

Both VanStone and Townsend have emphasized cultural persistence. Perhaps because change is a strong motif in our own culture, perhaps because anthropologists have reacted against the assumption of stability expressed in the old "living ancestors" view of preliterate peoples, ethnologists and social anthropologists have not handled *persistence* in a dynamic, fruitful way. Helen Codere, with a larger amount of material available, in a longer and more detailed paper, has summarized Kwakiutl culture change in terms of "persistences and non-persistences" (Codere: 509). Her type of analysis is not common in writings on acculturation and sometimes indeed is very difficult because of lack of data.

Yet in all the present papers, surprising to me and probably to the writers, the question of cultural persistence is a common theme. Moreover, without the quantity of detail available on Kwakiutl Indians and many other North American groups, they have tried to assess persistence as well as change.

Both Ackerman and McClellan in testing cultural persistence in details have made the concept a methodological problem and are experimenting with the tools for its test. Archaeologists have given due attention to persistence and some specialists in ethnology, for example mythologists, have examined *persistence with variations,* but most social anthropologists have not been so concerned about it, possibly because they have not had the necessary methodology. The present papers should help and encourage them. A few can follow the leadership of these writers to the geographic frontier of southwest Alaska and the Yukon-British Columbia border. Many can follow them to the frontier of uses of ethnohistory.

Reference

Codere, Helen
    1961   Kwakiutl. *In* Perspectives in American Indian Culture
            Change, ed. Edward H. Spicer, pp. 431-516. Chicago.

Part Two

*The Aleut Social System, 1750 to 1810,
from Early Historical Sources*

BY MARGARET LANTIS

PREFACE

Part II presents the stuff of ethnohistory: a composite ethnography of Aleut social life in a period now nearly two centuries past, compiled from—I think and hope—all published sources. In short, here are the data, which can be used in various ways: to fill a big gap in our record from prehistoric to modern times; to answer questions regarding Aleut relations with Asiatic and American neighbors; to add the social to the already better-known material part of total Aleut culture.

The sources are identified and placed in historic sequence; then the early observers' ethnographic, that is, descriptive, notes and comments are given verbatim. These observers were amateurs, living a hundred years before anthropology was born as a separate discipline, but they were there. Most of them were educated men—naval officers (at least navigators, if not more), physicians, naturalists—in an era often referred to as an age of enlightenment and tolerance, and they were members of internationally assembled crews.

Through the second half of the eighteenth century and the first quarter of the nineteenth, there were more accounts and better ones on the Aleuts and the Koniag (Eskimo) of Kodiak Island than on other Eskimos for two reasons. First, there was competition between European maritime nations to circumnavigate the globe and explore the Pacific. Second, the ships of the period, while pitifully small and crowded by modern standards, nevertheless were better than any land vehicles. The ship provided not only transportation on an open highway but also housing for men and storage for food, weapons, trade goods, and biological and anthropological collections. Finally, it gave the intellectually diligent persons a place to write. We salute the ships as well as the men.

THE SOURCES AND THEIR USE

The Aleutian Islands, now so end-of-the-line and so thinly populated that they are considered appropriate for United States atomic explosive tests, were the eagerly traveled Russian route to the New World two hundred years ago. That time, the period of the exploration and first conquest of Russian America, is the subject of this paper. Although Russians had seen the New World at Bering Strait, it was only after Bering's voyage along the south coast of Alaska (1742) that the stampede to Alaska began. The objective was the Aleutian Islands' treasure of furs, yielding an almost unbelievable catch of fur-bearing animals, as documented in Bancroft's *History of Alaska* (99-126, 169-74).

The fur traders of the Okhotsk area were, fortunately, not the only ones interested in the newly discovered lands. By Imperial order there were exploring expeditions in which naturalists participated. Then came missionaries, administrators, and higher status merchant-managers than the crews of the small early vessels outfitted by stay-at-home Siberian merchants. On the expeditions, educated men from England, Germany, and Russia made famous voyages and left accounts of their observations on their travels that were translated into two or three languages other than the one originally written. The second half of the eighteenth century and the beginning of the nineteenth century constituted a period of great interest in natural history. This was, after all, the period of Carolus Linnaeus, 1707–1778. Explorers evidently obtained great satisfaction in correctly identifying some bird and bringing back the skin to prove it.

Among the curiosities to be observed in the new lands were the people. Their appearance, houses, boats, and tools were described over and over, as if one were describing plumage and nests. After reading several of the early journals in search of ethnographic data, the ethnologist is likely to feel that if he reads once more about the bone pins through Aleut nasal septums and toothlike ornaments in Aleut chins, he will quit the whole undertaking; then of course he reads once more about facial ornament, underground houses, and kayaks. Anything on the aboriginal social system is hard to come by. Dances were witnessed, household habits were observed and not infrequently shared by over-wintering crews; but the system that held all the customs together was not sought and probably therefore not seen. Considering the type of education and the interests of the period, probably we should not grumble but should be pleasantly surprised that anything relevant to social culture was recorded. It was not so labeled, of course. It must be dug out of the matrix of a naturalist's or a physician's or a naval lieutenant's general observations of the customs of the aborigines.

Aleut culture, early described, is still little known, not only for the above reason but also because the historical sources have been available, at least in the United States, in only a few large libraries. Also, the culture was greatly changed so early that reconstructing a picture of it in the eighteenth century has seemed hopeless. Finally, Aleut culture was considered a geographically isolated offshoot from the Eskimo, a cul-de-sac not important in the study of any other culture. Now the Aleutian Islands are seen as a prehistoric pathway between the Old and New Worlds, a unit in the chain of cultures of the North Pacific rim. Although we come to our task rather late, it is not too late to assemble as much as we can about the people who may have been survivors of an old, submerged Bering Sea culture area or on a late western frontier of Pacific Eskimo and even Tlingit cultural expansion, or both. The reader can look at the evidence and make his own interpretation.

Ethnographically interested naturalists' and scientists' visits to the Islands and their reports fall naturally into five almost completely separate periods. George Wilhelm Steller of the Bering expedition, the first scientist to visit Russian America, did not write about the Aleuts. The two people who dominated the first period were a mystery man, J.L.S., and a man who never visited the Islands, Gerhard Friedrich Müller.

1755–1785

Gerhard Müller, member (1733–1743) of Bering's second expedition on which he went as far east as Irkutsk and Yakutsk, professor of history, member of the St. Petersburg Academy of Sciences, Archivist of the Foreign Office, official historiographer of the Russian Empire, in 1758 presented "the first connected narrative of the Russian discoveries in the northern Pacific" (Masterson and Brower:3; hereafter cited as M. and B.). More important (to us) than this was his influential position enabling him to control the release of information about the new territory. It was charged even before the end of the century that Müller had edited or withheld manuscripts to protect the Russian reputation (M. and B.:15). We can surmise today that such action probably related to the Russian conquest and colonial administration, not to reports on flora and fauna and social customs. Also, apparently we can be grateful to him for an act of just the opposite sort: "there is reason to believe that the material for [*Neue Nachrichten*] had been made available to J.L.S. by Müller himself" (M. and B.:8).[1] Prior to the reports issuing from the Billings expedition, the fullest and most accurate source was the little book *Neue Nachrichten von denen neuentdekten Insuln in der See zwischen Asien und Amerika, aus mitgetheilten Urkunden and Auszügen verfasset von J.L.S.*, 1776.

There have been several guesses as to the identity of the

---

[1] For brevity, Masterson and Brower is referenced as M. and B., the *Arctic Bibliography* as A.B.

author, but Masterson's evidence in rejection of the guesses
and assumptions is convincing to me. J.L.S. evidently is
still a mystery (M. and B.:6-7). In any case, with whatever
help he received, he presented the first reasonably accurate
map of the Aleutians. "The volume summarizes twenty-four
voyages of Russian hunters and merchants to Bering and
Copper Islands, the Aleutian Islands, and Kodiak, 1745–
1770, with facts concerning the identity of the Islands, their
natural history, and their natives." The author obviously
had access to logs, journals, and other manuscripts "in ways
unknown" (M. and B.:7).[2]

Among other reports in the period of the *Neue Nachrichten* was the one by Stählin von Storcksburg (1710–1785),
originally printed in the *St. Petersburg Geographic Calendar*
for 1774.[3] According to the *Arctic Bibliography*, the first
forty pages contain "an account of the commercial voyages
of discovery along the Aleutian Islands, and the islands in
Bering Sea, carried out 1765–67; with extracts from reports
on individual islands" (2:2460). Masterson and Brower (5,
9) regard his account as confused and inaccurate, and I
add that it is of little use to an ethnologist.

The next two contributions were by Englishmen, William
Coxe (1741–1828) and James Cook (1728–1779).

In 1780, before the survivors of Cook's last voyage had arrived
in England after their circumnavigation, the Reverend William
Coxe published his *Account of the Russian Discoveries between
Asia and America. To which are Added, The Conquest of Siberia,
and the History of the Transactions and Commerce between
Russia and China. By William Coxe, A.M., Fellow of King's
College, Cambridge, and Chaplain to His Grace the Duke of
Marlborough*. The writer had visited Russia in 1778 as tutor

---

[2] Coxe, in his Preface, wrote that Müller had compared the *Neue
Nachrichten* with the original Russian journals from which its contents were
taken and had pronounced it accurate (vi-vii).

[3] Life dates are given if I have been able to find them. The *Arctic
Bibliography* has been most useful in providing life dates.

to a young English nobleman and had made the best of his opportunities to meet the scholars of Moscow and St. Petersburg and to collect oral and manuscript accounts of the Eastern discoveries. He gave to the English public its first (and for more and to collect oral and manuscript accounts of the Eastern discoveries since 1745. His work consists of an almost complete translation of J.L.S., an abstract of the journals of Krenitsin and Levashev (not previously known even to Russian readers), and a number of other documents, with useful introductory and editorial matter and four maps. It is difficult to recall any volume published in the eighteenth century that made available to English readers—or, in translation, to French and German readers—a larger accession of geographic knowledge that was entirely new to them. There were three revised editions, and another is needed (M. and B.:10-11).

Captain Petr Kumikh Krenitzin and Lieutenant Mikhail Levashev, whose voyages were accomplished 1764 to 1771, were important among those to whom we are ultimately indebted for any record of eighteenth-century Aleutian culture. Men like Coxe performed essential editorial duties, but there would have been nothing to edit without people like Krenitzin and Levashev. By order of Empress Catherine, these naval officers undertook a voyage of exploration. After a wreck, they finally sailed from Kamchatka, June 1768, for America and returned to it the following summer. Krenitzin drowned in the Kamchatka River in the summer of 1770; Levashev returned to St. Petersburg, October 1771.

The travel accounts by four others who visited the Islands in this period were not published (at least not identified in a publication) for nearly two hundred years, then only in Russian, and I have not consulted them. They may well have been used by J.L.S. and later writers. S. T. Ponomarev and S. G. Golikov were in the Aleutian Islands 1758–1759, M. Lazarev and P. Vasiutinski 1764. The *Arctic Bibliography* note on the contents of their reports (hereafter cited as A.B.), published by Aleksandr Andreev, suggests little information for an ethnologist. Nevertheless, any future ethnohistorian of the Aleuts should consult this Russian source.

The giant among explorers of this period was James Cook (1728–1779), who began his work in the Newfoundland-Labrador area in 1763 and finally reached southwest Alaska in 1778 on the third of his great voyages to the Pacific Ocean. It was on his return from the voyage along the coast of Alaska that he was killed in the Hawaiian Islands: "The manuscript of Cook's journal, together with dispatches of Captain Clerke dated in Avacha Bay, Kamchatka, June 8, 1779, was received by the Admiralty Office Jan. 11, 1780. . . . These papers, sent by courier across Siberia and Russia, had apparently been available to Pallas, who [December 1779] . . . addressed to Anton Johann Büsching a somewhat detailed summary of Cook's voyage to the time of his death." The earliest volumes on Cook's third expedition were published in both England and Germany in 1781, but the full official edition did not appear until 1784 (M. and B.:1, *n.* 38).

What Cook recounted of his passage through the Aleutian Islands is graphic but short. If he had lived to complete his journey and had written a full memoir, we might have had more.

The last person who must be mentioned is Peter Simon Pallas (1741–1811), born in Berlin, doctor of medicine who became a naturalist. After six years of directing a scientific expedition in southern Siberia, 1768–1774, he devoted the remainder of his life to writing and editing others' writings on philology and ethnology, geology, botany and zoology, at a time when one man could do all this. "The contributions of Pallas to Alaskan studies are contained in his *Neue nordische Beyträge zur physikalischen und geographischen Erd- und Völkerbeschreibung, Naturgeschichte, und Oekonomie.* Issued in seven volumes between 1781 and 1796, this work consists chiefly of articles by Pallas (occasionally by

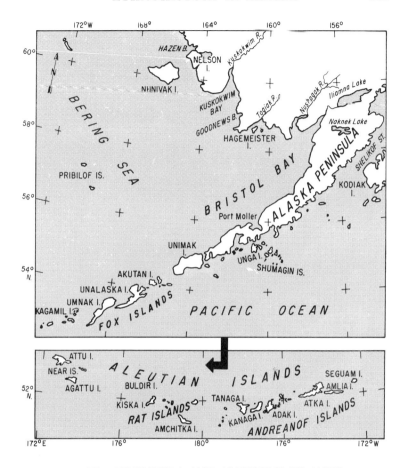

ALASKA PENINSULA AND ALEUTIAN ISLANDS

others) pertaining to the geography and the natural history of the more remote and obscure parts of the Russian Empire." Included in its first four volumes (1781–1783) are nine items relating to Alaska in some way, translated and published by Masterson and Brower. Of these, four are of some interest to us: "Remarks on Coxe's book, introducing an annotated translation of his abstract of the journals of Krenitsin and Levashev. . . . Translation of a narrative by Dmitri Bragin of his fur-hunting voyage from Okhotsk to Kodiak, 1772–1777. Abstract of the journal of a fur-hunting voyage of Ivan Soloviev from Okhotsk to the Alaska Peninsula, 1770–1775. Abstract of a report by Potap Zaikov of his fur-hunting voyage from Okhotsk to Unimak, 1772–1778" (M. and B.:11-13).

Among Ivan Petroff's manuscript translations from the Russian, deposited in the Bancroft Library, is one from a source identified by Petroff as *Literary Collections,* Part 5, St. Petersburg, 1790. It contains "Account of the Voyage of Master Zaikoff, on the boat St. Vladimir, to the Islands situated between Asia and America" (147-64) and "Extract from the Journal of the ship 'St. Michael' during its voyage among the islands situated between Asia and America." (I failed to record the total number of pages translated from the latter. The section that I have used covers pages 304-17.) Title, date of publication, and page numbers are different from those of the Pallas publications translated by Masterson and Brower, yet Zaikoff and the Bragin (*St. Michael*) reports in the *Literary Collections* cover much of the same material. The most important discrepancies occur in the extract from the *St. Michael* journal. Not so important to us, nevertheless arousing curiosity, is the statement in the Petroff manuscript that the ship was under the command of Dmitry Polutoff, whereas according to the Pallas article it was under Dmitri Bragin. Perhaps he had two names. Both sources have been used here, with an effort made to reconcile discrepancies, which are not merely different wording by the translators but evidently somewhat different versions in the original publications.

All these reports are short and generally tell more about the writers than the subjects of their writing. They do indicate the relations, whether hostile or amicable, between the Aleuts and these long-term visitors, and provide a starting point for a study of interethnic relations and culture change.

1785–1810

Although the interval between the early explorers (and their editors) and the next group was short, the change in scientific value was great. Dominating the second period was the Geographical and Astronomical Exped'tion to the Northeast Parts of Russia 1785–1791, under order of Empress Catherine and under command of the English naval Captain Joseph Billings, which reached Kamchatka and Alaska 1789–1791. Billings apparently wrote no public account, but three worthwhile reports were published in due time: by Sarytchev, Sauer, and belatedly by Merck. Billings had been the astronomer's assistant on Cook's third expedition, 1776–1780 (Sauer: vii-ix) and now headed a 141-man expedition, including Robert Hall, commander of the *Chernyi Orel*, Gavril Sarytchev, commander of the *Slava Rossii*, Martin Sauer, secretary and interpreter (Russian-English?) of the expedition, Luka Voronin, artist, and Carl Heinrich Merck, physician and naturalist (A.B. 6:721-24).

Gavril Andreevich Sarytchev (1763-1830), who incidentally called it the Geographical and Astronomical Maritime Expedition under Command of Captain Billings in 1785–1793, provided the fullest account (published in Russian 1802, in English 1806–1807), with a separate atlas containing maps and plates. (All maps and most plates were omitted in the English edition.) Sarytchev, a naval lieutenant, was responsible for the nautical-cartographic observations (Jacobi:113), but fortunately he did not limit his report to these. His ship cruised the Aleutians and the south-central coast of Alaska as far east as Prince William Sound in 1790 and traveled as far east as Unalaska in 1791. Both *Slava Rossii* and *Chernyi Orel* over-wintered 1791–1792 at Unalaska after Sarytchev's 1791 voyage from there to St. Lawrence Island, Bering Strait, and the Chukotsk Peninsula, and return.

Martin Sauer's account, published in 1802, contained

fourteen plates and a folded map, as well as a report of observations by a reasonable man, a conscientious observer. These books begin to sound like modern scientific reports. Sauer wrote in his preface that he took notes as he went. "My object has been to travel with my eyes open, and to relate what I have seen in the simple language of truth" (x-xiv). He wrote, moreover, in English so that we do not have to question and check the quality of translating and editing (A.B. 6:724-25). Sarytchev's account, for example, was not only translated but also abridged in the English version (A.B. 6:721-23).

Some of the work of the German-born doctor of medicine, Carl Heinrich Merck, was used by Pallas (the botanical and zoological notes); then after the death of Pallas in Berlin in 1811 Merck's journal disappeared, reappearing in a Leipzig bookseller's shop in 1936. Merck is now best known for his observations on and collection of birds, through a publication by Erwin Stresemann in 1948 (A.B. 2:2521) and for his ethnographic observations, published by A. Jacobi in 1927 (A.B. 5:398-99). The journal was started in Okhotsk in August 1789 (Merck visited Alaska on two voyages, 1790 and 1791) and covers, according to Jacobi, 162 folio sheets, hard to read because of the fine script and the use of German to which Merck was no longer accustomed after several years in Siberia. Jacobi evidently modernized and somewhat smoothed the German (Jacobi:114). We are glad to have this journal but it is not of the magnitude of either Sauer's or Sarytchev's production.

About ten years after the Billings expedition there began an even more ambitious one, the first Russian round-the-world voyage, 1803-1806, from which came a report by one of the best observers, Lisianski. The expedition was made on behalf of the Russian-American Company by order of Alexander I. It was led by Ivan Fedorovich Kruzenshtern (von Kruzenstern in German) (1770-1846) on the *Nadezhda*, while Yuri Fedorovich Lisianski (1773-1837) was in command of the *Neva*. Each published his own account, Kruzenshtern writing (regarding the north Pacific) chiefly on Kamchatka (A.B. 1:1406-1409), Lisianski on Alaska, unfortunately for us much more on the Koniag Eskimo and Tlingit than on the Aleuts. Lisianski's two-volume work was published in Russian in 1812, and in English only two years later (A.B. 2:1526).

The "Yudin Collection" in the "Documents Relative to the History of Alaska" contains material from and about N. P. Rezanov, indicating that the leaders of this expedition could be petty men, not exactly glamorous explorers. Rezanov, Actual Chamberlain of the Imperial Court, Knight of various orders and shareholder of the Russian-American Company, was sent by the Emperor as Envoy Extraordinary and Minister Plenipotentiary to the Japanese court. The Company also made him a plenipotentiary. Unfortunately for him, he was made chief of the expedition: His report to Alexander I states that Kruzenshtern and Lisianski resented him. According to his description of their behavior and that of Berkh, they showed the greatest disrespect and, he thought, even tried more than once to have him murdered. (In contrast, he spoke well of Kvostov and Davidov, whom he encountered in Kamchatka.) That he was not merely paranoid or a pompous man who expected too much deference is shown by a report from an employee of the Russian-American Company, F. I. Shemelin, to its Board of Directors, detailing his and Rezanov's experiences. He claimed that a man named Tolstoi turned Lisianski and others against Rezanov, but the naval officers were not innocent: they were accused of criticism of the government, disloyalty, atheism, debauchery, and misuse of money and supplies. Kruzenshtern apparently was the chief offender on the last count (Documents 3:170, 195-96, 247-48). Any high official or conscientious and independent outsider must have threatened the comfortable status of Company officers and Royal Naval officers alike. They undoubtedly ap-

preciated the advantages of being 10,000 miles from the
Russian Court without a representative of that Court
watching them. Some of the men in the employ of traders
seem to have been fairly good observers and at the same
time to have practiced severe mistreatment of the Aleuts
and the Koniag of Kodiak Island, to the point of tyranny.
This case, with its petty mistreatment of men of one's own
race, appears to have been different.

The physician of the expedition, Freiherr Georg Heinrich
von Langsdorff (1774–1852), presented his original two-
volume report in German the same year as Lisianski's
(1812), with an English translation published 1813–1814,
and he did report on the Pribilof Islands and Unalaska
Island. "The author left the expedition at Kamchatka 1805,
visited the Aleutian Islands, the northwest coast of America,
and returned, via Kamchatka, overland across Siberia to
St. Petersburg. The second volume of this narrative is a
record of his travels after he left Kruzenshtern" (A.B. 1:
1449). Like many of the early visitors, von Langsdorff
devoted many pages to material culture but not many to
the social culture. He should not be faulted on this, since
he not only observed but was willing to publish his unflattering view of the policies and methods of the Russian-
American Company, unlike most of his contemporaries.
His view, more judgmental than that of Merck and several
of the other early writers, led him occasionally to write
moralistically on local customs. He also said what he
thought about his contemporaries: a bit disparaging of
Sauer, praising Davydov.

Aleksandr Andreev has included with the reports by
Golikov and other early visitors to the Aleutians, already
mentioned, N. I. Korobitsyn's narrative of his "commercial
travels," 1795 to 1807. The last five years he was on the
Neva under Lisianski's command and like his commander
wrote about Kodiak and Sitka (A.B. 1:115).

A contemporary of Lisianski and a competitor for honors

as recorder of observations was Gavril Ivanovich Davydov (1784–1809) who, with another naval officer, Khvostov, made two voyages to America, 1802–1804 and 1804–1807, on behalf of the Russian-American Company. Like Lisianski, he wrote about the Eskimos of Kodiak Island and the Tlingit Indians (A.B. 1:575). In this period there is more and better information on the Koniag Eskimos than on the Aleuts.

Andreev included in his book of documents on the Russian discoveries in the New World various papers by and concerning Grigorii Ivanovich Shelekhov (1747–1795), one of the founders of the Russian-American Company, which became in the ninteeenth century virtually Russian government in Alaska. These documents as annotated in the *Arctic Bibliography* (1:115) do not appear to be the personal report translated by Ivan Petroff, which was consulted for the present paper. The manuscript translation in the Bancroft Library, University of California, is titled "Voyages of G. Shelekhoff. From the year 1783 to 1790, from Okhotsk, through the Eastern Ocean, to the American Coast and his return to Russia, etc. St. Petersburg, 1812." Shelekhov, the trader who became more than a trader, recorded what he knew about the "Koniagi" and "Kuriltze" and what he had read about the Aleuts. Because he seems to have depended heavily on J.L.S.'s *Neue Nachrichten,* one need not reject his notes on Aleut customs, but one cannot always take them as independent observations.

Another voyager of this period who is today virtually unknown is Archibald Campbell, a Scottish sailor who early in his voyage around the world, 1806 to 1812, was shipwrecked in the Islands. (He was on a ship out of Boston that was chartered by the Russian-American Company to take a cargo from Chinese ports to its various stations.) Although his account is that of an untrained adventurer, it is personal and adds graphic reality to our picture of that time.

1815–1855

Russia evidently had to recover from the Napoleonic invasion, and officials and influential citizens had to absorb reports like Lisianski's (1812) before undertaking further exploration and missionary work. After a lapse of about fifteen years (approximately 1806 to 1820), interest in Russian America flowered again.

The only big exploration before 1820 was von Kotzebue's search for a "northeast passage" from Bering Strait. Lieutenant Commander Otto Evstafevich Kotsebu or von Kotzebue (1787–1845) commanded two voyages around the world, in 1815–1818 and 1823–1826. The first one, privately financed, is interesting to us because of a few observations by the expedition's naturalist, Adelbert von Chamisso. The English translation of Kotzebue's three-volume account amazingly appeared the same year, 1821, as the Russian edition, evidence of the demand for this type of literature in the early nineteenth century. The second voyage, made for the Russian-American Company, yielded a description of the Kamchadals and the Tlingits of Baranof Island but not of the Aleuts (A.B. 1:1380).

Chamisso mentioned documents of Müller, Coxe, and Pallas, from which expedition members had learned of Dezhnev's voyage to Bering Strait in 1648. He also had read Sauer, Sarytchev, Cook, Davydov, Langsdorff, Kruzenshtern, and others. "We have found their reports on the customs and practices of these peoples very true, insofar as we could learn about these, and must contradict them on only one point," namely, the peoples' physical characteristics (Kotzebue 3:217, 246; reference is to the 1825 German edition, from which this translation was made).

Vasili Stepanovich Khromchenko (d. 1849), accompanied on some of his journeys by A. K. Etolin, made useful exploring voyages in Bering Sea from 1821 to 1833 for the Russian-American Company. He recorded vocabularies in various places and also a few observations, the most valuable work done between Bristol Bay and Norton Bay, but seems to have contributed nothing to Aleut ethnography. In this period others were exploring the interior, even farther from our locus of interest, hence are not considered here.

Baron Ferdinand Petrovich Vrangel (von Wrangell in German and cited as Wrangell) (1794–1870) as a naval lieutenant led a Russian government exploring expedition along the north coast of Siberia east of the Kolyma River mouth, 1820-1824; later, as a vice-admiral he was administrator of the Russian colonies in Alaska, 1830-1835, for the Russian-American Company. Miscellaneous materials that he had collected were edited and published in German by K. E. von Baer. They contain, however, little that is new, that is, not available in Veniaminov's material, quoted by Vrangel, or elsewhere.

Our best source was Evan Evsievich Popov Veniaminov (1797–1879), who was an Orthodox missionary for ten years on Unalaska Island, 1825–1834, and five years at Sitka. (Barsukov said 1824–1833 and 1833–1838 respectively.) His three-volume *Notes on the Unalaska Islands District,* published under auspices of the ubiquitous and powerful Russian-American Company, "give the first detailed description of a part of the Aleutians, Pribilof Islands and Alaska Peninsula" (A.B. 2:2771), "the only ethnographic study made before their original culture deteriorated" (2772). (To be fully accurate, one should say "completely deteriorated," since it was already partly destroyed but could be recorded as a memory culture.) Besides ethnography, they contain a description of the islands, their fauna, history, weather observations, and miscellaneous other data. Veniaminov became the first Bishop of Alaska, then Archbishop of Kamchatka, the Kuriles, and the Aleutian Islands. He was transferred to Yakutia and from there to Moscow where (1867) he became Innokenti, Metropolitan of Moscow. His letters and a short biography were published by Ivan Barsukov, 1897–1901 (A.B. 1:196).

What kind of man would advance like this? H. H. Bancroft quoted descriptions as follows: "Father Veniaminov, whom Sir Edward Belcher, writing in 1837, describes as 'a very formidable, athletic man, about forty-five years of age [actually he was forty], and standing in his boots about six foot three inches; quite herculean, and very clever.' 'When he preached the word of God,' says Kostromitin, who was baptized by Father Joassaf in 1801, 'all the people listened, and listened without moving, until he stopped. Nobody thought of fishing or hunting while he spoke, and nobody felt hungry or thirsty as long as he was speaking—not even little children'" (Bancroft:701).

Ivan Petroff, Bancroft's principal assistant in the preparation of his history of Alaska, used Veniaminov's *Notes* liberally and included in his (Petroff's) 1880 census report a translation of long excerpts from the famous work. Since there still is no complete and accurate English translation from the Russian, nearly all English-speaking writers and students have depended on Petroff's version of Veniaminov, which they have seen as a manuscript translation in the Bancroft Library or more likely in the Tenth Census. The former begins as follows:

Letters about the Islands of the Ounalashka District, compiled by I. Veniaminoff. Parts I, II, III. St. Petersburg, 1840.

The first volume of Veniaminoff's "Letters from the islands of the Ounalashka District" contains principally geographical description and meteorological observations and will therefore not be translated in full. For an explanation of its contents a translation of the preface will be sufficient, while such items in the volume as have any historical bearing will also be extracted.

I. Petroff, translator.

In the preface, one reads (Petroff's translation), "Having lived 10 years in that country, and traveled over it in the line of my duty several times and having had occasion to become intimately acquainted with the inhabitants of this distant coast of our country, to study their disposition and capabilities, to learn as far as possible their language, character, customs and their whole being, as well as the productions and climate of the country, I think it my duty to give to my dear countrymen the result of my ten years' labors. All I could see, observe, remark and collect that is curious and worthy of attention and remark, connected with this country, I present" (Veniaminov 1:ii). After telling from whom he had obtained climatological and other technical data, he continued, "In describing the moral peculiarities and character of the Ounalashkans I have not trusted the observations of others, but have only made use of my own impressions; especially their traits of character have been drawn by myself and from nature, and only in a very few from description of the Ounalashkans themselves, and then I ascertained its truth as far as possible. In order to become better acquainted with their character I endeavored to observe them when people become more open and more talkative, i.e. when they are a little drunk, but I found nothing that is not in accordance with my subjoined remarks or indicative of any secret traits of their character." Dated St. Petersburg, December 6, 1839 (Veniaminov 1:iii-iv).

The literary style may be different but the message is the same as the modern ethnographer's, stating his fieldwork credentials and evidently feeling rather pleased and self-righteous about them. We cannot begrudge Veniaminov whatever satisfaction he may have felt: as the work of a not-especially-well-educated priest in the first half of the nineteenth century, the report is excellent.

(Having become suspicious of some passages in Petroff's translation and wanting to quote Veniaminov as exactly as possible, I obtained the assistance of Andrae Malazemoff, then [thirty years ago] instructor in the Slavic Languages Department, University of California. He corrected Petroff's translation or in some cases translated de novo those sections that might be needed for this and for my previous publications on Alaskan Eskimos and Aleuts.)

In this period three other voyagers briefly visited the

Aleutians. Navy Captain Graf Fedor Petrovich Litke (in French and German, Lütke) (1797–1882) went around the world 1826–1829 on the navy sloop *Seniavin*, by order of Emperor Nicholas I, after four voyages along the north coast of Russia and Siberia, 1821–1824 (A.B. 1:1527-28). His few pages on Unalaska culture—he wrote much more on the Kamchadals—need not be considered, since they coincide chronologically with Veniaminov's volumes, except for some bits of information on changes then under way. He was inevitably, like other casual travelers, able to write about kayaks but not about kinship.

Georg Adolf Erman (1806–1877), who journeyed around the world in 1828–1830 for geographic studies, visited Alaska in the latter part of 1829. His report forty years later gives much firsthand information on the Tlingit of Sitka but, as the *Arctic Bibliography* states, "describes the ethnography of the Aleuts largely on the basis of Russian and German publication" (1:715-16). Erman's observations can be useful for an account of cultural changes under Russian influence but not for the pre-Russian culture. He commented on the fact that by this time the Aleuts had, for the most part, a European substitute for the aboriginal way of life (Lebensweise) (3:159-60). For information on the latter, he had used chiefly Shelekof and Veniaminov.

Alcide d'Orbigny left France in 1841; exactly when he arrived in the Aleutian Islands is not stated. Since the 1854 edition of his *Voyage dans les deux Ameriques*, the one consulted, is a compilation of personal observations and material from historical sources, it is difficult to evaluate as an original source. Evidently most of the material on Aleut culture was taken from Veniaminov.

The period can be closed with Henrik Johan Holmberg (1818–1864), a Finnish naturalist who published in German an ethnological and historical study "based chiefly on printed Russian sources and on . . . [his] own observations during his stay at Sitka, Kodiak and other places in 1850–

51" (A.B. 4:425). Unfortunately, what Holmberg has given on the other places adds almost nothing to our Aleut data. His information on Kodiak is, however, valuable and should not be overlooked in any comparison of Koniag and Aleut.

Although there is in the Bancroft Library a manuscript translation by Petroff of the "Tabular Statement of the Present Condition of the Russian American Colonies, 1860, by Actual State Councillor Kostlivtzoff," this and other documents like it, prepared, one surmises, in anticipation of a change of administration or sale of Alaska, need not be included in our résumé of sources. The "Statement" gives an interesting picture of the condition of southwest Alaska in 1860, not in 1800.

1870–1915

Alphonse Louis Pinart (1852–1911), known to specialists in our area almost solely for a paper illustrating a few Aleut masks that he found in a cave on Unga Island in 1871 and better known to American ethnologists for his work in California and Mexico, should be remembered also for field notes written in Alaska 1871 to 1872. The notes, deposited in the Bancroft Library, record chiefly religion and mythology and in regard to area deal chiefly with Kodiak. Parmenter, who has published an annotated Pinart bibliography, says that James C. Pilling's *Bibliography of the Eskimo Language* (1887) mentions a "Manuscript of about 700 pages, in Alaskan and Russian, Collected by Mr. Pinart in 1871 in Unalashka, Belkofsky, Unga and Kodiak" (Parmenter:3-4). This description does not fit the manuscript that I have used; it must refer to another. Pinart, a wealthy Frenchman, went to Alaska before he was twenty years old. Instead of merely adventuring, he industriously recorded vocabularies, myths, and tales. His material has a directness and sincerity that unedited field notes are more likely to have than a later publication.

Only a few years after the purchase of Alaska (1867), William Healey Dall (1845–1927), the most prolifically published scientist in the early days of Alaska as a United States Territory, began his work in the Aleutians. ("Between 1870 and 1884, he published some 400 papers"—Sherwood: 54.)

After heading the scientific corps of the Western Union Telegraph Company Expedition 1866–1868, he made the Smithsonian Institution his headquarters while writing his first book. Sherwood, who has written a chapter-length biography of him, said: "Dall's book, *Alaska and Its Resources,* was a narrative of his adventures and researches in Alaska with the Telegraph Company and a compilation of geographical, historical, and scientific information on the country. It established his reputation as an expert, though Dall knew the volume raised more questions than it settled" (39).

Dall next directed United States Coast and Geodetic Survey explorations in Alaska, 1871-1880, with the Coast Survey's work in the Aleutians and around Kodiak Island done early in this period: 1871–1874. In 1884 he transferred to the Geological Survey. To complete the highlights of his career, one should note that Dall was a member of the International Polar Expedition to Pt. Barrow, 1882–1883, and the Harriman Alaska Expedition, 1899.

Dall's own specialty was marine invertebrates, but he published papers on birds, Aleut mummies, and a great variety of subjects besides mollusks. In 1873 he began publishing notes on his prehistoric and early historic finds in the Eastern Aleutians (A.B. 1:553-561). Dall had the disadvantage of writing when the theory of evolution was the new creed: he could not simply present his observations and finds but had to assemble and explain them in terms of evolutionary stages that he thought he saw in his excavations of shell-heaps. The result is that he appears to us a rather wild theorizer, but perhaps in saying this one is too hard on Dall. He was at least the first to attempt modern archaeology. He located sites and told the general nature and extent of them, to the benefit of later archaeologists; and in 1878 summarized their prehistoric relationship to the mainland soundly enough: "The evidences of the shell heaps are conclusive as to the identity with the continental Eskimo of the early inhabitants of the islands, as far as implements and weapons go, but their insular habitat, and the changed fauna and climatic conditions under which they existed, gradually modified their habits, and their manufactures, of every kind. With these changes, it is probable, the language changed" (Dall 1878:2).

Lucien M. Turner went to the Aleutians in 1878 after Edward W. Nelson relieved him as weather observer at St. Michael. "Turner trained voluntary observers and traveled about collecting additional specimens until he was relieved in 1881 [by the Signal Service]" (Sherwood:93). He collected, according to the U. S. National Museum Report of 1881, ethnographic and archaeological specimens, vocabulary, and stories and legends during his travels with Unalit and Malemiut Eskimos, Nulato and Ingalik Indians, and Unalaskan Aleuts (Caswell: 194). However, social culture as usual was slighted.

A valuable short biography of Ivan Petrov (b. 1842), who usually Americanized the spelling as "Petroff," has been written by the historian Morgan Sherwood (57-69). As a reluctant soldier, Petroff had been in the Kenai and Kodiak areas before 1871. In 1878, after becoming an assistant and translator to Bancroft, the historian, he went to Unalaska, among other places in south Alaska, examining records in preparation for the *History of Alaska.*

The principal work under Petroff's own name is *Population and Resources of Alaska, 1880,* published as part of the Tenth Census. Of it, Sherwood has written:

It was only natural that Petroff, the census taker, should discourse at length on the natives. He relied on the old authorities and on Dall, whose ethnological work he credited as the most valuable since acquisition of the territory by the United States. The implication of Petroff's language, however, is that his own labor was an original study by an expert. The differences between his ethnographic map and Dall's were slight, he felt, "and give evidence only an extension of the field of investigation. This result is all the more gratifying because Mr. Dall and myself have arrived at very similar conclusions through entirely different channels and without consultation upon the subject." The language must have infuriated Dall. At several points, Petroff seems even to paraphrase the "Dean": "All that can be done at present in the way of classifying the natives of Alaska is to divide them into four distinct families or tribes. . . . The numerous subdivisions of each family . . . can only be vaguely indicated, in the hope of furnishing to future investigators a framework upon which to build a more satisfactory structure." The "four distinct families," Petroff fails to mention, had been suggested by Holmberg and outlined by Dall. Petroff used different labels than Dall. The former explained: "I have adopted the terms Eskimo and Athabaskan, in lieu of the Innuit and Tinneh of recent writers, purely in the interest of uniformity, and in deference to the action of both the American and British science associations, which have decided that priority must prevail." In a later article, Petroff said he retained the older terms on the advice of Otis T. Mason of the National Museum, and of Powell and Baird. Further, Petroff "agreed" with Dall that the Aleutians were peopled from the east, not Asia, but probably not before the invention of the kayak. Snorted Dall: The Tenth Census report on the Alaska Peninsula "is retrograde in many particulars rather than an advance, being the work of a person unqualified for the task."

Ivan Petroff, though well qualified as a regional specialist, was no ethnologist or for that matter a scientist. He was a journalist, and occasionally a pretentious one at that. His ingenious composition employed techniques he probably derived from Dall, techniques that implied he was at least the equal of Dall as an anthropologist. The implied expertise in turn disguised his reliance on old sources and his wholesale use of Dall's own material. Though a good general treatment of the subject, there was nothing scientifically new in Petroff's ethnographical report. His writing was chiefly the result of bookish research and casual travel and not the result of original investigations (60 62).

We can be grateful to Petroff (and to the Bancroft Library) principally for his voluminous translations from the Russian. They need checking for strict accuracy but probably no more than the specialist would expect to do with any translation by an early—and self-confident—nonspecialist. Regarding his other work, Sherwood refers to Petroff's casual travel. For the 1880 census, he went from Unalaska west to Atka and east to the Shumagin Islands, besides travels on the mainland which may well have been exaggerated. In directing the census of Alaska in 1890, Petroff "allegedly covered 12,000 miles" but recorded no exact itinerary (Sherwood: 63). In the early 1890s he was discredited for fabricating and interpolating statements into his translations for the Department of State, and he was thereafter given no credit for the Eleventh Census of Alaska. The date of his death is unknown (Sherwood: 68).

The physician, Irving C. Rosse, whose "Medical and Anthropological Notes on Alaska" was included in *Cruise of the Revenue-Steamer Corwin in Alaska and the N. W. Arctic Ocean in 1881* (1883), has given us a few comments on the effects of contacts with the Russians and other newcomers to southwest Alaska that might be useful in a study of culture change but not of much use in the present work.

The next worker was a collector of folklore: Frank A. Golder (1877–1929). Our bibliography shows that the material in which we are interested was published from 1903 to 1909. In his introductory note to the first group of tales, Golder wrote, "The author has but lately returned from Alaska" (1903:16). To historians, Golder is better known for his archival work. Assisted by the Carnegie Institution of Washington and (later?) by the American Geographical Society and the United States National Archives, Golder spent eight months in Russia in 1914 and from its archives obtained logbooks, journals, and various reports of early Russian explorations between the mainlands of Asia and America. His *Bering's Voyages* was the first full account in English of the Bering expedition's explorations, notably the first complete translation (by Leonhard Stejneger) of Steller's journal (A.B. 6:313-16; Golder 1917 and 1922; Gruening:493; M. and B.:16). This 1922–1925 publication, after our fourth period, is mentioned only to complete Golder's record.

Reports on the only new, genuine anthropological work of the period, that of Vladimir or Waldemar Jochelson (1855–1937), also were considerably delayed. They were not published until 1925 and 1933 because of the Russian revolution. Jochelson explained regarding his "Archaeological Investigations in the Aleutian Islands":

During the year 1909–10, the author led the anthropological division of the Aleut-Kamchatka Expedition, sent out under the auspices of the Imperial Russian Geographical Society [and financed by the Moscow banker, F. P. Riaboushinsky]. . . . The original manuscript was prepared in Russian, was ready for the printer in 1916, and was presented to the Academy of Sciences of Russia, where it received the Akhmatoff prize. Its publication was, however, delayed because of the war. Later, in the autumn of 1917 when the Russian revolution broke out, the office of Riaboushinsky Brothers in Moscow, where the manuscript was to be printed, was destroyed by the mob, and it was with difficulty that the author succeeded in saving the Russian manuscript, drawings, and maps from destruction. Of the plates, however, but one copy of each was saved, from which the reproduction used here was made. After reaching the United States the author rewrote the manuscript in English and added new material, so as to include a comparative study of the Eskimo-Aleut collections in America (Jochelson 1925:v).

His report on the history, ethnography, and physical anthropology of the Aleuts, the last studied by his wife, a doctor of medicine, evidently was prepared in the United States "as a continuation of the archaeological report" (Jochelson 1933:v). This monograph, published toward the end of his long life, contains only forty pages of ethnography, of which about half are occupied by photographs. For our purpose the principal value of the work is the kinship terminology. It is a pity that Jochelson could not have visited Alaska earlier in his productive career and produced something like his big monograph, "The Koryak."

During World War I and the following decade the Islands were neglected while attention turned toward the Eskimos.

1930–Present

In 1930–1931, H. Dewey Anderson and his wife and Walter C. Eells, specialists in education from Stanford University, made "A Survey of Their [Alaska Natives'] Sociological and Educational Status" at the request of the United States Office of Education and supported by the Carnegie Corporation of New York. Although they visited six Aleut villages, where they tested a total of sixty-four children, the large section of the report on economy, health, psychosocial characteristics, and social relationships deals only with the Eskimos.

I spent 1933–1934 on Atka Island as a graduate student new to Alaska, presumably serving as a substitute teacher but actually spending most of my time (rather ineffectively) on village health care. The medical situation at that time was deplorable, as was community morale and organization. My field notes are used here for the first time, to help explain—where this seems possible—Veniaminov's and other accounts for the period covered in this paper. Jochelson's, Hrdlička's and other publications of this period are similarly used as footnotes to the early journals.

Aleš Hrdlička (1869–1943), the physical anthropologist, late in his Alaskan career studied the Aleuts, 1936–1938.

As we would expect, he concentrated on archaeology and physical anthropology. As the *Arctic Bibliography* states, his report, published two years after his death, includes ethnographic notes from the literature on the Aleutians: It covers "various aspects of material, intellectual and social culture as recorded in the literature" (A.B. 1:1120). Hrdlička generally traveled and lived aboard Coast Guard cutters; therefore he did not have much opportunity for extended interviews and observations on social organization even if he had been more interested in it.

After World War II, Gerald Berreman, Theodore Banks, a botanist, Gordon Marsh, a linguist, and William Laughlin and his students did field research in the Aleutians, Berreman and Laughlin principally on Umnak Island. Only Berreman has concentrated on the social system, and not all the results of his research have been published.

After 1910, little was to be gleaned regarding the pre-European culture. In fact, after 1850 or even after Veniaminov's time the memories of Aleut elders must have related to postconquest time. Although Veniaminov said that his report is based largely on his own observations, it appears that much of the information of greatest interest in the present connection was obtained from the old folks remembering what life was like in the late eighteenth century and recalling family stories of early and mid-1700s. Reports following Veniaminov's *Notes* have been used here principally to elucidate confused or contradictory accounts from the period prior to 1825.

Selection and Use of Ethnographic Data

Although a few technological aspects of the activities and systems reported here have been included, an effort has been made to limit the data to the nonmaterial. We need not know the details of construction of a house or a coffin or the exact type of weapons used in warfare unless these are stated to represent status or other social differences. Religion is excluded, since most of the historical data on this subject has been included in some of my earlier publications (Lantis 1938, 1940, 1947).

This is seen as a compilation of primary ethnohistorical materials, organized for much readier use by ethnologists than are the original old, often rare publications and the even less accessible manuscripts. Explanation, where it appears to be needed and possible to supply, has been added, but no attempt at a modern functional or structural analysis of the data has been made. That is a separate operation which may be undertaken at another time.

It has been tempting to compare the Aleut social system with those of neighboring peoples both east and west (Tlingit, Pacific Eskimos, Tanaina and Bristol Bay Eskimos; Koryak, Kamchadals, and Ainu) and further to essay a historical reconstruction of their relationships from the data at hand. Such a historical interpretation—like an analytical one—would make this publication too long.

The third temptation was to present the early writers' recording of and comment on changes effected by Europeanization of the Aleuts and the later writers' statements on their Americanization. This has not been completely resisted.

For cross-cultural comparison, historical reconstruction or use of any other method, one must be sure first of the basic data to be used: one must have confidence in the accuracy and completeness of the record.

Although it is always possible that a valuable source has been overlooked, I have tried to present the full ethnohistoric record, the first step toward rediscovery of Aleut society and proper placement of it among the societies of the North Pacific.[4]

---

[4] All sources cited have been consulted by me unless stated otherwise. Although I may quote an A.B. note on the contents, I have also read the original.

Glossary

Baidar—umiak, open skin-covered boat; by some early writers applied
to any skin-boat

Barábara—underground sod-covered house

Bidarka—kayak (decked skin-boat), with one, two, or three cockpits

Kalé, kalgi—slave, servant; Aleut term

Kamley, kamleika—waterproof parka made of strips of sea-mammal
intestine casing sewed together

Kantag—wooden dish or platter

Parka—fur or birdskin outer garment with only neck opening, with
collar and without hood as on Eskimo parkas

Peredovshik—a leader (Russian or Siberian)

Pood—unit of weight equal to about 36.1 pounds

Promyshlenik—a hunter (Russian or Siberian)

Reindeer—caribou

Tookook, tukuk—chief; Aleut term

Toyon, toyoun, toion—chief; said to be a Yakut word

Verst—a Russian "mile" equal to .663 miles

Yurt, yourt—underground sod-covered house, barábara

THE ETHNOGRAPHY

Setting, Settlement, and Household

Exactly forty years ago W. Jochelson's characterization of the Aleutians was published, a statement that I might improve only in minor details:

For about one thousand miles the Aleutian Islands stretch from the Alaskan Peninsula in a long bow-shaped chain of seventy treeless islands, excluding the numerous islets. All of the islands are of volcanic origin, and are covered with high mountains, among which are both active and extinct volcanoes. The shore line is irregular, the rocky mountains sloping abruptly to the sea. The bays are shallow, full of reefs, and dangerous for navigation.

The vegetation is luxurious though limited to grasses, berry-bearing shrubs, creeping [plants], and varieties of low willows [and fields of flowers, ten or a dozen species in bloom at one time]. On the mountain slopes we find an alpine vegetation and various species of mosses and lichens. In the narrow valleys between the mountain ridges and on the low isthmuses with insufficient drainage are fresh-water lakes with hummocky shores, such as characterize the Siberian tundras. . . . The absence of arboreal vegetation is due not to the climate, which is comparatively mild, but to the constant gales, and to the fogs and mists that are encountered in Aleutian waters, and that deprive the plants of much sunlight.

[(Paraphrasing:) The fogs and gales result from the meeting of two waters: from Bering Sea on the north side and the Japan Current on the south.]

For the period from March 1, 1909, to March 1, 1910, the annual mean was 3.9 (39°F.), with a maximum of 16.5 (62°F.) . . . and a minimum of –13.0 (9°F.). . . . There are only two seasons: a long autumn and a short, mild winter. But the incessant winds and gales cause the slightest cold to be felt and, in summer particularly, the constant fogs hide the sun.

Throughout my nineteen months' stay in the islands, the sky was clear only nine days (1928:413).

Slightly lower temperatures have been recorded and the sun may shine a few more days; yet fittingly Jochelson titled his article "People of the Foggy Seas." We know today that the turbulence of wave and wind, the frequency of rain and fog are heightened by the difference in sea depth on the north and south sides of what Alaskans call "The Chain": the continental shelf under at least the eastern Bering Sea, the very deep Aleutian Trench under the Pacific paralleling the Islands. Even the land is unstable, like other mountain zones along the Pacific rim given to strong earthquakes. Sudden williwaws knock down chimneys, great heavy storms build up just south of the Aleutians and sweep eastward. The land is beautiful, wild, and at one time was rich in natural resources. These were renewable resources, namely, the animals, but neither the Russians nor the early Americans bothered to renew them.

Population

Estimates of the aboriginal population seem fancifully high (15,000 to 30,000), yet since we do not have exact demographic data, we cannot with certainty refute them. The only statement on which the early sources agree is that the population declined drastically in the first fifty years of contact with Europeans and Siberians. Following the Discovery, nearly a generation passed before population figures for specific islands were recorded and, of course, even longer before they were published. Coxe, quoting Krenitzin and Levashev, says only that Unalaska had in 1768–1769 "upwards of a thousand inhabitants. . . . and they say that it was formerly much more populous" (214). Figures obtained soon thereafter (1774) by the crew of the *St. Michael* and quoted in two sources are only confusing: Petroff's translation of the *Literary Collections* containing an extract from the *St. Michael* journal lists eighty men for Unalaska (306), while Pallas's publication of Bragin's journal of the same voyage gives more than two hundred males for that island (M. and B.:69). The early writers usually recorded only the male population, so that "eighty souls" meant eighty adult males or in reality sometimes only heads of families. (They often stated further that the population included both tribute-payers and non-tribute payers.) Our biggest problem is to figure out the average number of dependents or the average size of kindred under an enumerated male.

Krenitzin and Levashev noted that "Six or seven of these huts or yourts make a village, of which there are sixteen in Unalashka" (Coxe:214; M. and B.:58). If one figures conservatively at six houses per village for a total of ninety-six and a population just under a thousand, then there would be ten persons per house. If one takes Bragin's figure of two hundred males and the same population, one has only four dependents per man. Both figures seem low, in view of general statements about the large number of inhabitants per dwelling. Sarytchev seems to have been the first to give specific data. He recorded that, on Unalaska Island, Makushinsk had forty-five people, male and female, in two houses, Koshiga, thirty-two in three houses, and Tschernowsk, thirty-nine in two houses (61, 64, 66). He said that the total for Unalaska Island (1790) was 323 males in fourteen "dwelling places," each with two or three houses (Sarytchev:72). If both reports can be credited, there was a decline between approximately 1770 and 1790 in number of villages (by two) and in number of houses (by two-thirds or down from 95-100 to 30-35) but an increase in number of men (by a third or more).[1] (This increase may be explained by better knowledge of the island at the later

[1] Shelekof's account covers part of the period between Bragin *St. Michael* and Sarytchev-Sauer, i.e. 1783 to 1790, but he has obviously used the former source, hence is not a good independent authority.

date or by a different basis of enumeration: for example, all adult males in contrast with family heads only.) As we shall see when we assemble the data on settlements and on kinship, a village—at least late in the eighteenth century —usually had only two or three large houses, a few smaller huts, and twenty or more people per house, possibly as many as thirty (Krenitzin and Levashev, in M. and B.:58; Jochelson 1925:119). Probably these people comprised three to five nuclear families or even as many as ten, depending on age and circumstances, and one kindred.

Regarding total population of the Islands, the only census before Veniaminov's time was provided by the *St. Michael* journal. Both versions of it give the same numbers of males for fifteen islands but they differ regarding Unalaska. The Pallas version adds Umnak and Unalga but gives no population for Agadak and Attu, available in the *Literary Collections* version. Combining the two lists, we have 694 men, probably family heads, on twenty islands.[2] If we allow generously for an average of six dependents per man, we still have a total population under 5,000 for most of the large islands, extending from Attu to the Shumagins. If we triple the number to correct for underenumeration on these twenty islands and for omission of villages on the Alaska Peninsula and on unlisted islands, the total population would be just under 15,000.[3] This appears to me to be the maximum estimate, with 12,000 a more reasonable figure.

Sauer, like Sarytchev writing of 1790 conditions, said that

[2] The islands with their adult male population: Attu 27, Agadak 10, Amchitkha 30, Ouniak (Seven Mountains) 25, Tanakh (Tanaga) 30, Kanaga 30, Adakh 20, Sitkhina 2, Egitki 3, Tagalakh 5, Amlia 30, Atkha 35, Ougamok (Naugaman) 7, Kigalga (Kigalda or Tigalda) 40, Avatanak 20, Akun 50, Unalga 10, Akoutan 40, Oumnak 80, Ounalashka 200. Spellings vary: Amlia is sometimes Amlakh or Amlyn; Egitki is now Igitkin; Sitignak (uninhabited) is now Little Sitkine.

[3] Most of the Aleuts were hostile to the Russians and evidently wanted to conceal the true number of hunters who might be impressed into service. Later, after the population decline they wanted to conceal their weakness, according to Langsdorff (32).

the number of males including children "of all the Aleutian islands," evidently meaning the Fox Islands in the Unalaska district, was 1,100 (272). Since this was, according to all accounts, the most populous of the groups of islands, this figure is not inconsistent with other data. Langsdorff wrote that Sarytchev had reckoned the Fox Island male population at 1,300 in 1790 whereas in his time, about 1805, it was not over 300 (32).

Veniaminov as usual gave more detail: He notes Sarytchev's statement (2:156) that by 1790 only one-third of the pre-Russian population remained.

From the tables appended to his work we see that at his time the male population was 1,235 souls. If we add to this the female sex at a little higher figure, the inhabitants of the Ounalashka District [exclusive of the Pribyloff Islands] . . . must have counted over 2,500 souls. When we take this number as a third part . . . the number of inhabitants here in 1750 . . . was not less than 8,000 souls.

A tradition of the Aleuts says that previous to the arrival of the Russians their number was more than ten times as large, . . . Old men tell that in olden times and long before the advent of the Russians the inhabitants of the Ounalashka District were so numerous that every island and every convenient spot on each island were settled, and that in each village were from 40 to 70 one-hole bidarkas, i.e. so many grown men, able to go out in bidarkas, and if we add to this as many women, and twice as many children and old people, it follows that the inhabitants of each village must have numbered from 150 to 280 souls, or an average of 215. From personal observation and accounts of the Aleuts I must suppose that there were as many as 120 villages in this district, and if we assume that all these villages were inhabited at one and the same time, it follows that the Aleut population, at its best time, amounted to 25,000 souls (2:176-77).

The priest then commented, "Without doubt this number is a little too high"; and he estimated that it probably was between 12,000 and 15,000 (2:177). Despite his attempt at

careful reconstruction, he did not question the number of
adult males per village, although he did indicate some
doubt as to whether all the villages were occupied at the
same time. The number and size of house pits per settlement lead one to question whether the villages were so
large, and certainly there is no evidence that so many
villages were occupied at one time. Jochelson gave some
indication of the size of the thirteen sites on four islands
that he excavated (he apparently looked at others, too),
although he did not in all cases publish the full number of
pits counted. A list can be assembled as follows:

Attu	Nanikax	15 pits
	(Two others, apparently post-Russian, sites excavated.)	
Atka	Atxalax	25 pits, all of moderate size, some rather small
	Halaca	8 large pits, plus small ones for storage, apparently a summer village
Umnak	Aglagax 1	8 large, 10 small pits
	2	8 very large pits
	Nutxakax	15 pits, mostly burial, evidently summer village
	Ukix	14 dwelling pits, plus small burial pits
	Ugludax	small site (4 pits excavated)
Unalaska-Amaknak-Hog Isl.	Amaknax	small site (1 large, 3 small pits excavated)
	Xatacxan	small site (1 pit excavated)
	Tanaxtaxax	about 12 pits, none large
	Uknadax	2 large pits, several smaller ones

(Jochelson 1925:22-40)

The descriptions of the sites show clearly that some were
winter villages, others summer villages, hence not fully

occupied simultaneously even if of the same age; that not all house depressions in a given site were of equal age, that is, twelve or fourteen houses were not occupied at one time; that not all villages were coterminous (Jochelson 1925:119).

The loss of population under early Russian rule—better characterized as nonrule and laissez faire exploitation—is indicated by comparison of the above figures with the first ones in the "Documents Relative to the History of Alaska," from the reports of the Governors of the Russian-American Company.

Population, Aleutian Islands, January 1, 1845*
By Ethnic Classification, Age-Group, and District

		Russians	Creoles	Aleuts	Total
Unalaska	Adults	16	55	606	677
District	Minors	11	69	653	733
	Total	27	124	1259	1410
Atka	Adults	19	62	410	491
District	Minors	3	98	173	274
	Total	22	160	583	765
Total		49	284	1842	2175

* Documents 4:61.

This table compared with the following one for the Unalaska District only and for a period about fifteen years earlier indicates a still declining population after the period of atrocities had ended. By the 1830s and 1840s, disease probably was the dominant demographic control. If Veniaminov (in the following table) did not include creoles with Aleuts and if the same islands were used in both counts, then the Unalaska District population declined from 1485 to 1259. If, however, creoles and even Russians were included, the decline was small: from 1485 to 1410.

People who claim that the Aleut population shows little ethnic infusion should note that in 1845 9 percent of the non-Russian population in the Unalaska District and 23 percent of that in the Atka District were creoles.

Regarding sex ratio, there are no exact figures until Veniaminov's time. For the Unalaska District he reported (year not given but probably about 1830):

Island	Number of Villages	No. of Males	No. of Females	Total
Ounalashka	10	214	256	470
Oumnak	2	49	60	109
Akouna	3	42	43	85
Borka	1	17	27	44
Ounalga	1	10	13	23
Avatanok	1	24	25	49
Akautan	1	6	7	13
Tigalda	1	38	59	97
Ounimak	1	38	53	91
Alaska Pen.	3	93	113	206
Ounga	1	52	64	116
Pribyloff	2	88	94	182
	27	671	814	1485

(Veniaminov 2:202-203)

This amounts to one-fifth more females than males. The dangerous life of the fur hunters, into which the men were forced, probably explains the difference between numbers of males and females. Although in nearly half the fourteen years for which Veniaminov has given Unalaska birth statistics there were more female births than male births, nevertheless in the total period (1822–1836) 288 males and 284 females were born, including what the priest considered illegitimate births (2: Table 1).

These and other data from Veniaminov show also that by 1825–1830 the size of village ranged from 13 to 196 persons, the largest—as we would expect—on Unalaska Island. After assembling the early explorers' observations of the villages, we may understand the demographic situation better, although we do need to exercise care regarding their tendency to accept without question the Aleuts' accounts of their former numerical strength.

Only one firm conclusion can be drawn from the available data: at least 80 percent of the Aleut population was lost in the first two generations of Russian-Aleut contact. A few were taken to southeast Alaska and California; most, however, were not merely lost to their homeland, they were totally lost. It is not surprising that those who survived this human devastation tended to exaggerate their preconquest numbers. It also is not surprising that by 1825 Aleuts were describing to their ethnographer, Veniaminov, a culture that was largely of the past, a memory culture. For this reason, the earlier reports by Cook, Sarytchev, et al. are invaluable.

The Village

"The greater part of the villages are now, as they were formerly, situated on the northern side of the islands, facing the Behring Sea, as being more abundant in fish, driftwood and especially whales cast upon the beach" (Veniaminov 2:200). Dall's and Jochelson's archaeological reconnaissances, while sketchy, do show nevertheless that there were a few villages on the south shores, with apparently more numerous ones facing northwest or east.

All the ancient Aleut villages were situated on the sea-shore, not on the high land above the sea, and usually on land between two bays, so that their skin boats could easily be carried from one body of water to another at the approach of foes. Thus the usual location of villages was on narrow isthmuses, on necks of land between two ridges, on promontories, or narrow sandbanks. An indispensable adjunct to a village was a supply of easily accessible fresh water—a brook, fall, or lake. River-mouths were never used as permanent dwelling-places, because the topographical conditions were conducive to unexpected attacks. The underground dwellings of the old Aleut were much like traps; if an attack were made when the inhabitants were within, they could leave it alive only through the single opening in the roof. For this reason villages were built on open places, whence observations could be made far out to sea. Near every village was an observatory (*agi'sax‘*) on a hill where constant watch was kept. The sentry was called *amgi'gnax‘*. Here, too, hunters watched for the appearance of sea-mammals, and in turn the people of the village watched for the return of the hunters, greeting them with songs and dances.

At the time of our investigations [1910] the Aleut villages were situated mainly in valleys at the river-mouths, where they were settled by the Russian invaders. This change had some advantage, since, with the advent of the Russians, internal wars ceased; moreover, the Aleut were in a position to take advantage of the annual spawning migration of salmon, which they caught and dried in the summer for winter use. In ancient times the Aleut visited such rivers to catch salmon, but never had permanent villages on their banks; moreover, they caught sea-fish, chiefly halibut, cod, and sculpin, from skin boats out on the open sea. (Jochelson 1925:23).

Veniaminov's descriptions of specific villages show various differences between them: some had good landing places or an abundance of fish or good order and prosperity, while others did not. He remarked that the good villages were "under the management of their hereditary Toyouns" (2:201). "The distances between villages vary greatly (from 7 to 70 and more versts), and it is not possible to go from every village to the nearest one on foot. For this reason the communication between them is kept up only by means of bidarkas exclusively" (2:200). Formerly, baidars, the large open skin-boats, would also have been used.

To understand some of the early trader-hunters' observations, one must note Jochelson's statement: "Settlements with a population of 200 to 400 men were established by the Russian conquerors, who segregated small scattered groups of Aleut hunters in certain spots in order to facilitate control over them" (1925:119).

Soloviof (Soloviev), who treated the Aleuts harshly and in turn fared poorly at their hands, told of villages and camping places that he saw on Umnak and Unalaska islands in the fall of 1764, as published by J.L.S. The following passages are examples:

"This was called Makushinsky Bay; and on an island within it they found two Tojons, . . . with about an hundred and eighty people of both sexes employed in hunting sea-bears [fur seals]. . . . He remained there until the 10th, when the Toigons[4] invited him to their winter quarters, which lay about five hours sail further East: there he found two dwelling caves [underground houses]. . . ." At another village, Totchikala, "Some of them listened to his representations; but the greatest part fled upon Soloviof's approach; so that he found the place consisting of four large dwelling caves almost empty, in which he secured himself with suitable precaution. Here he found three hundred darts and ten bows with arrows, all which he destroyed, only reserving one bow and seventeen arrows as specimens of their arms." Later, "about an hundred men and a still greater number of women returned" (J.L.S. in Coxe:160-62).

In July 1765, on Unalaska Island he visited Igonok which consisted of only one dwelling cave. "The inhabitants amounted to about thirty men, who dwelt there with their wives and children." (Large barrack-houses were built under Russian domination.)

"Upon the shore of the same bay, opposite to the mouth of this rivulet, lay two villages, one of which was inhabited; it was called Ukunadok, and consisted of six dwelling caves. About thirty-five of the inhabitants were at that time employed in catching salmon in the rivulet. . . . After coming out of the bay, he went forwards to the summer village Umgaina, distant about seven or eight leagues, and situated on the side of a rivulet,

---

[4] Coxe's translation of the *Neue Nachrichten* was compared with the original. In the original German, Toigon was Tojon.

which takes its rise in a lake abounding with salmon. Here he found the Toigon Amaganak, with about ten of the natives, employed in fishing. Fifteen versts further along the shore they found another summer village called Kalaktak, where there was likewise another rivulet, . . . The inhabitants were sixty men and an hundred and seventy women and children: they gave Soloviof a very friendly reception; and delivered two hostages, who were brought from the neighboring island Akutan [probably slaves]; with these he set out on his return, and on the 6th of August joined his crew" (J.L.S. in Coxe:166-68).

There is no evidence that Aleut communities had ceremonial houses (kashims, kazgis), so characteristic of Kodiak and other Eskimo villages (Veniaminov 2:201). Many Aleut houses were bigger than the largest Eskimo kazgis.

House, Household, and Home Life

House and heating.   Cook observed in 1778:

As these people use no paint, they are not so dirty in their persons as the savages who thus besmear themselves; but they are full as lousy and filthy in their homes. Their method of building is as follows: They dig, in the ground, an oblong square pit, the length of which seldom exceeds fifty feet, and the breadth twenty; but in general the dimensions are smaller. Over this excavation they form the roof of wood which the sea throws ashore. This roof is covered first with grass, and then with earth; so that the outward appearance is like a dunghill. In the middle of the roof, toward each end, is left a square opening, by which the light is admitted; one of these openings being for this purpose only, and the other being also used to go in and out by, with the help of a ladder, or rather a post, with steps cut in it. In some houses there is another entrance below; but this is not common. Round the sides and ends of the huts, the families (for several are lodged together) have their separate apartments, where they sleep, and sit at work; not upon benches, but in a kind of concave trench, which is dug all round the inside of the house, and covered with mats; so that this part

is kept tolerably decent. But the middle of the house, which
is common to all the families, is far otherwise. For, although
it be covered with dry grass, it is a receptacle for dirt of every
kind, and the place for the urine trough; the stench of which
is not mended by raw hides, or leather being almost continually
steeped in it. Behind and over the trench, are placed the few
effects they are possessed of; such as their clothing, mats, and
skins (2:512).

I saw not a fire-place in any one of their houses. They are
lighted, as well as heated, by lamps; which are simple, and yet
answer the purpose very well (2:514).

An Aleut village brought to Langsdorff's mind a different
image (32):

The habitations are holes dug in the earth, covered with a
roof, over which earth is thrown; when they have stood for
some time they become overgrown with grass, so that a village
has the appearance of an European church-yard full of graves.
Into these huts the inhabitants descend by the chimney, or hole
whence the smoke issues out. To some of the largest which are
inhabited by the Russians, a low door is made in the side. The
light is admitted through a little opening or window covered
over with seal's entrails or dried fish-skin. Several divisions are
made within by means of seal-skins or straw-mats, which separate
the domains and property of the different families that occupy
the habitation.

Langsdorff came relatively late. What do the earliest
accounts say? J.L.S. quoted Pushkaref and company who
were in the eastern Aleutians in 1762: "Their dwellings
under-ground are similar to those of the Kamtchadals; and
have several openings on the sides, through which they
make their escape when the principal entrance is beset by
an enemy" (Coxe:76). Korovin, who spent the winter of
1763–1764 in the Unalaska-Umnak area, reported: "They
light little or no fires within, for which reason these
dwellings are much cleaner than those of the Kamtchadals."
"They sleep upon thick mats, which they twist out of a

Figure 5. INTERIOR OF AN UNALASKA HOUSE

soft kind of grass that grows upon the shore; and have no other covering but their usual clothes" (Coxe:119-20).

Lasarof's journal also recorded that "they make no fires even in winter" (Coxe:86). Sarytchev and Shelekov commented on this remarkable fact relating only to heating, not to cooking. "They have no ovens and build no fires in their houses, for the reason that they are warm enough without" (Shelekov:82). "They seldom make a fire in the jurt, except to cook the flesh of the sea-animals, and some sorts of fish" (Sarytchev:72). The Aleuts' little flatiron-shaped stone lamps provided light and heat, probably not much of either per lamp. But evidently each family had its own.

Sarytchev, as usual, has given a good description (72):

The floor of such a hut is sunk somewhat under ground, and the roof is made of the floating wood which they fish out of the sea, covered with moss and grass. The light is admitted through some small openings in the roof, that serve also for the egress and ingress of the inhabitants, by means of a ladder, which consists of different steps cut out of a plank. About seven foot from the outer wall stakes are driven into the ground, which partly support the roof, and partly serve to mark out the partition for each family, in which, instead of beds, platted grass-mats are spread. They sit on these mats in the day-time to work, and sleep on them at night, using their cloaths for covering. They empty their dirty slops and every filth, into the middle of this common dwelling, which becomes by that means excessively wet and muddy; and were there no openings in the roof, would

---

The illustration of an Unalaska house is taken from the third volume of: Troisieme voyage de Cook; ou, Voyage a l'océan pacifique, ordonné par le roi d'Angleterre, pour faire des découvertes dans l'hémisphere nord, pour déterminer la position & l'étendue la Côte ouest de l'Amérique septentrionale, sa distance de l'Asie, & résoudre la question du passage au nord. Exécuté sous la direction des capitaines Cook, Clerke & Gore, sur les vaisseaux la résolution & la découverte, en 1776, 1777, 1778, 1779 & 1780. Traduit de l'anglois par M.D. Ouvrage enrichi de cartes & de plans, d'après les relèvements pris par le lieutenant Henry Roberts, sous l'inspection du capitaine Cook; & d'une multitude de planches, de portraits & de vues de pays, dessinés, pendant l'expédition, par m. Webber. . . . 4 vols. Paris: Hôtel de Thou, 1785.

soon occasion an insupportable stench and vapor. Each partition has a particular wooden reservoir for the urine, which is used both for dyeing the grass, and for washing their hands; but after cleaning the latter in this manner, they rince them in pure water, and dry them in the open air, by swinging them backward and forward.

Veniaminov, taking his informants' word, wrote: "Their ancient habitations (ouliagamakh) were never divided, as they are now, in separate compartments for each family, but were always in common, accommodating many families (from 10 to 40), who generally stood in close relationship to each other. Their ancient dwellings or 'yurts' were nothing but sheds from 10 to 30 fathoms long and even more, and from 4 to 7 fathoms wide. They say that in some villages there were yurts over 40 fathoms long" (2:204).

It seems likely that there was some kind of division (achieved by hanging mats, clothes, and other possessions), with each family having its place in the house, although there were not wooden partitions until after the Russians directed the construction of houses.

Regarding size of the communal dwellings, we have a typical ethnohistory problem, not completely solved by archaeology. Five writers gave house measurements, presumably for the interior although this was not stated. (Their measurements, given in feet, yards, fathoms, or Klafter [fathoms or hand spans] have been converted to feet.) Chronologically they reported:

J.L.S. from early journals		60 to 150 x 18 to 30
Staehlin from a 1765–1766 journal		30 to 180 x 24
Cook	(maximum)	50 x 20
Sarytchev		54 x 18
Veniaminov		60 to 180 x 24 to 54
Jochelson	average for pits excavated	56 x 35 x 14

If Jochelson dug out the walls, his excavation pits would have been larger than the usable interior of the houses, explaining especially the greater width that he recorded. Veniaminov gave massive proportions because, it is likely, he saw principally post-Russian houses and house ruins. Cook, a good observer, was the most conservative; he did not, however, see much of the Islands. The greater consistency of width than of length measurements probably is explained by the limits set by the building materials—whale bones and driftwood—and building design. Sections could be added to make greater length to accommodate more families but greater width would have been difficult to achieve. The eastern Aleuts, at least, expanded the household space by means that were discovered by Jochelson:

On Uknadax Islet, Unalaska, "We excavated the two largest pits on the shore; one was 28.3 by 5.5 meters, the other 20.4 by 5.2 meters. The longitudinal axis of both large pits lay from east to west. At the[ir] sides . . . was a row of smaller depressions. . . . In the large depression the refuse was only 2 feet deep, but the smaller pits seemed to have served especially for the reception of refuse.

The digging of the two large oblong pits revealed similar situations; on either side were 8 small pits, 3 to 8 feet in diameter. In the smaller pits on the southern side was kitchen refuse and whale-bones, which presumably had served as material for the ceiling. Three of the small pits, evidently for burial, contained quite decayed skeletons. The remaining 5 pits contained no skeletal remains. It is difficult to assign a use for them. They may possibly have been sleeping-places for children, which communicated with the main pit by an underground passage. According to tradition, such compartments were skillfully hidden and covered by mats, so that attacking enemies could not discover them. The pits to the north of the large oblong one contained no skeletal remains, but were full of kitchen refuse and may have been especially dug for this purpose. At the western and eastern walls of . . . [the house] was a pit somewhat larger than those to the south and north. These contained some kitchen refuse, but not in such quantities as in the small pits. These last two pits had evidently been storage-places or possibly special cooking-lodges (1925:40).

The small side-rooms might have served also for women during menstruation and for both sexes during mourning. However, Merck's account, which was not yet published in Jochelson's time, mentions only storerooms.

(Translated and condensed:) There were summer houses (Sakudaktschaluk) and winter houses (Kamuktschaluk), the latter somewhat warmer. Attached to both by low turf-covered passages were small storerooms, in which stomachs (what Alaskans now call "pokes") of oil, dried fish, roe, and other things were kept. The winter houses had a four-post support and were quadrangular with rounded corners. (Details of roof construction omitted here.) Broad planks attached to the supporting posts separated the sitting- and sleeping-places along the side, whose floor was somewhat lower than in the remainder of the house and covered with mats. Small containers hung here and there from the earth wall. In the roof were two holes, the smaller of which served for entrance and the larger for bringing in the skin-boats to dry (Jacobi:118).[5]

This description corroborates Cook's earlier observation.

Staehlin, on information from a party of promysleniki, wrote, "Behind, or adjoining to these great *Jurts*, they commonly build a few small ones, which serve as houses of office" (39). We do not know what he meant by that.

Bathing. Sweathbathing in special bathhouses evidently was well established by the Russians before the nineteenth century. The early authors, in writing of cleanliness, rituals and festivals, dwellings and special structures, or anything else that might have suggested a note on sweatbathing never mentioned it. Sarytchev said specifically, "Expert as these islanders are in the management of their baidars, they are incapable of swimming; and, from what I observed, are not in the habit of bathing, which may be owing to the severity of the climate" (2:74). From the elders' reports, Veniaminov wrote, "In the past, the Aleuts did not have

[5] The translations from French and German are mine.

any bath houses and never used them, and although they were acquainted with them and saw them among their neighbors, the Kodiaks, they considered them an unnecessary luxury, . . . which would weaken the strength of the body. In their place, they used cold baths, that is, generally everyone from youth to old age [reference is to men only] took baths in the sea or in the streams at all times of the year and in all weather" (2:114). Like Tanaina and Tlingit custom, this was not bathing for cleanliness but for hardening of youths and testing of manly endurance. J.L.S., the earliest reliable compiler of ethnographic notes, wrote, from Popof's and Otcheredin's observations, "In general, they do not observe any rules of decency, but follow all the calls of nature publicly, and without the least reserve. They wash themselves with their own urine." "If an infant cries, the mother immediately carries it to the sea-side, and be it summer or winter holds it naked in the water until it is quiet. This custom is so far from doing the children any harm, that it hardens them against the cold, and they accordingly [go] bare-footed through the winter without the least inconvenience. They are also trained to bathe frequently in the sea; and it is an opinion generally received among the islanders, that by that means they are rendered bold, and become fortunate in fishing [hunting]" (Coxe: 195-96).

The social composition of household and village will be given under the heading of "Kinship." Other than that, we have only bits and pieces on relations among members.

Sharing and entertaining. "The successful hunter of fish divides it with all. . . . If he, in the division, forgot someone, he must give him a part of his share" (Veniaminov 2:56). Whether "all" covered more than the household, we do not know. Langsdorff said more specifically but also from report, not from observation, that the "large open leather boat, called a baidar, which will hold fifteen or twenty persons," was "formerly the common property of a whole village" (2:43-44). Since all families in a small village were related, as we shall see, such ownership was reasonable.

J.L.S. in the *Neue Nachrichten,* apparently quoting Soloviev: "No stranger is allowed to hunt or fish near a village, or to carry off any thing fit for food. When they are on a journey, and their provisions are exhausted, they beg from village to village, or call upon their friends and relations for assistance" (Coxe:179).

After being shipwrecked in the eastern Aleutians in 1806, Campbell and his shipmates were visited by three men.

The chief himself remained, and most willingly gave us a share of his provisions, which consisted of a bladder of train oil, and a basket of berries, about the size of bilberries, preserved in oil. . . . This friendly Indian [Aleut] who had hooks and lines, went out in his canoe, and in a short time returned with a few small fish. He then kindled a fire. . . .

Next day about forty Indians, men and women, came and encamped beside us; they made huts for themselves, by setting up planks, leaning against each other at the top, and throwing earth upon them, over which they put a covering of grass.

They brought a supply of provisions, consisting of berries, oil, blubber, and dried salmon, and gave us a share of all they had with the utmost liberality (Campbell:48-49).

That Campbell's experience was not unusual is shown by Sarytchev's report. The promyshleniki who treated the Aleuts harshly were resisted and even murdered, but a person like Sarytchev was accepted for what he was, a friendly visitor.

The inhabitants are very quiet and peaceable among each other, at least as far as we can judge from experience, having never observed the least discord among them, during our whole stay.

On my journey round the island, they every where received

me with the greatest friendliness, and entertained me in the kindest manner, so that I may with justice place hospitality among the principal virtues of this rude people; it being displayed to all who pass through their places, without regard to relationship or acquaintance; for I myself was witness to their sharing the half of their own provisions with perfect strangers from other islands, and that too without receiving any compensation. At the same time they have the commendable custom of relieving every one from the painful necessity of asking for any thing, by setting before the weary traveller whatever they possess, as soon as he enters their jurt and is seated. In addition to this, the Aleutians form an exception to savages in general, and particularly those inhabiting the Eastern Islands, that they are not thieves. Nor have I observed any other evil propensities among them, but indolence and ingratitude. They never betray any vehement emotions, nor do their countenances ever indicate either vexation, melancholy, or joy, on any occasion, however extraordinary. On the return of a relative from a distance, he is received with as much unconcern as if he had never been absent. He likewise goes himself without saluting any one, or speaking a word, into his partition of the jurt, seats himself by his relations or wives, and takes off his travelling attire. If he asks for any thing to eat, it is set before him, and if he is cold he has a lamp given him; after which, he begins relating some particulars of his journey, and they on their part inform him of what has passed at home during his absence; but all this goes forward without the slightest indication of curiosity or interest (2:78-79).

Later, Veniaminov recorded that "in the past" invitations were not extended to individuals and single families, although travelers were received with hospitality, and there were no salutations (2:117-18). Whole villages were invited, however, for the festivals. It is not entirely clear whether Shelekov in the following passage was describing Aleut or Kodiak Eskimo behavior, but there is a good chance that he was writing about the former.

When guests are seen approaching they besmear themselves with red paint, put on their best garments, feather-cloaks, etc., and await the party, their weapons of war in their hands. The guests attire themselves in the same way. As soon as the bidars or bidarkas approach the shore the hosts jump into the sea, seize the canoes and drag or carry them ashore with shouts of joy and welcome. Then they lift the guests and their belongings out of the bidar, one by one and carry them to the house, where games are immediately begun. When they arrive at the house all sit down together, but keep silent, no questions being asked or answered. The oldest or most prominent man then gets up on his feet and offers the new-comers some cold water, and then a boy brings vessels with oil and such victuals as whale-blubber, seal-meat and dried fish. After this come berries of various kinds, huckleberries, cranberries, heatherberries, thimble-berries and others, accompanied by various roots. The berries are eaten without oil. Then comes dried fish again, which they call 'youkala,' then meat of different animals and birds, the best that can be obtained. Salt is unknown to them. At every meal and every separate course the host must eat and drink first of everything offered, without which ceremony nobody would eat anything. From this one might believe that they have used poison on some occasions. The host, when he has tasted of each dish, he offers it to the principal one of the guests, who takes some of it and the host passes it on to the next in rank until all are served and then he helps himself to what he wants last. When they rise from their repast they go to the place where the games are played, and all sit down there and begin to talk for the first time, and the games are commenced (78-80).

Merck recorded a good firsthand account by the physician Krebs of one such entertainment of visitors in the winter of 1791–1792 (Jacobi:125-26).

Veniaminov, as always, had the final word:

The accumulation of food cannot be said to be the only object or the exclusive end of their existence with the Aleuts as it is with very many Russians among the common people, who look at it in that light. Every Aleut lays up some provisions, but he seems to do it more for others than himself and when he has accumulated enough to last for two or three months he calmly awaits the winter, and though nearly every Spring he experiences the same pinching and starving he does never profit by the lesson. This carelessness is caused by a delusive opinion that, living on the sea-shore they can always obtain something to eat from the sea, which is inexhaustible and rich in edibles for all who live near it, and from which something can be taken at all times if they only make use of opportunities and means at hand. Therefore, this carelessness of the Aleuts with regard to their supply of food is from one point of view praiseworthy, because it is more or less a sign of trust in an All-providing God. On the other hand we cannot deny that this confidence is greatly aided by laziness, but then laziness is better, at any rate, than fretting and whining (2:234-35).

Division of labor. Several early travelers in Russian America commented on the Aleut women's work. Cook, for example, said, "All sewing is performed by the women. They are the taylors, shoemakers, and boat-builders, or boat-coverers; for the men, most probably, construct the frame of wood over which the skins are sewed. They make mats and baskets of grass, that are both beautiful and strong. Indeed, there is a neatness and perfection in most of their work, that shows they neither want ingenuity nor perseverance" (2:513-14).

Later, Langsdorff reported more fully:

The fabricating a sort of little drums, of rattles composed of the beaks of birds, of ornaments, wooden hats, wooden dishes and vessels with figures carved upon them, little models of their canoes, &c. &c. are only what may be called the amusements of their leisure hours (2:41).

The men make the wooden skeletons of the boats, and prepare the skins with which they are to be covered; the latter are sewed together by the women. The arrows, or rather javelins, with which they make war upon the whales, sea-otters, sea-dogs, and birds, are also made by the men, and are of different forms and sizes, according to the objects against which they are to be directed. The most remarkable thing is, that they are not shot from a bow, but slung from a little plank, nor are they pointed with a quill (2:44). [The "sea-dog" probably was a sea-lion.]

The women and girls are employed in summer in cleaning fish, and hanging them up to dry, and in collecting berries and roots for winter stores. They also sew the skins together, for covering the baidarkas, make clothes, boots, and shoes, draw thread from the nerves and tendons of the whales and reindeer, make slings for the javelins, and hooks for angling. In all their different kinds of sewing work, they display prodigious dexterity: the mode of sewing is very different for different objects. The rain garments, made of the entrails of sea-dogs, for instance, must be sewed in a very different way from the garments of birds' skins: another sort of work is necessary for sewing together the skins that cover the baidars and baidarkas; and still another for making the boots. At their leisure hours, particularly in long winter evenings, the women make fine mats, little baskets, and pocket-books, of straw, which are woven together with so much regularity, and in such symmetrical figures, that they might be supposed the work of very skillful European artists.

Though these people, therefore, must in general be allowed to be little cultivated, some taste for the beautiful cannot be denied them. They besides dye straw, leather, and other objects for ornaments, with very fine and gay colours, using, for want of better materials, urine mixed with a variety of different things, according to the colour wanted: they also use urine with a very good effect for many other purposes, particularly in washing, as a substitute for soap-lees (2:46-47).

The men, by hunting, provided the essential oil and meat. "The Aleuts call themselves in a really miserable condition only then when all the men in a whole village are sick, because in that case only extreme want stares them in the face" (Veniaminov 2:237-38). The men had their arts, too. They carved wood and ivory figures and presumably made the stone lamps. "In their festivals or parties, the songs are sung mainly by men only, and never and nowhere will women participate, although every one of them knows the contents and the melody of all the songs of her settlement" (Veniaminov 2:299-300). Women, however, danced in the ceremonials, taking an apparently prominent and important part (see, for example, Merck in Jacobi:126).

Child-rearing. There is not much on this subject, a fact
that should not surprise us, since all recorders were men
and eighteenth-century men were not much concerned with
child care and training. Something on the care of infants
will be given under the heading "Childbirth." In the same
passage in which J.L.S. reported the outdoor cold bathing,
he wrote also, "They feed their children when very young
with the coarsest flesh and for the most part raw" (Coxe:
196).

The preparation of children for their rugged life began
early: "Scarcely has a boy attained his eighth year, or even
sometimes not more than his sixth, when he is instructed
in the management of the canoes, and in aiming at a mark
with the water javelin. An old chief of Oonalashka, whose
confidence I had gained very much, informed me that the
making and managing their baidarkas is a principal object
of emulation among them" (Langsdorff 2:41-42).

Jochelson (1925:93) and I observed boys casting respectively lances with blunted heads and toy-model lances.
Their game of throwing toy spears at an object suspended
on a long string was a good test of markmanship and
strength, as the moving object was not an easy target. A
variety of skills had to be acquired: "According to an old
Aleut saying, a lad had no right to marry before he had
ground off a penis-bone flaker to its base in the manufacture
of stone implements" (Jochelson 1925:71).

The education of the boys consists mainly of an attempt to
make them endure anything. . . . Later they taught them how to
ride the bidarkas, how to navigate it in strong winds, during
the incoming or outgoing tides; how to save themselves and
others in dangerous situations and especially how to be skillful
in hunting and war. House duties hardly ever entered into their
education as they, outside of building houses and utensils, concerned themselves only with storing fish or hunting animals;
it was furthermore not considered a duty of men. It was
considered unnecessary to teach the boys petty household duties.

The education of girls consisted of moral education. Besides the girls were taught how to make any kind of clothing, to embroider designs with the hair of animals, to weave carpets [mats] and baskets, to clean fish, and to prepare for eating anything that her husband might obtain.

It was also her duty to collect roots, grass and other things. To clean houses and the general care of the houses was considered the duty of slaves.

Generally the parents do not try to accustom their children to work or housekeeping, saying "our children are not from the parentage of slaves (Veniaminov 2:72-73).

Which relatives reared the children is discussed under "Kinship."

Among the earliest and best reporters were Krenitzin and Levashev, who said, "When both parents die, the children are left to shift for themselves. The Russians found many in this situation, and some were brought for sale" (M. and B.:59). If later visitors to the Islands had written this, one would have assumed that the great social disruption caused by the fur hunters accounted for such treatment of orphans, and indeed even within the first generation of conquest there may have been enough loss of life and family breakdown to prevent the usual care of orphans. Yet in view of the paramount importance of the kindred, one suspects that even before the conquest, children without close kin may have been nobody's concern. Most of the early reports fit together remarkably well and have an understandable inner rationale. Occasionally, however, there is one that we cannot easily evaluate and understand.

Crises of Life

Birth

Everything surrounding the closing of an individual life has received considerable attention from all students of the Aleuts, but only Veniaminov and Merck have recorded the practices surrounding birth. The former's account will be given in full.

When a woman feels that she is pregnant, she must immediately inform her mother or her grandmother of this who naturally instructs her how to behave in time of pregnance, what to eat and what not to eat, where to go and where not to go. Among these instructions some are very senseless and often unhealthful. Of these advices and instructions, one particularly deserves attention, that if a woman wants the child to have the likeness of the father or any one of the relatives, she must think of that person only when she is eating or drinking. After two months of pregnancy, the old women periodically massage the abdomen of the woman and the further pregnancy progresses, the more it is done. At the time of birth, more care is shown to the mother than to the child. As soon as the woman gives birth, she is placed in a squatting position and they do not allow her either to lie down or to sit down. To avoid after-pains, she is bent back and her stomach is massaged or as they say, "they gather up birth." After a little while, they bind her with a belt or a towel across the stomach and carry her to another place, setting her down in the same position; so that she cannot lie down or sit down, they place around her sides and on her back, pillows. In this position, she must remain four days. On the fifth day, she is washed and allowed to sit down or lie down but always in such a position that she cannot stretch her legs. During the first five days every twenty-four hours, they massage her stomach . . . and after that they massage her and wash her twice a week. "A poor gathering" or "an injury to birth" according to them is the reason why a woman having once given birth will never give birth again and will always suffer internally. Such consequences are often seen, but as one doctor has said, this happens not because they gather up incorrectly but merely because they try to gather up.

Up to forty days after birth, the woman is considered unclean and she must not touch any eatables and must see men as rarely as possible.

Cases of delayed parturition were considered a sure sign of a woman's unfaithfulness, and if in such a case, the child by accident does not look like the father, this serves as the main cause of family misunderstanding, and previously was the reason of divorces or inhuman punishment or the like.

The newly-born child is taken care of by other old women, usually by more than one of them. Having tied the umbilical cord, they wash it and keep it warm under the parka or in the oil-container. After that, they massage the stomach of the child or as they say, they gather up all his entrails into the proper place. The child is fed at the breast after he vomits all the uncleanliness which according to them he was fed in his mother's womb and to assist his vomiting, the old women stick a finger down his throat. The remaining uncleanliness in the child later becomes the cause of many internal diseases and such a child will always be weak.

To preserve the health of the newly-born child or the woman, they use various concoctions prepared from roots and grasses with which they are acquainted (Veniaminov 2:67-69).

Veniaminov said that infanticide was very rare (2:61), but neither he nor any other early observer ascertained the Aleuts' attitude toward twins. I found that in modern times twins were allowed to live, although they did not seem to be welcomed. There was no suggestion of the convade.

A few explanatory notes on the above passage are necessary. First, there is the reference to the removal of the woman from one place to another. The delivery probably took place in the "woman's hut" where a girl's first menstrual period was passed, and it seems unlikely that the mother would be allowed to return to the barabara until after the period of uncleanness. Hence the exact significance of removing the woman from one place to another is lost, unless it was simply for cleanliness. The formal conclusion of the period of uncleanness, although not stated here, was probably the same as for the end of isolation of a girl at puberty: thorough washing and a change of clothing, as among the Kodiaks.

The tabus on a woman at this time are familiar: she should not contaminate the men of the community or the food supply. To carry out the latter tabu, she must have been restricted from preparing food for others, would have had to use her own cooking and eating vessels, and possibly even had to take food from a stick instead of directly from her fingers. Although Veniaminov did not mention it in this connection, we can surmise that it was unthinkable for a woman to touch a bidarka or hunting implements while she was unclean.

In 1933–1934 I found that it was permissible for a woman to take a position for delivery either resting on her knees and elbows or on her back, although one woman said the women were expected to take the ventral position for at least the first delivery. Hence we cannot say whether anciently there was any one rule. One thing that is certain, however, was the necessity of keeping the legs in the flexed position after parturition. Even in the 1930s a woman had to remain thus doubled up for at least three days after delivery. Jochelson commented at length upon the fact that in his time the Aleuts still squatted on their heels as the favorite position for resting, and the dead, according to his archaeological finds, were invariably flexed (Jochelson 1925:43). Moreover, a baby always was wrapped tightly in the uterine position and kept that way until the navel had completely healed (personal observation). This appeared to be typical Russian swaddling. A band around the abdomen of the woman probably was worn until the end of the forty-day period, still the case in the 1930s. We get some inkling from the modern practices as to the purpose, if not the nature, of the concoctions mentioned by Veniaminov. On the second day a woman would begin to drink hot chocolate in order to start the milk flowing and on the third day, after the flow had begun, she would take a laxative. Since the materia medica of the ancient Aleuts is supposed to have been extensive (Veniaminov 2:259-64), it is not unlikely that they had or thought they had medicines to serve these purposes.

One modern custom of Aleut women is not so easy to project into the past for practical reasons: a woman would not eat any kind of solid food until the baby's umbilicus had healed. If this was the ancient practice also, it must have restricted a woman severely in her diet. In the 1930s, the meat of sea-mammals, fish, and raw foods such as berries and wild celery in season were among the restricted although not entirely tabued foods for a woman during the forty-day period. Perhaps the modern requirement that a woman should eat cornmeal or rice gruel and similar foods reflects the old tabus on her handling or in any other way having anything to do with the meat supply while she was unclean. Aside from any such problems of origins, there is the concept that what the mother does influences the welfare of the infant. One woman said that she and her baby were both unwell because she had been forced to eat meat from lack of other more suitable food. Merck mentioned mussels and fresh fish. These may have been eaten raw or a fish soup may have been prepared.

The disposal of the umbilical cord and the afterbirth was by careful burial in the twentieth century as in the eighteenth. Women in the hospital at Unalaska objected strenuously to the burning of these parts of the body, for which attitude they would give no explanation. One woman, however, explained that the napkins used during menstruation should not be burned as this would cause the drying up of the woman's blood. Possibly this extended to everything containing the blood of a living person. The statement plus the fact that on one recorded occasion a midwife was at considerable pains to bury a placenta secretly and at night would indicate a fear of magic performed with things which were so intimate and vital to the woman. Immediately, however, we are confronted with this statement by Veniaminov: "They believe that all animals and even fish will fear the material used in periodic sanitation, and hence this material must be burned, otherwise all animals and fish will be driven out from the neighborhood of the community" (2:108). In the disposal of all unclean things, I surmise that if they were burned, this was done by the woman herself. That the woman's hut or corner of the large barabara was probably without fire is also to be considered.

Merck's report is valuable because it is earlier than Veniaminov's and because some of its contents are unusual. Something of family relationships and the supposed influence of each sex on the other is given, too.

The husband during his wife's pregnancy could not kill a resting sea-mammal with a club for fear of causing a stillbirth, or take anything from a stranded whale or work with a hatchet for fear of killing the foetus. At childbirth, one old woman attended. As soon as it began, all the males' clothing was taken to another house or laid in a heap and covered with matting, because (if contaminated) the men might have an accident in which a large sea animal would chew up the kayaks. All drinking utensils and food leftovers had to be covered, and all males, young and old, withdrew. The shell or arrowhead used to cut the cord was buried with the afterbirth. The newborn was washed first with urine, then with fresh cold water, then warmed over a grass fire. (One might add that on various occasions smoke was used for purification.) When this was finished, all the males had to bathe outdoors, even in winter. (Pallas, generalizing from early writers and probably to be doubted, wrote that "Newborn infants are washed in the sea, even in severe weather, and lie in the cold huts almost completely naked" (M. and B.:46). (Merck's observations only twenty years later than Krenitzin and Levashev appear more reasonable. Of course, Aleuts may have said that an infant should be washed in the sea, expressing the value of child-hardening, known from elsewhere in Pacific Alaska, then washed him indoors. Or old customs may have weakened in twenty years.) The mother was fed mussels and fresh fish for several days. On the third day she could go out to the water. If she was too weak to suckle the child, a little piece of seal fat on a cross-stick, to prevent swallowing, was given the infant to suck. (No mention of wet nurses.) Children received the breast until their teeth appeared, whereupon they were fed pap. Favored children drank water from the mother's mouth.

The cradle was an oval bent frame, held to shape with skin lashing, which extended up over the feet. The child was laid on moss, held fast by straps, with the head out. The cradle hung obliquely. For six months people hung on the cradle a piece from each game animal killed, and all birds, the snouts of sea-mammals, and a piece of fish. This was done for mother and child by the nearest relatives. (Implication that these were the nearest relatives of mother and child only, not the father?)

If an Aleut woman following a difficult delivery wanted future unfruitfulness, she would throw the afterbirth out to become the food of birds and animals instead of burying it (Jacobi:122).

If a woman from fault or lack of care (attentiveness) had a stillbirth or if to conceal an alien love affair she induced an abortion, this meant future misfortune for the family. Her parka would be then stuffed with grass and set up, and husband, brother, closest relatives or eldest of the settlement shot it with arrows, to show the people that the wife was killed while she secretly went home to her house. Or the shaman might impose the following punishment: Toward evening the stuffed parka would be set up between the house and a fire. The woman stood behind the parka so that only her face showed. Then the eldest pointed to her and said, "This is the evildoer," whereupon he would shoot the parka while she fell with it to the earth and old and young beat it with sticks. She, however, went home and remained hidden there twenty-four hours while her clothing lay outside, after which time she dared put it on again. The natives had the mistaken idea that without punishing the unfortunate one in this manner, a relative would drown or otherwise perish and the hunt would be unsuccessful (Jacobi 122-23).

The newborn was named by one of the most experienced people of the settlement from whatever first occurred to him—birds, sea animals, and the like (123). We can doubt whether the name had so little meaning.

Puberty

Concerning the period of seclusion for a girl at puberty, Veniaminov's statement is a little confusing.

A girl at puberty was put in a special barabara and could be seen only by her mother or other close female relative. The first period for a girl's seclusion was forty days, twenty days the second time and seven days the third time. Five days after the end of her isolation, she was washed. A girl who did not follow this custom would become black and would have all sorts of diseases and a married woman who did not observe the tabus placed on her would spoil her husband and infect him with disease. "Besides, her husband will be very unfortunate and will either be killed by an animal or will be drowned, etc."

Married women were excepted from complete isolation during menstruation but for seven days they could not touch their husbands and they had to wash three times (2:107-103).

According to Jochelson, a woman also was not permitted near a river or the sea, and men carefully secreted their hunting talismans so that a menstruating woman could never touch them (1933:78).

A girl at first menstruation, according to Merck, had the same requirements as a widow. She had to remain thirty days in a part of the barabara enclosed with matting, without going out or showing herself to anyone, since she was considered unclean for this period. Relatives passed water and food to her, and she relieved herself in a hole.

A widow did the same except that it was for only twenty days (Jacobi:124).

During regular menstruation, a woman could not sleep by her husband. (Although Merck did not specify, she probably slept in a separate cubicle of the large communal house.) Two days after the period, she washed and rejoined her husband (Jacobi:121).

Since forty days was the Russian Orthodox ritual period, we must question Veniaminov's constant designation of this as the traditional Aleut period. Yet, Merck's various ritual periods do not show a pattern or system which most cultures have because there is a basic rationale for such observances. Merck was in the Islands a generation earlier, Veniaminov stayed longer. The reader can take his choice.

There is no indication that any tests were required of the girl at puberty or that any operation was performed on her or on the pubescent boy, except that girls were tattooed on the chin. Evidently the women's extensive tattooing was only begun then. Whereas men were tattooed simply on chin or from nose across cheeks, women were tattooed on cheeks, hand, foot, forearm in single lines or dots, on forehead and nose with crosses and other designs (Jacobi:116-17). The men's designs illustrated in Merck's journal surely must be symbolic. An intriguing suggestion is that the further tattooing of women (on hands, feet, etc.) is done "zur Zierde." Does this mean in this context "for ornament" or "for honor"? (See discussion of rank.)

Marriage

Concerning the Unalaskans, Veniaminov wrote, obviously referring to a past time, the eighteenth century, described to him by the old people of his own time, "It sometimes happened that the parents of young children arranged a marriage for them so that when they grew up, they would absolutely be united. If the groom died before the marriage ceremony, many of such brides remained widows for the rest of their lives. The groom almost always had a right to marry again" (2:78).

How old the people had to be before they entered marriage is not known. One can only say that the men were not allowed to marry until their beard had appeared because they say that to marry in youth will bring a person to forget his relatives, as he will exchange them for his wife and children. Hence, early marriages were not allowed so that the children could be more useful to their parents and their relatives. A girl did not get married until she was proficient in her household duties.

A man and woman cannot enter matrimony without a general approval of the relatives, especially their parents and their uncles. A man breaking this rule is for a long time in disfavor among his relatives. It often happens that the parents without asking their son whom he would like to marry and even without the knowledge of the future bride decide among themselves whom he should marry and only inform their children of their decision at the last moment, at the same time asking their wishes. The groom then can never dare to oppose, but the wish of the bride is very often respected, because the choice of the groom is almost always left to her and she from her early childhood has been impressed with the fact that she must not marry a bad Aleut and hence shame all her relatives. On the choice of the bride, the parents and relatives of the groom take considerable care, trying to become acquainted with her as well as possible.

When the marriage was approved by all, the groom for two years after that hunted for the relatives of the bride. If the bride was from another settlement, he moved into her settlement so that he could personally show her his ability; but if, for some reason, he could not or did not want to work for his bride; then he had to give rich gifts to her parents and her relatives. Having fulfilled either the first or the second obligation, the bride was given to the groom but without any return presents or ceremony (except a small feast).

The data on the Atka Aleuts is supplementary and in one particular contradictory to the above.

Marriage was contracted at ten years of age, the time when a boy was considered able to manage a bidarka and throw a spear, and consequently was counted among the hunters, while the girl was able to sew. The parents betrothed their children to each other. As soon as such an engagement had been resolved upon, the parents presented the children with household utensils, clothing, hunting gear, etc., but the marriage was only considered as binding when the young couple had brought forth children. At that time it was the custom for the son-in-law to give the father-in-law a slave (3:9-10).

The statement that a lad was married at the age of ten is scarcely to be credited, except marriage in the sense of agreement between two families whereby the boy began the period of bride-service with his prospective father-in-law, who might be his maternal uncle.

In the 1840s, one generation after the period of our study, there were communications, preserved in the Alaska Church Collection, regarding appropriate and permissible ages of marriage for Alaska natives. In 1840, the administrator-general of the Russian-American Company recommended fourteen years for women and eighteen for men as the legal age for marriage, saying that the sixteen-year minimal age according to Russian law was inappropriate: girls matured never later than fourteen years except in cases of illness. The famous Etolin, when he became administrator-general, recommended setting the age at fifteen, with creole girls allowed to marry at that age only with a priest's permission. In 1841, Dean Hieromonk Misail instructed the Kodiak priest to set the minimal age at fifteen years for a boy and thirteen for a girl. In 1844, Bishop Innokenty, the former priest Veniaminov, petitioned the Holy Synod to allow girls to marry before age sixteen because 1) a native's exact age was not always known, 2) villages were too far apart to allow a free choice of mates of the right age, 3) a priest was not always available, 4) a girl might be an orphan or have dissolute parents (Documents 2:303). Although none of these men mentioned custom, the recommended lower age for marriage did agree with reported custom of Aleuts and many southwest Alaskan Eskimos both before and after this period.

The statement about the gift of a slave after childbirth shows that the Aleuts shared the widespread idea of marriage being a contract and bearing children part of the contract.

Veniaminov's statement that "the parents" presented the young people with clothing, implements, etc., is clarified by the following statement by Sarytchev indicating that the girl's father presented a dowry in return for the gifts from the bridegroom.

> They have no nuptial ceremonies. The bridegroom commonly treats with the parents for the bride, and promises what he thinks he can afford, either in cloaths, baidars, or what are termed Kalga [slaves]. . . . If the parties are agreed, the bridegroom begins to visit his bride, and frequently spends whole days with her, in the character of a lover. If they have any regard for each other, the bridegroom either takes her to his house, or repairs for a constancy to her dwelling. If they live in harmony, the father now on his part makes presents to the son-in-law; if, however, the husband be not satisfied with his wife, he can send her away, but has no right to demand his own presents back, on the other hand, if the woman will not live with him, he is at liberty to take from his father-in-law all that he had given for her (2:76).

This is what Veniaminov has to say:

> Polygamy was not forbidden but as wives were very expensive, most of the Aleuts had only one or two wives; very few had more than six. Strong and brave warriors could have concubines from their slaves, i.e. captured women. Children born of concubines were not slaves. Of all the wives and concubines, no matter how many there were, one had the priority over the others; she was

called aiagagamaga, "the real wife"; all the others were named aiagakh, "wife," or aiagada, "concubine." The priority or seniority among the wives was not held by the first wife but by the favorite and even more often the one who gave birth to the most children. [Footnote·] People say that among the polygamous, the wives lived very well with each other in spite of the fact that they were jealous.

On the death of one wife, everyone could get another. Furthermore, because of barrenness or unfaithfulness, the husband could drive out his wife and replace her with someone else but this was not in general use and was only done by the most dissipated who went under the name of the "angry or the quarrelsome" (2:77-78).

Merck wrote that marriage was a purchase from the parents or relatives; the payment consisted of boats, clothing, and slaves, from which the bride's parents returned a portion as dowry. Wealthier men took seven or eight wives; if one displeased him, he quite often would send her back to her parents, with or without the children. Rarely a woman would have two husbands. "Parents seek to keep their sons away from women until full manhood, the longer the better" (Jacobi:121-22).

On the question of the usual number of wives, there is some slight disagreement, but there is surprising agreement on the possibility of a man's returning a wife to her kin. Sauer, for example, said that a girl was purchased from her parents and that if a man was displeased with the deal, he could return her to her people and part of the purchase price was refunded to him (160). Langsdorff said, "The number of wives depends entirely upon the pleasure of the husband, and he commonly chooses to have as many as he can conveniently maintain. If his means decrease, he sends first one, then another back to their parents; and these women become perfectly at liberty to seek out other husbands" (47). Coxe, quoting from the Journal of Krenitzin and Levashev, undoubtedly was confusing concubines with wives in the following statement: "It is common for them to have two, three, or four wives; who do not all live together, but, like the Kamtchadals, in different yourts. It is not unusual for the men to exchange their wives, and even sell them, in time of dearth, for a bladder of fat. The husband afterwards endeavours to get back his wife, if she is a favourite, and in case he is unsuccessful he sometimes kills himself" (217-18). According to the *Neue Nachrichten* (Coxe), the number of wives rarely exceeded four (180). Finally, "the rich had several wives, and besides them, several concubines from slaves. The most sensual of them often exchanged those and the others under various pretexts, either barrenness or unfaithfulness." This awkward statement by Veniaminov evidently means that a concubine could be raised to the status of a wife and vice versa, which, if true, is further proof of the desire and esteem for big families and the disgrace suffered by a barren woman. How such a practice could be harmonized with matrilineal descent which would pull the children away from the father and his lineage is difficult to see unless an exception to the rule was made in the case of a slave-woman's children. That is, in such a marriage the children would belong not to the mother's kin group but to the father's, further indicated by the statement (see p. 245) that the children of a free man and a slave-woman were free.

Certain marriages within the kin group were not only permissible but laudable. Nevertheless, it was also desirable at times that a man should marry into another settlement "for political reasons" (Veniaminov 2:76). The residence evidently was patrilocal even in the case of the first wife, following temporary matrilocal residence as Sarytchev said, unless there was some special reason for prolonging the stay in the woman's settlement.

The lending of wives or slave concubines was noted by nearly all the early writers (*Neue Nachrichten* in Coxe: 180-81; Langsdorff:47; Coxe:217). Further, Pallas, from early sources, wrote that "both wives and daughters attach themselves without shyness to strangers" (M. and B.:46). Although this probably referred to relationships with Russian and Siberian crews rather than relationships within the Aleut society, women must have been able to change sex partners readily in either case.

Krenitzin and Levashev wrote, "When strangers arrive at a village, it is always customary for the women to go out to meet them, while the men remain at home: this is considered as a pledge of friendship and security" (M. and B.:59).

The most sensible report was given, as usual, by Veniaminov. He said that lending one's wife to a guest was conducted only among the chiefs and honorables "and furthermore they offered not their wives but their concubines or slaves and only in the case when the host could hope to be treated in a similar way" (2:60). A somewhat surprising statement in this connection by Sarytchev, when duly qualified, gives a clue to the working of another trait. After mentioning that a husband could "resign" his wife over to another "either for a term of years, or for a continuance, which is not unfrequent," he also said: "I was told, that formerly this custom was not practiced for money, but from a sort of compassion, and a cordial attachment to an individual, who, on his return after a long absence, was allowed to sleep one night with every female, married and unmarried, in the jurt" (77). There are two points to be considered: with patrilocal residence and a patriachal system whereby several sons and their families lived together in one barabara or jurt, the adult women with the exception of a man's own mother and young unmarried sisters would be his sisters-in-law and, by the levirate, eligible wives; or with a system of matrilineal descent, if he were a young man serving his maternal uncle, the women in the household would be uncle's wives, female cross-cousins, and male cross-cousins' wives, intercourse with none of whom would be considered incest (unless the women in this last category happened also to be his own sisters, which would be the case with one form of cross-cousin marriage).

It is interesting that a custom so strange to eighteenth-century Europeans as polyandry should have been overlooked by all except Merck and Langsdorff. The latter said, "Sometimes the same woman lives with two husbands who agree among themselves upon the conditions on which they are to share her" (2:47). Later, Veniaminov wrote,

Similarly women could have two husbands, of whom one was the main one and the other his helper. Such a woman was not considered dissolute but was even praised and famous as being skillful and able because she had to sew for two men and keep in repair their kamleikas and their bidarka cover. The second husband had all the rights of the first husband and equally with him had to hunt and help to support the wife and the family, but he was not the full owner of the house. In case the helper wanted to separate, which he could always do, he had a right to take a part (but not a half) of all that was in the house. The children always remained with the mother or more often with the uncle (2:78).

If there was matrilineal descent, the question of paternity would not figure in determining membership in the larger kinship group, but even so, there must have been some common understanding in the matter, to avoid constant confusion and to determine conduct toward the mother's husbands' relatives. Whether modern conditions can be taken as a relatively pure survival of ancient attitudes in such matters is problematical, and I give the following with this in mind. Of three households in the village of Atka which I observed intimately and in each of which there was a polyandrous situation and also a birth within the year of my residence, in every case the woman's legal husband regarded her infant with genuine fondness and was always referred to as the father. The Aleuts by that time had become familiar with the "Outsiders'" attitudes and might almost be called sophisticated; yet such things as a caressing tone of voice, concern over a sick baby, purchases of toys and other luxuries for the child were not entirely simulated to deceive outsiders and were, to my mind, indicative of an acceptance of paternity although each "father" knew that another man had been having intercourse regularly with his wife. (In one case the second husband lived continuously in the household; in another, he took up actual residence with the "wife" only when the legal husband had to be away for the fox-trapping season and the like; and in the third case the second husband was a Caucasian trader who had maintained an open liaison with a married Aleut woman over a period of seven years and had contributed considerably and frankly to the support of the family.) The difference in attitude of a man toward the children whom a woman had borne before her marriage and toward all children born since her marriage to him is another indication that when the man thought the children might be his, he was willing to deceive himself into thinking that they were his. At the same time, attention paid by the second husband to the children was not resented—at least outwardly—further proof of the continued acceptance in modern times of the legitimacy of a polyandrous marriage. It should not be overlooked that in all these households, the second husband contributed to the economic maintenance of the family.

Transvestism. Regarding the berdache relationship, Krenitzin and Levashev wrote the following clause which Coxe omitted in his translation: "and some [men] have also an object of unnatural affection, who is dressed like the women" (M. and B.:59). Merck said, "Here one finds, as on Kadjak, but more rarely, men-women (Aijahnhuk), who themselves have wives" (Jacobi:122). One must recall that his spelling was German. And Langsdorff observed:

Boys, if they happen to be very handsome, are often brought up entirely in the manner of girls, and instructed in all the arts women use to please men: their beards are carefully plucked out as soon as they begin to appear, and their chins tattooed like those of the women: they wear ornaments of glass beads upon their legs and arms, bind and cut their hair in the same manner as the women, and supply their places with the men as concubines. This shocking, unnatural, and immoral practice, has obtained here even from the remotest times; nor have any measures hitherto been taken to repress and restrain it: such men are known under the name of Schopans (Langsdorff:48).

Sauer, writing about the Kodiak Islanders, appears to have suggested a motive: "The women seem very fond of their offspring; dreading the effects of war and the dangers of the chase; some of them bring up their males in a very effeminate manner, and are happy to see them taken by the chiefs, to gratify their unnatural desires. Such youths are dressed like women, and taught all their domestic duties" (176).

Death

The details of the various methods of disposing of a corpse in vogue among the Aleuts will not be repeated here since they have been discussed at such length by Dall, Jochelson, and Weyer. A few summary statements are desirable, however. None of the early visitors to the Islands reported the method of placing a body in a side compartment of a large barabara and then filling in the compartment while the barabara continued to be used, Dall being the first to describe such burial (1878:7), but Jochelson's excavations confirmed Dall's report.

In some underground dwellings were uncovered lateral burial compartments which had been walled up by stones and earth and covered with grass mats while the underground house continued to be occupied. In a large dwelling one side often contained compartments for the dead, while the other was for the accommodation of children or for storage. These latter partioned spaces could also be used for burials of the members of the family and were then walled up.

"The greater number of skeletons was discovered through the excavation of the large pits, remnants of underground dwellings, where they were usually located at one side only." In addition, there were small special burial pits outside the houses (1925:49).

Since Jochelson's excavations indicated a homogeneous culture in late prehistoric time, we cannot postulate one type of corpse disposal supplanting another in successive periods. The rank of the individual, circumstances of his death, season in which the death occurred, and local preferences probably all contributed to determining when a person should be buried in a house compartment, in a cave, or in a coffin. As for isolating these factors, that would be unjustifiable at present.

The lack of fear of the dead on the part of the Aleuts, which, it seems to me, has been overstressed, nevertheless did exist to such an extent that the people usually saw no need of abandoning a house merely because a death had occurred in it and the body been interred close by (Dall 1878:7).[6] Modern Aleuts told me, however, they had heard that in the nineteenth century a house sometimes was abandoned following a death. Whether this was a custom introduced to the Aleuts by members of other tribes with whom they came in contact under Russian administration would be difficult to say. Since Jochelson did not happen to find any sarcophagus burials and could not obtain information of any from the Aleuts, he was inclined to doubt their existence (1925:45-46). However, in the eighteenth century, Sauer described briefly—and Merck in detail (Jacobi:124)—how "they buried men in a sitting posture, in a strong box, with their darts and instruments; and decorate the tomb with various colored mats, embroidery, and

[6] For references on lack of fear of the dead, see Sauer:161, Sarytchev: 77-78, Jochelson 1925:41.

paintings. With women, indeed, they use less ceremony"
(Sauer:161). Merck mentioned coffins big enough to hold
ten bodies.

Veniaminov also described—giving the impression that he
had seen such—a mausoleum "which for the rich and
honorable was nothing else than a tall quadrangular box
covered with boards and divided into two partitions and
painted on the outside with various colors" (2:81).[7] The
findings of the Stoll-McCracken Expedition vindicated both
Jochelson and Veniaminov, for it discovered just such a
coffin, but the isolated spot in which it was located and
the fineness and number of the grave deposits showed that
such interment was no common thing and not likely to be
located in the digging of a village site (Weyer 1929). Coffin
burial was common in southwestern and western Alaska, an
element of culture which apparently was diffusing northward in Nelson's time (Weyer 1932:263-66). It may have
been accepted by the Aleuts, not so long ago either, not
having had time to come into general use at the time of the
discovery, or, what is more likely, it had been known for
some time but was confined to the wealthy class because
of the scarcity and hence high value of suitable wood for
constructing a coffin. One item in Sauer's and Veniaminov's
descriptions of a "mausoleum" is interesting in view of
Nelson's statement that in the St. Michael region, near the
Yukon delta, totem figures or pictures of animals which the
father of the deceased had been skilled in hunting were
painted on the coffin (311). We do not know definitely
that the Aleuts had any kind of totemism but we do know
that being a great hunter was one of their peaks of achieve-
ment, hence the "paintings" become important, simply by
suggestion.

When the body of a great man was placed in a cave, it
was first put into a skin-boat, which was then hung upon

[7] Sarytchev also stated that such coffins were used only for the wealthy:
p. 77.

poles placed crosswise, according to the *Neue Nachrichten* (202). This possibly explains the use of a kind of cradle for suspending the body in several types of burials on the Aleutians; that is, it is possible that originally a boat always was used for this purpose, with a smaller, specially constructed contrivance later being substituted. At any rate, it would be appropriate for a noted and wealthy hunter to be laid in his boat. The *Neue Nachrichten* gives as the usual method of disposal that the body was "exposed to the air in a sort of wooden cradle hung upon a cross-bar, supported by forks" (181).[8] Veniaminov's account cites the use of a frame to hold the body, even when it was placed in a coffin (2:81), which was also verified by the excavations of the Stoll-McCracken Expedition. The "cradle" discovered in the latter case, as well as in the earlier findings by Dall, was a wooden hoop covered with skin, with a kantag placed at the hips, that is, at the bottom of this contrivance (1878:16-17).

On Atka, Jochelson found a shallow cave in which there were so many skeletons that he designated it the village cemetery. These skeletons seemed to have been laid one on top of another and without numerous accompanying deposits. On the other hand, he found no cave burials of any kind on Attu which, although not conclusive proof, did suggest the possibility that the Attu people never used caves for burial (1925:42-50). Evidently in the eastern and middle Aleutians, merely placing the body in a cave was the least respectful way of disposing of it, but placing a carefully mummified and wrapped body in a frame and then secreting it in a cave with an accompanying deposit of goods (and sometimes also the body of a slave) was the most honorable. If there was any reason why a corpse should be specially disposed in a cave rather than in a coffin burial, it probably was that this treatment was re-

---

[8] Possibly the person responsible for the first of these statements mistook the funeral frame for a boat.

quired for shamans or for members of a special status-group comparable to the whale hunters on Kodiak Island.

Pinart stressed the placing of masks over the faces of the dead and Dall acknowledged the practice, although he stated specifically that he did not find masks with the mummies discovered on Kagamil Island (1884:141). Merck's detailed description of coffin burial does not mention masks; Weyer in reporting on the mummies which he found in a coffin did not refer to masks, thus by negative evidence bearing out Dall's generalization which is given below. It could not have been a question of preservation in this burial because wooden bowls, a wooden shield, and other artifacts were found in a fair state of preservation. Pinart said of the deposits found in a cave on Unga Island, "These masks, which were used in funeral dances, were broken after the ceremony for which they had been made and thrown into the sepulchre. Along with the masks designed for the actors of the funeral ceremony, there were others which must have served another purpose. One rite of the ancient Aleuts consisted of the placing on the face of the dead person of a mask representing a human or animal figure" (1875:5). Dall's theory is as follows:

The practice of putting a mask over the face of the dead seems not to have been universal, since no masks were found in the Kagamil cave, but under what circumstances they were used is not known, except that they have been found with adults from one end of the Archipelago to the other, when the bodies were placed in rock shelters. Those buried in the earth did not have masks, as far as known, nor have any been obtained from underground caves, properly so-called. It may be that the custom had something to do with the placing of the bodies in comparatively open places, not secure against the visits of malevolent spirits; but this is merely speculation (1884:141).

Veniaminov did not refer to this funeral use of masks although they were still being used occasionally in festivals in his time, on the islands which were less dominated by Europeans (3:3).

Finally, nearly every writer on the Aleuts has commented on the special treatment of dead children. Dall said that mothers sometimes placed babies in a carved wooden box and kept it in the house for a long time. Also baby bundles were suspended from wooden frames in a rock-shelter like the mummies of adults (1878:6-7). Sauer made the statement which has been quoted with wonder ever after that a mother would keep an embalmed child in the barabara for months (161). Sarytchev even said that an adult's corpse might be so preserved, in speaking of a woman's mourning for her husband,

sometimes carrying it so far as to keep the body for weeks together in the jurt, for which purpose a frame is erected of a suitable size, in the shape of a prism, and covered with skins. The corpse is fixed into this case, as in a sitting posture, and remains there in a detached corner of the jurt, until the unsupportable smell renders it necessary for it to be buried. But little children for whom such a frame can be made firmer and closer, are kept sometimes a whole year and even longer, until another comes into the world to supply its place. Such coffins are decorated by the mothers with enamel beads, thongs, and bird's bills, and hung over their beds (77-78).

Merck mentioned thus keeping the body of a husband, a beloved relative, or a small child in the house, the last until the birth of the next child (Jacobi:124).

Zaikov said that the following custom was "currently observed" (he was in the Islands from 1775 to 1778): the body of a chief's favorite wife was mummified, put in a coffin, "and hung up opposite the place where the husband sleeps. All possessions left by the deceased are burned. A similar practice is followed when the favorite children die" (M. and B.:92). The statement, contrary to other reports, regarding burning deceased's possessions is questionable.

The extreme care lavished upon some dead Aleuts cannot be appreciated unless one reads a detailed account of the wrappings and the deposit of artifacts in and around a mummy bundle. The student, to gain some understanding of the high development of Aleut culture, should read Dall's description of the mummies found on Kagam-Ilan.

Here is a statement of the whole procedure following a death, according to Veniaminov:

The dead Aleut was not taken from the house for fifteen days while his relatives held a wake for forty days. A few days after death, the body was embalmed, i.e. his entrails were taken out and he was stuffed with dry grass and sewed up. Then he was dressed in his best clothes. A diaper was put around him and he was placed in an open frame covered with skins which is at first hung up in the place where the person died. During the first 15 days, his relatives wept over him, especially in the morning and in the evening, enumerating his noble deeds and his good qualities. On the sixteenth day, after embalming, the body was taken to the burial ground, and if the dead person was a toyon, all the villagers followed. The body was hung up in the same frame in the middle of the mausoleum, which for the rich and honorable was nothing else than a tall quadrangular box covered with boards and divided into two partitions and painted on the outside with various colors, and for the poor a plain and small barabara covered with grass and with earth. The poorest and the slaves were placed in caves. However, it seems that even the rich were sometimes placed in caves as is seen now in several. These graves or mausoleums were built on some elevated place according to the will of the deceased. After the body is hung up in such a manner that it will not touch the ground, various articles are placed with him, the number depending upon the love of the relatives for him or on the amount of his possessions, mainly such things as hunting or fighting weapons, assorted clothes, and household utensils, from which the bottoms were removed.

Until the end of the 40 days, the relatives continued to wail over the dead and after that period they had a memorial feast, making it as notable as possible (i.e. satisfying). This consisted of bringing out all the food, stores, which could be found in the house of the deceased and offering these to the guests who consisted of every inhabitant of the settlement, feasting them one, two or three days, i.e. as long as the food lasted. On the last day, the relatives of the deceased gave to the guests the various articles of the deceased, which were divided either according to his will or of the opinion of the relatives. With this, the ceremony over the dead was finished and was never repeated again. The relatives of the deceased and, if he was a toyon, then all of the inhabitants of the settlement went into mourning for a short time. This mourning consisted of their refraining from any games or any festivities and refraining from doing that which the deceased was particularly fond of unless it was necessary.

The mourning of the widow was not easy but also not very long. A week after the death of the husband, all joints of the legs and arms were bound with strips of sealskin, from which the hair was not removed. Then she was locked in a special barabara; or sometimes in the same house, a special corner was barricaded with hides and with rods, and she was not allowed to step out of this corner even for a single step and especially not on the beach. During all this time she was considered unclean so that no one could touch her nor could she touch anyone or anything. Even the food that was offered to her was always cut to pieces as she could not pick it up with her bare hand. All her excrements she had to bury in the ground in the place of her isolation. After forty days, she had to wash every other day, this lasting for a week. With the last washing, her personal mourning was ended.

The same mourning was observed by the husband for the wife. Among other relatives, no one had to follow this mourning. (Footnote: According to the ancient philosophy he who does not fulfill his part in the mourning will become insane in his old age and lose many functions of his body, dying before his time.)

Women hearing of the death of some loved person, i.e. their child, husband, father, mother or brother, would cut off their hair, would tear the clothes upon them, and tear to pieces, their best and most favorite clothes and then almost nude would begin wailing for as long as they had patience and strength.

It was also a custom among the Aleuts to beat the slaves during burials and memorial ceremonies but this was not considered necessary, especially in latter times just before the coming of the Russians.

If anyone wanted to kill slaves and place them with the deceased, he had to do it after forty days. The number of slaves killed was not definite. Sometimes they killed a husband and wife and all their children and sometimes only one of them but the latter case was more rare. The slaves were killed either by the instructions of the deceased, from among his slaves, or his relatives in their love for him stabbed or strangled any number of slaves that they wished. It often happened that the relatives would not kill their own slaves and even the descendants would not fulfill such a cruel and barbaric wish of the deceased. Sometimes it happened that the dying rich man willed that his slaves should not be killed and even ordered some to be freed and sometimes would send them to their own home, giving them bidarkas and everything necessary for their trip. Such people were very rare and for their humanitarianism they became famous among their descendants in their songs. On the contrary, there were such barbarians among the rich and honorable who in their grief for a beloved son or nephew who died by accident, for their own consolation, destroyed the children of their slaves, i.e. they drowned them, threw them from cliffs or stabbed them in sight of their parents, trying to find in the desperation and grief of these parents consolation for themselves (2:80-85).

Items of social or religious significance:

(a) The first item not previously mentioned is the widespread custom of "killing" a vessel used as a grave deposit.

(b) The number forty is a multiple of the ritual number of the region: five. Why forty should have been chosen rather than some other multiple of five is not clear. As their counting was by the decimal system, it might be just as accurate to say that a multiple of ten had a special significance. Veniaminov may have been accurate in specifying this number, since one of the earliest accounts (that of Krenitzin and Levashev) says, "When a man dies in the hut belonging to his wife, she retires into a dark hole, where she remains forty days. The husband pays the same compliment to his favorite wife upon her death" (Coxe:218). Since the period of uncleanness following birth or death in common practice in the Greek Orthodox Church is forty days, one might be skeptical of the antiquity of this as a ritual number among the Aleuts if it were not for the Coxe publication. (There is exactly the same wording in Masterson and Brower, from Pallas, p. 59.)

(c) The memorial ceremony was not an occasion for a potlatch as was true of the Tlingit. The Aleuts had another occasion for feasting and giving away goods, at which there were invited guests from other villages and which evidently constituted a true potlatch whereas at the Aleut memorial feast only one village took part.

(d) Unlike the memorial feast of the Eskimos farther up the west coast of Alaska (Weyer 1932:279-82), the Aleut ceremony was not—at least according to this statement by Veniaminov—the occasion for the conferring of the deceased's name on a living person. It seems quite likely, however, that such a naming ceremony did take place.

Whereas among the Eskimos of Norton Sound a very important motive for giving the feast was the representation of the dead by a living person who received the honor and offerings in the name of the deceased, among the Aleuts display and honor not only for the dead but for the whole family was a strong motive.

(e) Slaves were not killed immediately after the owner's death or at the time of interment but at the end of forty days, which was also the time when the feast was given. The slaves were wealth and deliberately to destroy that wealth was an ostentation. When a man ordered that his slaves, who were prisoners of war, should be set fee and sent home, he was also acting (probably sincerely) as a generous "great man." As Veniaminov pointed out, the relatives would kill slaves simply to show their love for the deceased and the magnitude of their grief (3:11), probably in the same way that modern Americans give costly floral arrangements as proof of their esteem and sorrow.

(f) The significance of the woman in mourning having food given to her already cut up was undoubtedly that she was not allowed to use any sharp implement, as was the custom among many Eskimo groups. The meaning of other tabus stated or implied in the above quotation is commonly known and will not be elaborated here. Not only was the woman unclean but everything that had once been in contact with her was unclean; she could not go on the beach because she would have come in contact there with harpoon and fishing gear and with bidarkas, and possibly the inhabitants of the sea would have felt her defiling presence; finally she evidently could not do work of any kind, an extreme tabu. The compass of the tabus is more apparent in this statement on Akta practices by the same authority.

Near relatives of the dead continued a general lamentation for several days, during this time they fasted; i.e. they did not partake of meat or oily food, such as fish heads, and they kept themselves clean; and even husband and wife did not cohabit during the time of mourning. Those who were very much attached to the deceased, if they did not commit suicide during the first paroxysm of grief, often fasted almost to starvation, and frequently visited the place of burial to mourn and lament, giving away to the people large quantities of valuables in memory of the dead. When children died, the parents did not mourn, with the exception of cases where children died before having any teeth; in that case the father fasted ten days and the mother twenty. The wife at the death of her husband, and the husband at the death of his wife, kept a fast and lament for sixty days, beginning from the eleventh day after death; but if the husband died on perished at sea the days of mourning and fasting were reduced by half. At the conclusion of the mourning period the widows or widowers might contract a new marriage (3:12).

(g) The tabu on meat and oily food gives the clue which is to be expected: uncleanness was considered especially obnoxious to the sea mammals and evidently also to the fish, which were a far more important item of diet here than north of the Arctic Circle. Therefore, the unclean person could not handle anything which had been or would be in contact with animals or fish. However, the person in mourning may have been allowed to eat shellfish, birds, and plant food in spite of Veniaminov's statements concerning the rigors of the tabu.

(h) Cohabitation of a man with his wife while she was mourning for her father, for example, would mean a contamination of the husband who evidently would not be in mourning himself. If both he and his wife were mourning, then the mere fact of cohabitation would be obnoxious. The purification by washing meant that the mourner was free to remarry immediately if he or she desired, or was obligated to by the custom of the levirate and sororate (see also Veniaminov 2:79).

The war leader endeavored to bring home the bodies of his warriors who fell in battle (see p. 263). This seems typical of the Aleuts in that they did not fear the influence of the corpse and did not try to get rid of it as soon as possible, but rather were willing to transport it a considerable distance; also it was considered sufficiently important that the customary ceremonial be held and the body disposed of in a way fitting to the deceased's station in society; and finally there was kin responsibility and solidarity. Another statement from the section on warfare (see p. 266) seems significant in this connection: trophies of war were sometimes placed in the grave of their possessor. This suggests that the hunting implements of the men, the special sewing equipment of the women, and perhaps other grave deposits were not just articles necessary to the soul on its journey into an afterworld but were rather—or in addition—trophies, testimonials of the wealth, skill, and brave deeds of the deceased.

Suicide. Regarding suicide in the Unalaska area, the indefatigable priest wrote:

They used to say that they were quite prone to suicide. I do not know on what this opinion is based. In any case, I have not heard of this and will not believe readily even an eye witness. Is it possible that they come to this conclusion because the Aleuts in their terrible year, hiding from the fear-inspiring Soloviof were discovered and attacked on one small island and in view of the impossibility to escape or to defend themselves, many of them threw themselves off the cliff? But it is not known whether they threw themselves so as not to surrender to Soloviof or because they were pressed by their attackers. Besides this event and other similar ones in the past, there hardly ever was an incident to show their lack of courage in such cases (2:28-29).

Yet of the Atkans, he said,

The Atkans, like other savages, did not know the value of their lives, and therefore in great emotion they were easily overcome by their feelings and deprived themselves of their lives. Grief over the death of relatives—a son, cousin, husband, or wife, etc. —often led to suicide; but there were no examples of children depriving themselves of their lives from grief over the death of their parents, no matter how dearly they had loved them. This was probably considered as a law. It occurred also that men committed suicide from disappointment at the failure of an undertaking. Sometimes they preferred death to capture among their enemies, to become slaves, or to be tortured to death (3:9).

On "Suicide and human sacrifice" Merck wrote,

If one dare trust the stories, the old men who are an encumbrance to themselves and others free themselves from the burden of life in this way. Such a one joins a sea hunt of younger people going out, under the pretext that he wants to accompany them. He fishes like the others, but on the homeward trip he stays back in a place where above an under-sea crag there is a higher [rougher] sea. While his fellow travelers are already on shore, to let the waiting hunters take [divide?] their catch, the old man seeks the most dangerous place. To the command of the Russians, by shouts to warn him, they oppose silence, secret smiles, or at most the explanation: "he wants to drown"; had they already on the outward trip noted his intention, (it was) without opposition; they rejoiced rather over this courageous [strong] act. The old man comes nearer the danger, his boat is overturned and he sinks, under the approving smiles of his friends (Jacobi:124).

Social System

Kinship

One of the most perplexing problems in Aleut culture has been the rule of descent. Was it matrilineal or patrilineal? It seems clear to me now that it was matrilineal. Strong evidence for this is contained in the avunculate which was so well developed. Jochelson gave some details of this relationship (1933:71-72) and Veniaminov referred to it again and again. The situation was summed up by the latter as follows: "Of all the relatives, the mother's brother, and after him, the father's brothers had a great control over their nephews and nieces. In the past, they were always their tutors, and hence the uncles were considered the most important relatives, especially the first, who was honored even more than the father" (2:108).

Sarytchev wrote:

Hence it is, that the man, who can never with certainty claim the children as his own, that are born by his wives, has not an equally unlimited power over them with the mother; nay, that the uncle on the mother's side has more authority than he.

The children of one father by different mothers are not

regarded as brothers and sisters, and are accordingly permitted to intermarry; but the case is reversed, with respect to those by one mother and different fathers (77).

Even if we are inclined to doubt the statement about half-siblings marrying, still this passage by one who lived with the Aleuts in 1792 indicates clearly that formal kinship was reckoned only through the mother.

Sets of kin relationships; preferred and prohibited marriages. Another social trait should be given full consideration particularly in relation to the avunculate: cross-cousin marriage, which no one recorded except Veniaminov but whose testimony alone is sufficient. "To increase their kin group, the bride was generally chosen from their own kin, most preferably the daughter of the first uncle" (2:76). In another place he said, "The Atkans allowed intermarriage between all relatives, with the exception of a brother to a sister, father with his daughter, and son with his mother" (3:9). The parallel cousins were considered as brothers and sisters to oneself and their children were.as one's own children; the mother's sister was a mother, the father's brother was a father, and the elder brother also (which as far as unallowable marriage was concerned was important in a man's relationship with his younger brother's wife), so that with these extensions, Veniaminov's definition of incest, which does *not* include the cross-cousins, is accurate according to information obtained by Jochelson and myself even a hundred years later (Veniaminov 2:137; Jochelson 1933; Lantis n.d.).

Here was the sequence of important events in the life of an Aleut lad. His training in paddling a bidarka and throwing a spear, etc., began when he was about eight years old, with the maternal uncle superintending this instruction. When he was about fourteen, he was betrothed, the arrangements occasionally being made without his knowledge and sometimes quite early in his childhood. He then began his service to the future father-in-law, which usually lasted two years. About the time the boy's beard began to appear, he was married (Veniaminov 2:74-76; Lantis n.d.). If he married the daughter of the "first uncle," he continued to live in the home of the uncle who had been supervising his education and treating him as his own son and now accepted him as a son-in-law. By recognizing the sister's son as a *possible* son-in-law, a man might educate and care for a boy even if he had no unmarried daughter to marry him. A lad might be reared by a maternal uncle in his own village and then marry the daughter of another maternal uncle or of a parallel cousin of his mother in some other village. So a tentative conclusion is that the avunculate as practiced among the Aleuts was connected with matrilineal descent but also was strengthened by cross-cousin marriage and service for the bride, one or both of which may have been far older in their culture than unilateral descent. There is, incidentally, no reference to marriage with the paternal aunt's daughter. (See below for relations with the paternal aunt.)

Next there is the relationship between a boy or man and his paternal uncle. When Veniaminov so often said "a man's son or nephew," he may have been using these terms as a European would use them, not as an Aleut. A man's brother's son was as his own son, not a nephew according to Aleut reckoning (Jochelson 1933:70; Lantis n.d.). This ties in with the levirate and sororate which were recorded by Veniaminov (3:9) and which were still recognized in the twentieth century, although of course seldom practiced (Jochelson 1933:72; Lantis n.d.).

A man undoubtedly could not have sexual relations with his mother's sister or with his paternal uncle's wife, but the relationship between the maternal uncle's wife and the nephew was different. It has come to our attention particularly because it was the cause of marital difficulties, according to Jochelson. In both the "Archaeological Investigations" and the "Ethnology of the Aleut," he referred to folktales dealing with such relationship and jealousy on the part of the uncle. He apparently accepted these in good faith as referring to actual occurrences. Whether or not he was right in this assumption, the tales do reveal attitudes and elements of the moral code. Golder recorded on Kodiak a typical version of the Jealous Uncle plot, so well known on the Northwest Coast (1903:90-95), and he recorded in such widely separated villages as Attu and Belkovsky two versions which were practically identical except that one featured a woman and her husband's brother and the other the husband's nephew (1905:220-22; 1907:139-40). Both were influenced undoubtedly by the Aleut version of the brother-sister incest theme. Certain attitudes are apparent: a man may have been jealous of the love between his wife and his nephew (Aleut definition of nephew), but such love evidently was not considered incestuous. (Indeed, the supposition of the seniority of crosscousin marriage over the avunculate may be wrong: this type of marriage may have been a substitute and development from the relation between the young man and his aunt-in-law, the uncle's daughter being substituted for the uncle's wife. This, however, is theory which goes beyond the evidence at hand for the Aleut.)

The kinship terminology (pp. 237-39) reflects the marriage rules such as levirate and sororate. Jochelson obtained a terminology which agrees well with everything else that is known of Aleut marriage and kinship. He apparently, however, did not have in mind cross-cousin marriage when he published his material, since he did not comment on the fact that the term for cross-cousin, asagax, has what may be the same root as asanqax, the term for son's wife or brother's wife (latter used by women only), a root which appears in no other term. With rules of matrilineal descent and exogamy, X's cousin-wife would belong to a different sib from his mother's and sister's, just as it would be different from his own. If there were moieties, his wife would belong to his father's moiety; if there were multiple sibs, her kin-group probably would be different from those of both parents.

Another argument in favor of matrilineal descent lies in the fact that when a polyandrous marriage—and possibly any kind of marriage—broke up, "the children always remained with the mother or more often with the uncle" (Veniaminov 2:78). In Veniaminov's report there seems to be no question of the children's being cared for by the father's sister although in one folktale when a woman leaves her husband because of his treatment of her, the son is given to his paternal aunt who rears him, treating him very well (Golder 1905:217). In another story, a father's sister's son is referred to as a brother (Golder 1907:136). Of course, one cannot lean too heavily on such casual references. As already stated, there is no specific reference to marriage with the paternal aunt's daughter.

The relationship between a person and his grandparents described by Veniaminov, although interesting in itself, does not help much in the solution of this problem. For example, a child's name always was given by "the grandfather" if he was alive. If not, then the uncle conferred it, the name usually having been suggested by the father. A child was named from either the side of the mother or the father, sometimes both, but in any case the name always referred to some exploit of an ancestor (Veniaminov 2:70). Was the grandfather in this case the mother's father or the father's father, or either one according to circumstance? The mother's father would not have belonged to the same sib as the mother and her brothers if there were sibs and matrilineal descent; but he would have belonged at least to the father's group if there were moieties and matrilineal descent. There is, however, no good evidence either for or against moieties in Aleut culture. This individual was not unlikely the paternal grandfather, since naming was not infrequently in other tribes a courtesy and an honor carried out by another kin group than that of the child; for example, the father's sister or some other important relative of the father would confer the name, even in a case of matrilineal descent. The reference to names perpetuating famous deeds of the child's ancestors, taken in consideration with other aspects of their culture, would indicate the ancestors of the particular grandfather who conferred the name. Thus the child could have been tied to the father's group as well as the mother's.

The grandmother's role seems not to have obtained much notice aside from one item of interest: "The upbringing of the boys was always the duty of the mother's brother unless he was dead, in which case the boy's father took the duty. The upbringing of the girls was the mother's and grandmother's task under the supervision of the uncle" (Veniaminov 2:71). The mother's mother probably is the one indicated here, but marriages between villages and even between different islands were not uncommon and although there was temporary matrilocal residence, it seems to have been the rule for the wife to go to the husband's home after the birth of the first child, if not before, unless there was some special reason for continuing to live in the woman's village (Veniaminov 2:76). In some cases, therefore, the father's parents and elder brother and the father himself of necessity must have been the authorities in the life of young children. When the marriage was contracted within the village, the woman's relatives would be dominant.

As for significant relationships with more distant relatives, Veniaminov said that "the prohibition of marriage referred only to persons of the immediate family and no other relationship or other reasons could serve to prevent it." This certainly does not sound as if there were a distant kinship which was respected and abided by in the form of clan exogamy. It seems inconceivable that true clans would have escaped the attention of the very observant priest. It is true that he told of a strong feeling of kinship with people in other villages and of a belief in descent from a common ancestor (see pp. 251-52), but these might have existed without clan exogamy. Veniaminov also said that even in his time, the Aleuts were "very careful and fastidious" about their relations (2:79), apparently meaning that they were careful to remember their kin relationships accurately, always a necessary feature of strict exogamy. In the section on government and in the details of kinship just surveyed, there is good but not conclusive evidence that the Aleuts had, according to the Lowie definition of "clan," true clans.

In regard to kinship tabus and license, Jochelson secured examples of indirect address which showed respect (1933: 70-73). Veniaminov said that respect was shown by the kinship terms as follows: a man called his beloved wife "mother," a woman called her beloved husband "son" or "father." They called their first child always "father" or "mother" according to sex (2:31). The caressing expression for son obtained by Jochelson was la'dax, derived from lax (son) and adax (father). Among the Atkan children, brothers and sisters were not allowed to play with each other (Veniaminov 3:10), and there were some restrictions on married women, not clearly defined by Veniaminov. He said that sometimes women would not speak before men strangers even though they were not ashamed to bath in the bathhouses with them or openly to feed a child at the breast (2:116). There is no suggestion of a mother-in-law or father-in-law tabu. We know that the Aleuts often applied more or less derisive nicknames to each other (Veniaminov 2:71; Lantis n.d.), but what restrictions, if any, may have been imposed upon their use—except for specified close kinsmen—was not revealed.

In behavior toward kinsmen, a seniority principle was in

effect. Even though Jochelson was in the Aleutians a hundred years after the end of our period of inquiry, a century during which Aleuts had increased contact with Pacific Eskimos and Tlingit Indians and might have learned from them new practices, his information on this subject probably represents the aboriginal as well as early twentieth century system. He said that he learned the Aleut language and he did seem to get many data firsthand. Jochelson reported that a younger brother or sister would not look at the face of or address directly an older brother or sister, and a younger person would act similarly toward an older cousin. Father and son, uncle and nephew would not address each other by name or kin term, and a son, daughter, nephew, or niece could not have a direct request of a parent (father or mother) or uncle. The younger person could not say, for example, "bring my coat," but "a coat may be brought to me." Even a grown son and daughter would not address their mother by her personal name or the appropriate kin term: "they use an indirect form" (Jochelson 1933:73). What is meant here probably is—among other indirect forms—teknonymy.

Since the elder brother was a substitute father, he could not have intercourse with the younger brother's wife, but the younger one, if unmarried, had access to the elder's wife. She evidently was not regarded as a substitute mother, and, as appears again and again, the levirate (both simultaneous and successive) was in effect.

Although the essentials of my conclusions as to what must have been the rule of residence have been given, the matter should be discussed in more detail. Dall, Golder, and Jochelson all referred, in connection with supposedly historical tales, to the custom of a young man living most of the time with his parents but going occasionally to visit his wife who was living in another village because she was supposed to stay in her father's home until the birth of the first child (Dall 1878:9-11; Golder 1907:134; Jochelson 1925:45). Golder obtained his information from Veniaminov; both Dall and Jochelson were dealing with the same legend, the one which was supposed to explain the mummies found on Kagamil (or Kagam-Ilan) Island. That these stories are a true reflection of the general Aleut residence practice is doubtful. The situation depicted in them may indeed have occurred only in special cases, like these involving the daughter of a chief. In fact, Veniaminov said that although it was customary for the newly married couple to go to the husband's home to live after the marriage, they might even settle for good in the bride's village, "if his wife strongly wanted it" (2:76). As women seem to have been treated quite well in Aleut society, the rule probably was tempered with kindness as well as expediency.

Inheritance. The question of inheritance of property or of office is not easy to solve. Any question concerning inheritance of a house must have arisen very rarely, as a number of related families lived together in one big barabara (Veniaminov 2:204; Cook:512), which probably belonged to the oldest man in the kin group if to anyone in particular. It seems plausible that it might pass from him to a brother, a sister's son, or a son-in-law, depending upon circumstance and providing that inheritance conformed to the avunculate. (On this last point we are not at all sure.) There was supposedly no question of inheritance of personal property, especially among the people having the most property, since it was buried with the corpse, destroyed, or given away upon the owner's death (Veniaminov 2:81-82). Sarytchev said, however, "The distribution of the property on the death of the father is regulated by the relatives, who usually leave the greatest part for the widows and children, and take the rest for themselves" (2:77).

Regarding certain incorporeal items of wealth, Veniaminov said, for example, "Such surgeons were very famous for their skill, which they taught to no one except their most beloved children and grandchildren" (2:263). On the other hand, it was rare that the son of a shaman was also a shaman. The priest thought that possibly a man frightened his son by telling him of the dangers of the profession, but this seems unlikely. Since the common belief was that a boy was plagued by the spirits until he accepted his calling, nobody bothering to train him until after he had shown some manifestation of unusual relationship with spirits (Veniaminov 2:125), it would seem likely that a specific mental and emotional type was necessary to make a shaman. In such case, not a simple rule of inheritance but the complex of heredity and family experience would operate.

An old man when dying would bless his grandsons and give them some of his gray hairs or fragments of his clothing or arms which he had carried in war and would order them to preserve these charms against misfortune (Veniaminov 2:134). The *Unalaska Notes* discloses nothing more about the inheritance of amulets or the inheritance of crafts, but it does say that human fat from corpses was used in the whale hunt, that talismans such as the hollow stones picked up on the beach were very highly valued as hunting charms, particularly in the sea-otter hunt, and also that poison was used in whale hunting (Veniaminov 2:130-33) —all of which are identical with Kodiak practices. It seems reasonable in this case—even though the acceptance and rejection of culture does not always appear reasonable— that the Aleuts had the whole whale-hunting complex of the Kodiaks, including inheritance of being whale hunters.

Summary. If there were clans, they did not form a prominent complex in the community. There is, for instance, almost no evidence of animal totems linked with kinship with a religious connotation. The reference is always to human progenitors, "the great heroes." The rule of residence was patrilocal (technically matri-patrilocal) but it was not strictly enforced. Whether a man's sister's children or his own children succeeded to his position in the kin group and to any office in the larger social unit is the one question that we cannot answer with certainty, although we can surmise that the avunculate was stronger in the former than in the latter connection. Descent was evidently matrilineal. We are safe, I think, in attributing some of the importance of the avuncular relationship to cross-cousin marriage, in connection with service for the bride, regardless of rule of descent.

Kinship Terms as Recorded by Jochelson (1933:69-71)

forefather, ancestor   kada′lax‛
consanguineal relatives   kiŋla′xtix‛
G-F, 5th generation   qitnuču′dax‛, qitču′ŋix‛
G-F, 4th   ″   qi′txux‛
Gr G-F, Gr G-M   sagux‛
F's F, M's F   la′tux‛
F's M, M's M   ku′kax‛
my parents (lit. both my mothers)   ana′kiŋ
F   a′dax‛[1]
F's B, M's Si's H, step-F   adaxta′nax‛[2]
F's Si (see nephew-niece)   nix‛
M's B   a′mix‛
M   a′nax‛, agu′nax‛
M's Si, F's B's W, M substitute   anaxta′nax‛
M's B's W   quli′gax‛
man's B, wo's Si   agitu′dax‛
wo's B, man's Si, i.e. brothers and sisters   a′ŋan-a′gan
man's elder B, wo's elder Si   lu′dax‛
middle B   alux‛[3]

[1] On Attu Island, a′yax‛.
[2] On Attu, ayaxta′nax‛.
[3] Jochelson gives uyuŋ ludagi′—my elder brother, uyuŋ alugi′—my middle

younger B kiŋux'³
wo's B u'yux', hu'yux'
man's Si u'ŋix', hu'ŋix'
F's Si's S or D, M's B's S or D asa'gax'
man's F's B's S or M's Si's S, agitudaga'nax', agitutaxta'nax'
  wo's F's B's D or M's Si's D,
  substitute sibling
man's F's B's D or M's Si's D uŋiga'nax', huŋiga'nax'
cousin, caressing term of address a'yax', a'čax', anaqi'dax'
my cousin, related or unrelated member of com- a'yaŋ, a'čaŋ⁴
  munity, term of address; caressing term
S lax'
S, caressing term la'dax'
man's B's S, wo's Si's S laxta'nax'
D asxi'nux'
man's Si's S or D u'mnix'
wo's B's S or D nix'⁵
man's B's D, wo's Si's D asxinuxta'nax'
G-child i'lgux'
G-S taya'gum ilgugana'
G-D aya'gam ilgugana'
H and W iŋača'gix' (dual)
H u'gix'
H's B, wo's Si's H or H's B ugixta'nax'
lover ugi'dax'
W, wo aya'gax'
W, spouse, old wo. uyi'kux'
W's B, man's Si's H čiki'dax'⁶
man's B's W or W's Si, W's Si ayagata'nax'

---

brother, uyuŋ kiŋugi'—my younger brother, sex of speaker not designated. By analogy of ludax' and ludagi', I have postulated alux' and kiŋux'. I obtained on Atka Island luda'n·iŋ—my elder brother and kiŋi'n·iŋ—my younger brother. Jochelson's uyuŋ must be from uyux, a woman's brother.

⁴ Jochelson: Similarly, my mother, my grandfather, my uncle may be used.

⁵ Jochelson: taya'gum nigana'—nephew, anagagi'nam nigana'—niece, speaker not designated. Note that terms for F's Si and wo's B's child are reciprocal.

⁶ This may have been a reciprocal term between a woman's brother and her husband, the men who shared responsibility for rearing her sons. Bergsland recorded sa·tivi- for brother-in-law in the Attu dialect. See note 7.

H's F, W's F   sati'mgix'
H's M, W's M   satika'yax'[7]
S's W; wo's B's W   asana'qax', asa'nqax'
S's W's Si; wo's B's W's Si   asanaqaxta'nax', asanquaxta'nax'
D's H   na'gux'[8]
D's M's B   naguxta'nax'
partner: wo's Si's H, man's W's Si's H, wo's H's B's W   aŋayi'kux'

Terms Indicating Social Concept, Status,
or Group beyond Specific Kin Relationships,
Recorded by Knut Bergsland at Atka

man, person (homo):   anrari-na-r = living one, having breath. na is an agent noun.

people: anrarirs

man (vir):   tayaru-r   Formerly used also for homo, person.

old man, male animal: alir

woman, wife, female animal: ayaga-r

old woman: iqana-r = object of tabu

family: ila·nu-m tgin su-rta-· = relatives who keep together, or, keep itself = themselves (collective sing.). See: ila·nu-niŋ = my relatives (to one informant: including "distant relatives"). ila = part, one of, some of. ila-, ili-, il-, = by, with.

relative: ila·za-   (Recorded also by Lantis at Atka.)

kin: kiŋulir-.   kiŋ = subsequent, later. See: kiŋi-·· = his/her younger brother/sister.

friend: ila-rta- = to have as an ila, or possibly = to be together with, to be a part of.

my partner, my friend, my spouse: agita·da-ŋ   agi·ta- = be together with, accompany, take along.

man's brother, woman's sister: agi·tuda-   agi- = cognate of Esk. ai ? E.g. Esk. aipaq = the other of two, mate, fellow, companion.

cousin-partner: asaga- = cross-cousin. (One informant used this for Russ. bratan, best friend.) Cognate of Greenland Esk. asa- = love? Might asa- indicate possible marriage?

[7] Bergsland gives sa·timg- for both father-in-law and mother-in-law, for husband's or wife's parents (personal communication).

[8] Bergsland: son-in-law, ŋaru-r (Atka), narur (Eastern dialect) (personal communication).

village: tana dg usi-r   tana- = ground, land, island, settlement
settlement, village: tana-r-a-r = being had as a tana-

The terminology is most noticeably consistent with the
levirate and sororate. The clear distinction between
parallel and cross-relatives could come from the substitute
husband and substitute wife institution or from unilineal
descent. According to my interpretation of the historical
sources, the Aleuts had both. Descriptively, one can say
that the terminology tends to be bifurcate merging.

The question of a kinship basis of other relationships is
hard to answer at the present distance from the aboriginal
system. If we seek an answer in analysis of the language,
we find interesting suggestions in the accompanying list
of terms; but without more than these terms, one can say
only that a village or settlement was not—linguistically, at
least—a kindred and a partner not a kinsman, except possibly
a cross-cousin.

Partnerships

In view of the importance to Alaskan Eskimos and
Tanaina Indians of various kinds of partnerships, one must
be alert to any clues indicating partner relationships among
Aleuts. Since there is no direct reference in the early
literature, one must depend on kin terms and other terms of
relationship, in the hope that the usual conservatism of kin
terminology will suggest the aboriginal practice, even though
the terminology was recorded in this century. Because cross-
cousins were potential marriage partners and probably
joking partners, special attention should be given to cousin
terms. The terms that seem to be relevant are the following, in addition to those obtained by Bergsland, given
above:

Partner: man's wife's sister's husband, woman's
    husband's brother's wife, woman's sister's husband   aŋayi′kux‘
    (In the sense of a rival in cohabitation—Jochelson 1933:71.)

Cousin, close friend, member of community   a'yax, a'čax
(Term of address, usually caressing term—Jochelson 1933:70.)

Regarding aŋayi'kux', one should note the term given by Jochelson for "brothers and sisters": a'ŋan-a'gan. a'yax is the root for "woman" but a'čax is not the root for "man." I have not been able to place a'čax among the kin terms.

Of special interest is the only eighteenth-century recording of a relevant term: kinoghtaka (which probably today would be written kinuxtaka) for "friend" (Sauer). These terms do not help us much, but perhaps we can wring a few inferences from them.

aŋayi'kux', used reciprocally by two women married to brothers and by two men married to sisters, could indicate not only partners in the sense of substitute spouses, as stated by Jochelson, but also work partners. Men married to sisters probably worked together in their bride-service, and women married to brothers and living in the latter's house after the period of bride-service would have to work together. This term applied by a woman to her sister's husband would indicate him as a potential husband in accordance with the sororate or, if she already had a husband, as a partner of her husband. Beyond this, we can infer little. As shown in the discussion of kinship, there were designated substitute marriage partners and substitute lineal relatives. How far the bonds of obligation and privilege were extended beyond these, we do not know.

Secret Society

The evidence of a men's secret society, which seems to have comprised all free males of the community, was published some time ago (Lantis 1947:28-33). There is some evidence that on Kodiak Island the whale hunters formed a cult-group having special observances and privileges, also dangerous powers in their use of human remains as "poison," and that there was a group of male elders, the kasets or kaseks. "Next in rank to the shamans are the kaseks, or sages, whose office is to teach children the different dances, and superintend the public amuse- ments and shows [religious ceremonies], of which they have the supreme control. The islanders generally call our priests by this name" (Lisianski:208). Whether Aleuts had the same or similar keepers of knowledge of ritual, we do not know. That they had the whole Pacific whale-hunting complex, including the esoteric elements, is better sub- stantiated (Lantis 1940).

Chamisso, naturalist of Kotzebue's expedition who had read most of the literature on northern peoples available in his time, wrote that Aleuts, like Greenlanders, had a different speech for men and for women (245). We probably never will know whether—if indeed there was such a difference—it was everyday speech or only the speech of ritual occasions or esoteric communication among one sex.

Class and Caste

The Aleuts supposedly were divided anciently into three classes: honorables (Veniaminov's term), common people, and slaves.[9] If Veniaminov's designation of the con- stituents of the highest class is correct, some interesting problems are raised. He said that *the Toyouns and their children and nephews composed the highest class; their renown for war-like deeds and skill in hunting conferred upon their posterity the rank of the so-called honorable class* (2:165). If we had only the first part of this state- ment, we might assume that this caste was composed of the immediate family of the chief, which would mean that

[9] Of the numerous spellings of the Aleut word for slave, the most common is kalga (sing.). Although the Aleut word for chief is tukux, many early accounts used the term widespread in northeast Siberia: toyon (German: toijon). The glossary of *The Peoples of Siberia* (Levin and Potapov, eds.) identifies toyon in translation as "gentleman, Russian official, official from clan nobility" (923).

chieftainship was eligible to only a small group. (Chieftainship was, according to the rules, hereditary but the
chief on occasion might be chosen from a group having
the proper status.) However, the second part indicates
that probably all those people who were descended from
or were supposed to have descended from the great
leaders of past generations could belong to the highest
stratum. There must have been a limit somewhere to the
claim to nobility on the basis of kinship, but at what degree
of kinship this limit was set, we do not know. (See "Chieftainship" for further details.)

The second class was composed of "all ordinary Aleuts,
who were not distinguished for anything, and liberated
slaves" (Veniaminov 2:165). Veniaminov referred in several
places to enslaving and to liberation of slaves, i.e. shifts
in and out of the third stratum, but the only suggestion
of descent of individuals or families from the first to the
second is contained in his statement that among the Atkans
if a chief had been a poor leader in a war expedition, he
was deprived of his share in the division of the spoils
(Veniaminov 3:13). Since rank depended not only on
inherited position but also in part on wealth (see p. 252), it
seems plausible that any disgrace similar to this, and
particularly being deprived of possible additional wealth,
might degrade a man. It is possible, too, that degradation
in social status occurred as a form of punishment or in
conjunction with physical punishment, but I believe the
discussion of crime will show that it was not the specific
crime or form of punishment which stamped a man as
common or honorable but his conduct toward his judges,
his attitude in defending himself. It is possible also that
people lost class simply because they could not uphold
the prestige of their ancestors and themselves.

Conceivably men could lift themselves from middle to
high class by great deeds in battle or by leadership in
other affairs, but this must have occurred rarely indeed

as positions on hunting parties, war expeditions, and in
community affairs evidently were assigned on the basis
of rank, the most fruitful of glory being retained by the
great people. There are other factors: Not only one's own
kinship ramifications (apparently even mere size of kin
group) but also the status of one's relatives by marriage
seems to have been important in class placement, too (see
p. 250). Veniaminov said that "warriors of the lower classes,
i.e. slaves and the Aleuts without relatives," could never
share in the distribution of captives following a battle
(Veniaminov 2:103).

Regarding the social status or the remuneration of
shamans and curers, we have very little. Our earliest
reliable source, J.L.S., recorded from Popof and Otcheredin,
"Several persons indeed pass for sorcerers; pretending to
know things past and to come, and are accordingly held
in high esteem, but without receiving any emolument"
(Coxe:195). Veniaminov said, "Such surgeons [who practised bleeding] were very famous for their skill, which
they taught to no one except their most beloved children
and grandchildren" (2:263).

The relative numerical status of these two classes, if
judged from the reports of the early writers alone, was that
the middle group was not large and certainly not notice-
able. For instance, Sauer, one of the better authorities
among the very early ones, overlooked them entirely. He
spoke of the island chiefs being chosen from the chiefs of
villages, all the other people—except for the immediate
families of the chiefs—being Talha or vassals to them (272-
73). In spite of Veniaminov's statements concerning the
division into two free classes, his further analysis of the
community makes it difficult to figure out the distinctions
between these two classes and their relative numerical
strength, for he said, "Every village was invariably composed of relatives and almost formed one family, where
the oldest of the family, called Toyoun (toukkoukk) had

power over all" (Veniaminov 2:166; Jochelson 1925:119). Now if the village chief was only the head of a lineage, with all the people being related to him except for the slaves, who were originally prisoners of war, then who were the middle-class people? Were they, after all, the bulk of the population except for the immediate relatives of the chiefs on the one hand and the slaves on the other hand? Or was the middle class just a handful of people belonging to nearly extinct lineages, plus a few free captives? The most plausible explanation is that there tended to be just one large wealthy kin group which was related to the chief (possibly a joint family or even a true clan, for which there is some evidence) dominating each village. But this does not mean that there was actually just one lineage or whatever was the fundamental unit. Also, even though the village might appear technically complete in itself, the individual would have many bonds of relationship outside his own local group because of the tendency to marry outside one's own community. Moreover, my suggestion is that the fundamental units, whatever they were, had varying rank and were not rigidly divided into two free classes. Lineage solidarity or true clanship could accord with such a condition of gradation as among the Tlingit, for example. Also, what were originally regarded as castes appear more and more like classes rather than true castes.

"The leaders among them, or toyons, have three or four men as slaves" (Zaikov, in M. and B.:91). Most slaves were prisoners of war. Except in the case of the offspring of free men and their slave concubines (Veniaminov 2:77), slavery was inherited. Slaves could be liberated, and occasionally were, by the generosity, pity, or appreciation of their owners (Veniaminov 2:84, 165). Sauer mentioned an addition to this group: "Not only their prisoners, however, are their labourers or slaves, but orphans become the property of those who bring them up, and are frequently redeemed by the relations of the parents; especially such as are inhabitants of other islands" (Sauer:175). Conceivably, after the conclusion of peace between hostile groups, relatives of prisoners could redeem slaves by generous payment, particularly if the latter were children. In fact the above passage probably refers chiefly to "orphans of war." Sarytchev said slaves were "prisoners made in the other islands, or destitute orphans, who are consigned over to a rich Aleutian, to labour for their bare sustenance, and may be transferred to another on the same conditions" (76). Earlier Krenitzin and Levashev had written, "When both parents die, the children are left to shift for themselves. The Russians found many in this situation, and some were brought [to them?] for sale" (M. and B.:59).

Despite some contradictions as to what were the duties and privileges of these classes, certain points seem clear enough. First, wealth was connected closely with class. Although the Aleuts were said to have been unable to understand why the Russian fur traders exacted a tribute of skins to be given to the Crown, as they themselves made no outright gifts to their chiefs (Coxe:221-22) or, in another translation, "their Tookoos have no revenue" (M. and B.:61), the chief and his family nevertheless had opportunities to obtain possessions which in turn enabled them to live better than their neighbors. This is implied, for example, in the following passage: "Formerly, according to the laws of the country, when a whale was taken, the chief of the village, the person by whom it was killed, and every individual of the society, had his regular portion assigned to him" (Langsdorff:45). Because the man who was chief of a whole island had an equal share with the inhabitants of any one of his villages, of every whale, seal, etc., cast upon the beach, he had an opportunity to be "richer than all others and consequently stronger" (Veniaminov 2:167-68). (However, the chief's individual share was no larger than that of the others, according to Veniaminov.) Another opportunity for obtaining wealth was through the labor or the sale of one's slaves. "Slaves could not hold any property; all they acquired belonged to their master. He was always obliged to accompany his master, take care of him, and in case of an attack to defend him. For this the master was bound to support the slave as well as his family in a satisfactory manner, otherwise it was considered a disgrace to the master. Good and kind masters kept their slaves, and especially the good and useful ones, like their own children, and the name of kalgi was the only distinction between the slaves and the children of the master." On the other hand, "the power of the master over his slave was almost unlimited. He could punish his slave with death for crime without being held responsible; sell him or trade him for articles; give him away, lend him or set him at liberty. The prices of slaves were nearly always as follows: for a bidarka and a good parka they gave a pair of slaves, i.e. a man and wife; for a stone knife, a pair of tzukley beads, or a sea-otter parka[10] —one slave each" (Veniaminov 2:165-66; Sauer:175). Although common people could and rarely did own slaves, in practice the latter were possessed only by the "honorables." In spite of the fact that the high-class people had slaves to work for them, they themselves hunted, fashioned implements, and built houses along with the remainder of the community, only escaping the menial labor of such tasks as carrying water. The "Journal" of Krenitzin and Levashev said that even the chief labored like the rest when on land, although when he went on voyages the slave rowed the "canoe" (Coxe:218). "This is the only mark of his dignity" (M. and B.:59), which was untrue. The Masterson and Brower translation says (58), "Some of their boats hold two persons [two-hole bidarka]; one of whom

[10] Tzukley beads were dentalium shells, which were precious. Parkas made of sea-otter fur were the finest.

rows, and the other fishes: but this kind of boat seems appropriated to their chiefs."

In social as in economic status, the nobility had advantages. The high-caste man could have more wives than a common man, not simply because of his rank but because he was in a position to capture and support slave-concubines and to purchase wives with gifts (Veniaminov 1:60, 76). And, in turn, large families were profitable. (For a similar condition on Kodiak Island, see Lisiansky:198).

Another mark of distinction was the kind and size of the burial and memorial feast which the wealthy man could have. Jochelson said, "An old Aleut informed us that not all Aleut were embalmed, this being the privilege of noted hunters, especially whale-hunters." "Corpses of honored people and of the families of chiefs were also mummified" (1925:44). As only the honorables ordinarily owned slaves, it was only they who could enjoy the honor of a sacrifice of slaves to accompany them to the grave (Veniaminov 2:84). (For a similar situation on Kodiak Island, see Lisiansky:200.) Earlier, Zaikov had reported quite temperately, "When a toyon's wife or an eminent man died, it was formerly customary on certain islands to kill the favorite male or female slave to be buried with the dead, but since the Russians have undertaken to wean them from this custom it has passed almost entirely from use" (M. and B.: 91). In addition to the permissible although not requisite killing of slaves at the time of their owner's death, "it was also a custom among the Aleuts to beat the slaves during burials and memorial ceremonies, but this was not considered necessary" (Veniaminov 2:83). The great difference in the number and quality of wrappings and grave deposits from one corpse to another even in the same burial is shown by the contents of the mausoleum uncovered by the Stoll-McCracken Expedition (Weyer 1929:231-34).

Among outward evidences of rank, Ivanov mentioned the large and much ornamented wooden hats worn on hunting expeditions. He said that only the chiefs and honored class could wear these whereas the wooden visors were worn by ordinary people (481). Veniaminov's explanation is that the chiefs and honorables were the only ones who wore the big hats because only they could afford them (2:217). Also, the women of these high-class families could have amber and dentalium ornaments which were quite beyond the reach of poor people (2:112-13). Tolstykh said that the long thin bone ornament, about four inches long, which was thrust through the nasal cartilage demonstrated "the wealthiness of the clan and their mode of life" and was worn by men as well as women (quoted in Jochelson 1933: 10). Of the use of anything that might be called a crest, there is only one hint: The most beautiful women and the daughters of rich and famous families tried to express by the designs of face tattooing the deeds of their ancestors (Veniaminov 2:113). On the other hand, if there was any permanent physical mark of slavery, we are not informed of it.

The famous discoverer, Cook, gave this account of class distinction and honor shown by etiquette:

I was once present, when the Chief of Oonalashka made his dinner of the raw head of a large halibut, just caught. Before any was given to the Chief, two of his servants eat the gills, without any other dressing, besides squeezing out the slime. This done, one of them cut off the head of the fish, took it to the sea and washed it; then came with it, and sat down by the Chief, first pulling up some grass, upon a part of which the head was laid, and the rest was strewed before the Chief. He then cut large pieces off the cheeks, and laid these within the reach of the great man, who swallowed them with as much satisfaction as we should do raw oysters. When he had done, the remains of the head were cut in pieces, and given to the attendants, who tore off the meat with their teeth, and gnawed the bones like so many dogs (511-12).

That their code of ethics made numerous other distinctions between high and low cannot be doubted in spite of the meagerness of details on this subject. An incident in the early history of Russian colonization shows how strict was their system. According to the account of the murder of Drushinin's crew on the Island of Unalaska which was given directly to Veniaminov by an old Aleut, one of the strongest reasons why the Aleuts turned with such bitterness against these Russians, whom they had at first welcomed, was that the newcomers flogged the son of a chief. Such punishment was given only to slaves and people who had committed a crime, hence was the greatest dishonor to a member of the honorable class (1:120-21).

(As late as 1830, the priest stationed in the Atka District reported [Alaska Church Collection] that on sea-otter hunts the chief occupied a separate tent or shelter. This was a generation after the Atkans had been converted to Christianity and about the time that a boarding school was built on the island. The hunting party under one chief that was observed consisted of ten single-oared and two three-oared kayaks [Documents 2:36]. The sixteen hunters probably included one or more creoles working for the Russian-American Company, but they still might have been considered members of one kin-group or one village.)

Political Authority: Chieftainship

The functioning of the class system cannot be understood without a knowledge of the status, powers, and duties of the chief and elders of the community. The "Journal" of Krenitzin and Levashev says that the office of chief was not hereditary, "but is generally conferred on him who is most remarkable for his personal qualities; or who possesses a great influence by the number of his friends. Hence it frequently happens, that the person who has the largest family is chosen" (Coxe:218-19; M. and B.:59-60). Veniaminov partially confirmed this as follows: "He who has large family ties through marriage is so powerful that no one will dare to offend him (2:76). The priest's description of the working of Aleut government, however, indicates that an actual choice was made only when no one was available in the direct line of descent. To do justice to his description of Aleut government, I shall quote it in full, also pointing out Sauer's statement that, on Unalaska at any rate, there was one chief for the whole island who was chosen from among the various village chiefs, without any reference to right of inheritance of the office (272).

The former government of the Aleut may be called patriarchal. Every village was invariably composed of relatives and almost formed one family, where the oldest of the family, called Toyoun (toukkoukk) had power over all. But his power was almost the same as that of a father over his separated children, i.e. he had to watch over the common welfare, protect his boundaries (every village had its separate hunting grounds); allow no outsiders to hunt within limits belonging to them, as well as prevent his men from infringing upon strange grounds and thereby give cause for hostilities; he had to command in time of war; but he had no right to take anything from his subjects but his equal shares (according to his family) of cast-up whales and drift-wood, and no matter whether he was present at the division or not, his share was no larger than that of the others. With regard to public affairs his power did not go any further than that he could send whom he liked, with his son or nephew, to explore, reconnoitre or do anything concerning the common welfare; but to do anything for himself, for his own benefit, he could order nobody. Outward honors or respect were never shown him nor expected, except that in case of insult or abuse of the Toyoun, his command was bound to make his case their own. The Aleuts had punishments and even capital punishment but sentence could not be pronounced by the Toyoun alone without consent of all the honorables. A Toyoun could not begin war with his neighbors without the consent of other chiefs living on the same island, and without permission of the oldest among them.

Several villages descended from one ancestor or one kinship

group composed a state or community, where the older Toyoun, descending in a straight line from the first forefather who settled upon the island, or if such a one was not to be had— one chosen among the chiefs for his wisdom, bravery and prominence in skill at hunting—held the same power over all the chiefs and villages composing the community as the subordinate Toyoun had over his village; he had to protect them all and stand up for the safety and honor of his subordinates; in case of war he was commander-in-chief of them all, and with consent of the other Toyouns he concluded peace; without his will and consent no one of his subordinate chiefs could either engage in war with his neighbors or even undertake a voyage to Kadiak or start on any important hunting expedition. Of everything cast upon the beach he always had an equal share with the others and therefore these Chiefs were richer than all others and consequently stronger; and the very respect of their neighbors for them depended upon their power and influence over their subordinates. The Head-Toyoun, holding such powers and rights, might be called the ruler of his island or district, but there never were any toyouns or rulers among the Aleuts who has the right to govern several or all communities (2: 166-68).[11]

In short, first, beyond the village and island chiefs, there was no toyon for several or all islands; second, the chief usually had prestige and power but not formal authority. Bragin, a fur trader who got along better with the Aleuts than most of the others, writing of the period around 1775, said, "They yield little obedience to their toyons or leaders, but they show no little reverence toward the elders" (M. and B.:76).

After the arrival of the Russians and Siberians, chieftain-

[11] For a statement on the Atkans specifically: "They had hereditary tribal commanders, like other American nations, but their power was limited and conditional; they were only obeyed by those who chose to listen. Their power consisted principally in the office of selecting men to perform certain labor for the common welfare; to divide whales cast up by the sea, to collect the forces in case of emergency, and act as leaders during battles with the enemy. But on such occasions it was necessary that they should conduct themselves bravely and be ahead of everybody" (Veniaminov 3:13).

ship became a serious disadvantage: In the "Fox-islands" the hunters "lay their ships up for the winter. They then endeavor to procure, either by persuasion or force, the children of the inhabitants, particularly of the Tookoos [chiefs], as hostages. This being accomplished, they deliver to the inhabitants fox-traps, and also skins for their boats, for which they oblige them to bring furs and provisions during the winter. . . . In the spring they get back their traps, and deliver up their hostages" (Krenitzin and Levashev, in M. and B.:60-61).

Regarding the proportion of chiefs to population, we have little information. Soloviev, who did not get along so well as Bragin, nevertheless probably can be trusted on the following item. His ship encountered a party from Sannaga (Sannak?) Island. "These islanders were 51 men strong and had five toyons among them. Each had a small leather bidar, in which only one man could sit; but they also had five large bidars. In these boats they row [paddle?] with all their belongings from one island to another" (M. and B.:79).

Regarding public participation in government, Veniaminov said, "Concerning important matters or in those where there is necessity for a general opinion, they do not indulge in long discussion, but on hearing the matter from the toyon or from one of the old men and knowing their opinion, they, having kept a short silence, say yes or no and immediately drop all conversation about the matter" (2:40).

This gives a clear picture and there is no reason to question any aspect of the priest's report except that concerning kinship (or supposed kinship). One might believe that a village was synonymous with a lineage (i.e. a deme?), but that several villages composed no more than one big kinship group, while possible, is still rather difficult to believe. Although it is not known whether these large kin groups were strictly exogamous, the idea that people in different settlements were descended from a common ancestor is suggestive. The following statement also fits into the picture: "People who were interrelated by marriage into other settlements were famous and were sung about in their songs, especially those who could be considered the progenitors of many settlements" (Veniaminov 2:76).

One must remember that the Aleut system seems to have included matrilineal descent and patrilocal residence. A man, his young sons and daughters, a married son, and an adolescent nephew or two, his wife or wives, and, if he was a wealthy man, a slave concubine constituted his family. This explains the reference more than once to a man's "sons and nephews." Let's say that an Amlia Island woman marries an Atka Island man and after the birth of a child goes to Atka to live. Her eldest son later returns to Amlia to be trained in hunting by his uncle and to serve as the betrothed of one of the uncle's daughters, who is a niece of the young man's mother. (Presumably all youths were trained by their uncles. If the woman had an older brother, her elder sons would join him. If, however, her brother was much younger than her husband and herself, it is likely that the eldest son at least would go to the grandfather or to the mother's parallel cousin or other suitable male in her settlement.) In due time, the niece also comes to live on Atka. Meanwhile, the Amlia woman's own daughters may marry into an Atka, Amlia, Tanaga, Kanaga, or other village, depending on political as well as social relations between the islands and the availability of potential spouses. The system would bind the intermarrying communities closely through succeeding generations.

The statement in the first passage that "every village had its separate hunting grounds" was testified to by Staehlin's account, published in 1774: "Whenever any one has fixed his habitation, nobody else dares to hunt or fish in the neighborhood, nor appropriate to himself what the sea has cast up, unless he has previously agreed with him for a part of the produce. If a man happens, on his way or in hunting, to come upon another man's territory, he must take up his lodging in their *Baidars*, unless he is a relation, for in that case he takes him into his hut" (37).

Now to return to the rank of chief—it is important to remember that one family claimed direct descent from "the first forefather who settled upon the island," but if no one was available in this family, another man was chosen. Such a choice probably was made by the men of the honorable class and possibly only by the old men of this group although in another connection, that of fixing punishment for crime, Veniaminov said that all the honorables *and* the old men (of the middle class?) formed the court (2:168). So many of these questions seem unanswerable. Social rank, kinship, government—all are only facets of the same gem; chip off any one of them and the gem loses its particular and characteristic appearance. Hence some of these points which are still obscure, like the faces of the stone which are turned away from one, will be seen more clearly as all faces of the culture are turned to view.

Administration of Justice

Although we are primarily interested in the mechanism of determining guilt and fixing punishment, we must ascertain first what came under the jurisdiction of the elders. Veniaminov, probably because of his interest in moral instruction, seemed to pay special attention to this subject and certainly published a full account.

Renegades, murderers, traitors, slanderers, and those who had betrayed a common secret were punished with death, he was told. In the case of any such offense, which evidently was considered an offense against the group, the chief called together the honorables and old men and tried the case, as will be described later (Veniaminov 2:168). Although murderers were included in this group by Veniaminov, there is evidence that they were punished by feud retaliation on the part of the victim's relatives, not by a court. It was part of the code that the accused should not excuse himself or ask for clemency. In fact, he maintained a proud behavior and even spoke of his crimes as if he were boasting of them. "It was not necessary to keep the culprit under guard or bind him on the way to his execution, because every criminal endeavored to display the greatest possible coolness and fearlessness at his death." Many of these fearless criminals received admiration and honor by means of songs (Veniaminov 2:169), which explains the motivation of their behavior. Not only was the criminal (or rather his memory) not infrequently accorded respect but also, according to Golder, the man who executed the sentence was greatly honored by being chosen for the deed. The higher the rating of the man whom he had to execute, the greater was his own honor (1907:136).

Other smaller offenses were punished at first with reprimand by the Toyoun before all, and then, to make it more disgraceful, he was bound as tightly as possible and kept in that condition for some time, and sometimes they were beaten after being bound.

The punishments of slaves were more varied and much severer: for disobedience their ears were cut off; for betraying their master's plans, the lips were cut off, but if he did not heed and especially if war sprang from his busy tongue, inevitable death was his fate. For a first flight they inflicted corporal punishment, i.e. they beat him with whatever was at hand; for the second attempt his hands were tied back and he was kept in that position for some time; for the third attempt he was hamstrung, and the fourth was punished with death. The mode of death inflicted upon the slaves was entirely different; they were not speared like the others, but beaten to death with clubs. For the first theft, as a most disgraceful act, and especially if the slave stole from outsiders, he received a whipping; for the second some fingers of his right hand were cut off; for the third he lost fingers of his left hand or his lips, and the fourth was punished with death (Veniaminov 2:170).

Stealing committed by free people was as great a crime as among slaves. Everything was left unlocked and open, except the precious amulets, special hunting gear, and religious paraphernalia which were kept secluded, probably as much to prevent contamination as to prevent thievery. Since there was a communal sharing of whales and of the fish catch (Veniaminov 2:56) and probably also other food supplies, there was no imperative motive for stealing. Also the sanctity of caste and wealth might cause a theft of a wooden hat, with all its symbolism, for example, to be regarded more as a sin than a crime, to be punished by the Supernatural. Of course, thievery did exist in spite of the code. Veniaminov said that a man would steal food in time of necessity or, after the coming of the Russians, would pick up tobacco or other little things, "so to say, while passing by" (2:24-26).

The preceding statements all pertain particularly to the islands in the Unalaska District, that is, roughly from Four Mountains eastward. Concerning the approved attitudes in the Atka District, he said:

The Atkans . . . strictly prohibit the betrayal of secrets to other tribes as leading to quarrels, murder and war. They also prohibit laziness, theft, willful abuse; to avenge a wrong even by the most violent means was not only considered praiseworthy, but an unavoidable duty; obedience to parents and to the aged and gratitude to benefactors were considered virtues. To kill a man for cause was considered just and allowable. Such causes were a violation of the marriage bed, a refusal in betrothal, theft, or secret hunting in the territory of others, and sometimes envy. . . . Theft was not suffered among them at all; a house in which theft occurred was immediately and completely vacated and cleaned (3:7-8).

Although these seem harsh punishments, there is no reason to refute them, but it should be added that the object of theft in which the above procedure was observed was probably a sacred object or something of very special value.

Certain acts seem not to have been formally punished either by the community or by the individual but involved gradual loss of esteem, in the end a severe form of chastisement. Because this gives a good indication of the tone of Aleut culture, we shall digress slightly to consider the standard of ethics (again returning to the Unalaska District) (Veniaminov 2:137-40).

(1) Parents should be respected and helped. "To abandon one's parents was considered the greatest and most dishonorable of crimes." (2) The oldest brother should be respected and served if the father was dead. A person who lived apart from his family and disregarded these obligations would be discarded by his relatives in case of attack or storms. "Such a dishonorable one would perish and be held in general contempt." (3) Very old men should be cared for by the young men and their advice should be heeded. "Whoever acts thus will be longlived, be fortunate in the chase and in war, and will not be neglected when he becomes old himself." (4) The rich must not despise the poor but should care for them; and (5) on the other hand, the poor should be humble and respectful and not offend the rich who divide with them. (6) "One should be hospitable; every visitor should be received as liberally as possible, and feasted in order that he, on his return to his people, may speak of us with praise." (7) People who move from one village to another should not be abused by their new neighbors but should be welcomed as additional defenders. (8) People should not be talkative. (9) Children should be instructed "to be kind in their intercourse with others; to refrain from selfishness; to be bold in case of hostile attacks, and disdain death, and strive to accomplish some famous deed, such as avenging the death of their relatives," (in other words, one had to maintain the honor and prestige of one's family). (10) In addition to the crimes mentioned above, such as murder, the following were to be regarded not only as crimes but also as sins: "to grumble at severe weather, cold, wind, or heat of the sun; to talk unnecessarily and unfavorably of stars and clouds;

to defile in any manner a sacred spot, or a stream of running water, so as to prevent fish from coming up, or to defile the sea in the vicinity of the village, and thereby drive away the fish or game." If a girl killed and concealed an illegitimate child, she was treated very severely, this also being a sin because the spirit of such a child would haunt the village and cause misfortune.

Sources of shame rather than or more than guilt have been given elsewhere by the same authority:

According to them, the following actions were considered shameful: to fear inevitable death, to beg for mercy from the enemy, to preserve life or gain freedom by treachery, to die without killing an enemy, to steal and be caught for it, to be overturned in the bidarka when landing, especially during the meeting and the parting, to be the first to weaken and ask for a tow during long trips, to show greed in the division of booty, to tell his wife or his mistress a general secret, to keep the best trophies while hunting with a comrade, to boast especially without reason, to reprimand someone in misfortune. Especially disgraceful, the Aleut considered the following: to beg for something even in dire extremity, to caress his wife in public, to come out into the center of the circle and dance even if he were proficient in this matter, to blush when he was praised publicly, etc. Women were ashamed of not knowing how to sew, to dance; of caressing their husband or children publicly, and sometimes even of speaking before strangers. They were not ashamed to bathe in bath-houses with strangers (men), to openly feed the child at the breast before strangers, etc. (Veniaminov 2:115-16).

There are other examples of an automatic retribution in addition to the socially administered punishment. Incest, which was a very grave offense, "was believed always to be followed by the birth of monsters with walrus tusks, beard, and other disfigurement" (Veniaminov 2:141); and "according to the ancient philosophy he who does not fulfill his part in the mourning will become insane in his old age and lose many functions of his body, dying before his time" (Veniaminov 2:83).

The degree to which the Aleut code of ethics had developed is well illustrated by the following: "The Aleuts never had any oaths except giving a word of honor before witnesses or the repeating of the word of honor a second time." To break it was a disgrace, for the person who did not keep his word was called a " 'common woman,' and even his relatives spoke badly of him" (Veniaminov 2:114-15), which would be a disgrace indeed, in view of their kinship loyalty and pride. The effectiveness of the system can be judged from the following (perhaps too enthusiastic) statements by the priest who had come to minister to the timid and by then thoroughly subdued Aleuts: An Aleut considers an undeserved reprimand, even a slight one, as if he were being sworn at. "However, a deserved reprimand, no matter how severe, never insults him, but, so to say, destroys him" (Veniaminov 2:42). "During the last ten years which I have spent at Oonalashka, there has not been a single murder or even an attempted murder or even a serious fight or a quarrel although many of them and many times were in a drunken condition" (Veniaminov 2:54).

Now that we have ascertained what crime consisted of among the ancient Aleuts, we shall consider their formal treatment of it. The earliest statement says only that the chief "decides differences by arbitration and the neighbors enforce the sentence" (Krenitzin and Levashev in Coxe: 218-19, in M. and B.:59). The fuller and later account:

When it was reported that any one among the Aleuts, regardless of his descent, had done anything deserving death, the Toyoun formed a court of justice of all the honorables and old men, taking part himself and after explaining the facts of the case asked their opinion, and when all unanimously adjudged the culprit to be deserving of death, all the men proceeded to an open place with their spears. The culprit was produced and immediately surrounded by several young men who, upon the Chief's command, made a circle at an appropriate distance, and suddenly all threw one of their spears at once; and if after this the culprit was still alive, the Toyoun or the chief judge ordered some one of the adroit Aleuts to stab him or club him to death (Veniaminov 2:168-69).

To execute such a sentence singly and unaided was a great deed. After the sentence was carried out, "the nearest relatives of the dead, i.e. his uncles and cousins, with weeping took his corpse" (Golder 1907:136). Thus the criminal was buried and mourned for like anyone else.

In the Atka district divination was used, and very likely it was considered part of the evidence in the other districts as well. At Atka after a theft the shaman assisted by a few other men entered "the building," apparently the one where the theft had taken place, "burning a torch, and went through various ceremonies, in order to find out the guilty one. They say that always, after several shamanistic actions, the image of the thief appeared in the light of the torch. Finding out in this manner the criminal, people went to him and took away the stolen goods" (Veniaminov 3:8). Any record of other methods of divination has not been preserved.

Veniaminov wrote an eyewitness account of the inflicting of punishment by the community, in this case for theft, which does not agree with the dignified procedure that he has given in abstract any more than the average court scene in modern American society agrees with the textbook description of a court trial. In his time, the Aleuts had already experienced over fifty years of European influence and also in this case possibly they were being especially vehement and ostentatious in order to impress the Russian authorities with their ability to handle such matters themselves.

In a large meeting of the Aleuts in their main settlement one young Aleut stole a pair of boots and was immediately uncovered. The agent of the Oonalashka District turned over the guilty one to the judgment of the Aleuts. One should have seen this comical scene. The poor guilty Aleut stood without answering, with bowed head, and the furious judges, i.e. all the old men and the adults, separately and all together, like roosters, rushed up to him, and with certain gestures similar to nervous jerking, gave him a severe reprimand; saying that he shamed all Aleuts, that now it would be a shame to go into other harbors, etc. In the end, they wished to punish him if they would be allowed by their agent. The guilty one for a long time was in virtual ostracism and tried to appear in the main settlement as rarely as possible (2:26-27).

This system of justice on the social plane rather than upon the personal, individual plane was evidently either a local development in the Unalaska District, a copy from the Russians, or a new importation from the high Indian cultures to the east. At any rate, the Aleuts to the westward were said not to have had anything of the kind. In the Atka region "they had no punishment for crimes; each one was supposed to deal with his own offender." "To avenge a wrong even by the most violent means was not only considered praiseworthy, but an unavoidable duty." "Vengeance was sometimes carried so far as to include the wife of the offender, but children, especially small children, were always spared" (Veniaminov 3:7). Perhaps such orphans of feuds (in accordance with the statement by Sauer, given earlier) were treated as slaves if they had no wealthy relatives to help them. Veniaminov really attested unwittingly to the fact that revenge on a wholesale scale was prominent in all parts of the Aleutians in spite of the presence of more temperate means of dealing with crime. In the past, "for an insult made by one person, they revenged themselves upon the entire family" (2:44). And, according to his account, war seemed to spring most often from feuds; in other words, their wars were feuds. So we are brought to another aspect of Aleut life.

Feuding and Warfare

Very rarely the inhabitants of the entire island joined in one war-party; usually it was composed of people of the same family group. The leaders of the war-parties among the Aleuts were always the Toyons, or their sons or their nephews. Furthermore, the warriors did not choose their leader but the leader collected warriors. He would make a general suggestion, "I wish to go raiding," and warriors would join him fully armed. Not everybody could collect warriors, but only those famous for their bravery or their skill in war, their knowledge of the enemy country and their ability to command. To such a person even those outside of his family group were eager to join. When a sufficient number of people had joined him, then he told them his purpose, which was usually to avenge the blood of his forefathers fallen in the enemy territory or an insult given to him and to his people. The warriors after hearing his reasons and purpose gave him their word of honor to obey him as a father instead of making an oath, at the same time giving him the right to do whatever he wanted. . . .

After this the leader chose several assistants (from four to eight) from his closest relatives or experienced warriors who commanded the various units in his group and constituted his war council.

Before starting out on the expedition, the leader in the presence of all (warriors and people gathered to send them off) pronounced an heroic speech in which he declared that he who feared death in battle or who did not trust his own powers of endurance would do better to stay at home and not bring shame and disgrace on his tribe. He said further that in case he was killed, his warriors were to obey his oldest assistant. If a brave warrior fell in battle, the leader promised to bring the body back home. The speech ended with a pledge to stand together, fight bravely, etc. (Veniaminov 2:99-100).

Statements made in various connections all show the anxiety of an Aleut to protect his own honor and that of his kin. The familiar group-responsibility on the part of both the aggressor and the victim appeared in the sentence quoted above ("For an insult made by one person, they revenged themselves upon the entire family"); and in a folktale, a man calls upon his sister's son to avenge the death of his own son (Golder 1907:136). What could call forth such hazardous rebuke, that is, what was the definition of insult, can be figured out from the code already discussed. In addition, the following have been mentioned for the Atkans: "The refusal of an offer of marriage was considered a great insult, for which the most severe measure of vengeance might be instituted, even death" (Veniaminov 3:10). This may refer not to a rejection of the first tentative offer of marriage but to an unjustified or uncompensated breaking of a bethrothal, for instance, after the suitor's service for the girl. Also "adulterers were subjects of cruel vengeance, and this crime often led to trouble and fighting" (3:10). Evidently there was always cause enough to keep the most ambitious warrior busy.

The prominence of these feuds is attested particularly by the folklore. One supposedly true tale, which is indeed free from the magic and supernaturalism so common in heroic tales, is given to show the nature of Aleut warfare. It must be borne in mind throughout the following discussion of warfare that a statement made by the earliest observers of the Aleuts was one of the shrewdest ever made, namely that they "always endeavour to gain their point by stratagem" (Krenitzin and Levashev, in Coxe: 216).

Synopsis: Two men from Akutan saw an umiak floating offshore. When they investigated, they found people from Umnak who were half dead from hunger and thirst. Instead of helping them, the men killed these people, took some of their belongings and sank the umiak. Some time later, Umnak people visited in Akutan and recognized certain articles which they saw. The wife of one of these two men was an Umnak woman and informed her friends that it was her husband who somehow had obtained the articles. They managed to find out how he had got them. They showed no sign of revenge then,

but returned again, offering him a fine parka as a gift. When
the man, his wife and son were in the barabara, they gave the
parka to him, which he immediately tried to put on. The collar
was fixed in such a way that he had difficulty pulling it over
his head. While he struggled with it, they fell upon him, killing
first him and then his son. No resistance was offered to them
then but later the brother of the murdered man made a wooden
effigy of him which he dressed up and kept in his barabara.
After a time, he proposed to the Akutan and Umnak people
that they made war upon the Kodiak Islanders and that they
should meet at Tigalda. He got many followers as he was
considered a brave man. When the Umnak people arrived at
Tigalda, the Akutan people attacked them and killed them.
The further prosecution of this feud was stopped by the arrival
of the Russians (Veniaminov 2:96-98).

Although there is interesting material concerning the
actual conduct of battle, no one has told how the warriors
were painted or dressed or whether they were painted at
all; but the following passage may be taken to apply to
"warpaint." "In proof of their achievements, 'they would
mark their bodies in some way to indicate that they had
been on some inaccessible cliff, or that they landed un-
assisted with their bidarka at some spot where nobody had
yet landed before. But still more praiseworthy it was to
be brave in war'" (Veniaminov 2:142).

The attack is described as follows:

"Coming near the enemy settlement, they tried to go only at
night. Arriving at the appointed place, the leader disposed of
the group, saying who should be where at the moment of assault,
who should remain in the bidarkas, etc. He himself had always
to be at the front. . . . To attack the enemy and fight with him
during the daytime openly was considered honorable, . . . but
it was considered better to attack them by surprise and secretly.
The best time for this was considered the early dawn." In
contrast to the secrecy of the approach and preparations, tam-
bourines were beaten during the actual attack (which may be

a good primitive example of martial music or more probably an adjunct of the shaman's part in the battle). Being the first to enter an enemy barabara and capture its inhabitants was considered the greatest feat in the assault of a defended location (Veniaminov 2:101-102).

Among the Atkans also, the chiefs were the war leaders and it was incumbent upon them to "conduct themselves bravely and be ahead of everybody. Good and brave chiefs were readily obeyed, and in the division of spoils, all gave him the full power to divide as he chose. Poor chieftains, in the division of spoils, were even deprived of their share" (Veniaminov 3:13). Among the Unalaskans, too, there was punishment for the unsuccessful war leader. Ordinarily the leader had unlimited command over his men. However, if he was cowardly or inexperienced and through his inexperience lost many men, then his followers condemned him to death by unanimous decision and chose a new leader. The people claimed that they were themselves never cowardly. If a war party failed, it was through the mistakes or lack of experience of the leader (Veniaminov 2:105).

If they were able to take the settlement in one charge, which in this type of warfare happened almost always, the old men and women were slaughtered without mercy, and the young of both sexes were taken prisoners and after the battle handed over to the leader (Veniaminov 2:102).

The person taken prisoner was marked on the face or on the forehead with a bloody spot and those who were to be killed had one ear cut off or sometimes another part of the body, as for example, some hair with the scalp, and they even cut off the genitals from the men as well as the women. These amputated parts and the weapons of the enemy were the most important trophies of the conquerors, which were treasured for the descendants, to give greater fame to the race and to remain as living proof of their great military exploits. Some of these conquerors ordered that these trophies be placed in their graves (Veniaminov 2:103).

Jochelson added an interesting detail when he said that "the ancient Aleut warriors used to bring home the head of a slain enemy, which they set up on a pole on the roof of their dwelling" (1925:28). "The prisoners, especially the males, were treated by the Atkans with great cruelty, and those who were made slaves were fortunate indeed; the others were burned alive in fire, roasted on heated rocks, and beaten with straps" (Veniaminov 3:18).

An interesting statement by Sauer about Kodiak treatment of prisoners may have applied equally to the Aleuts, especially since it is not an uncommon trait (known for example among Plains Indians): The prisoners were often subject to ill treatment from the women (175).

Continuing the account of Aleut warfare: "After a successful encounter, the warriors placed all their booty before their leader who, taking his part as agreed upon, gave the rest back to them. Prisoners belonged only to those in the action who showed their fearlessness and were their actual captors. Warriors, however, often gave their prisoners to those who by the rules of war were not in a position to obtain prisoners" (Veniaminov 2:103). Such people were evidently those who stayed beside the bidarkas, the sentries, and so on. Poor people and slaves could never obtain prisoners, i.e. slaves, but they could share in the division of the other booty. The most highly valued plunder consisted of ornaments of amber and other precious substances. These were the share only of the leader and the bravest warriors.

The Aleuts had battles on the sea but very rarely and only in accidental encounters with the enemy. The Aleuts, having the advantage over the Kodiaks in the skill of handling the bidarkas, tried to hunt them out on the sea. . . . A victory on the sea hardly ever brought them any booty but mainly fame.

[When a community found that they could never win a decisive victory over a certain enemy group, they made a truce for a definite time, exchanging hostages to bind it.] Sometimes through negotiations by leaders, they concluded permanent peace, but the latter was made only with people of their own race or with the Aglegmutes and never with the Kodiaks (Veniaminov 2:104).

Holmberg's statement on Kodiak warfare can be used as a general summary of Aleut warfare also: "The wars of the Kanjags in ancient times consisted altogether of ambuscades and surprises, and prisoners were sometimes tortured and sometimes kept as slaves" (Holmberg:130).

Now we shall retrace our steps and consider other aspects of their warfare. It was stated that the Aleuts relied more upon stratagem than upon force to win. In addition to the example from folklore given above, other instances in the folktales demonstrate considerable ingenuity. For example, there is the story of the enemy lured into the village and trapped in an oil-soaked barabara that is set afire (Golder 1905:218-19). A historical example, at least according to the local account, concerns the murder on Unalaska of Drushinin's crew, one of the earliest parties of fur traders. The Aleuts laid plans to kill some of these Russians by falling on them when they were busy looking over furs that the former brought in for trade. One Russian happened to see a weapon concealed in an Aleut's sleeve and warned his companions, but even so, the Aleuts had the jump on them and were able to kill them (Veniaminov 1:122). The same trick was used, according to tradition, on Umnak in killing the crew of a boat the name of which has been lost but in whose crew was a very big and powerful man named Yakof. In this case, the Aleuts prepared even more carefully by wrestling and holding sham battles in secret and by assigning so many men to deal with each Russian (Veniaminov 1:128). This story is still being told today by the Umnak people and with even more elaboration concerning the preparations (Lantis n.d.). Four pages of Soloviev's diary recount the stratagems and deceits of the eastern Aleuts against the Russians in what was, from the Aleut viewpoint, justified retaliation for mistreatment but was, to the Russians, simply murder (M. and B.:81-84). (Several early travelers reported that the Russians were hated.)

Regarding the Koniag, Petroff said, "In warlike disposition, strength of body, and treachery they appeared to the Russians very different indeed from the meek and humble Aleuts" (228). The best proof of the correctness of this estimate lies in the fact that the Aleuts seem to have hated the Kodiaks more than any other adversaries. "They speak of the Kodiaks in unflattering terms. They say that the Kodiaks are the first instigators of the quarrels, they do not know the rules of honor, that they are brave only in words and before the beginning of the action, while in battle they are cowardly and yielding; they are boastful and yell like crows over carcasses and garbage. About the Aglegmute and the Chugatsch, they speak in different terms, as of brave and fearless people (Veniaminov 2:98).

The Aleuts occasionally could conquer the brave Agleg-mute (Petrof:83), but they must have had a hard time with the confident and yelling Kodiaks. The Aleuts never concluded peace with the Koniag, evidently because they felt that they never could cease fighting with them. However, as Veniaminov said, the Aleuts were much superior kayak men and could carry the war well into Kodiak territory. The Kodiaks never dared attack farther west than Unimak (which is east of Unalaska), but Unalaska and Umnak people went as far east as Kodiak. Veniaminov agreed with the Aleuts' claim that the Kodiaks suffered more from the Aleuts than vice versa (2:105).

A story told to Holmberg by an old Kodiak man, Arsenti Aminak, gives an interesting sidelight on the relations between the two peoples and in one detail contradicts Veniaminov in that it mentions a Kodiak raid on the Unalaskans. Although it may be simply a pretty tale, I believe it is worth repeating:

When the very first Russians landed at Kodiak, Arsenti was about ten years old, having already been allowed to paddle a kayak, and he supposedly remembered clearly the following incidents. The Koniag had traded with the Aglegmute, Kolosch (Tlingit) and Tnaina (Tanaina) and had even heard of the California Indians (!) farther down the coast, but they were totally unprepared for the appearance of the Russians. From many circumstances pertaining to these strange people, they were made much afraid. At first they thought the Russians were spirits but found that they were human traders in search for furs and had brought with them some Aleuts. Some years previously Arsenti's father had participated in a raid on Unalaska Island and had taken as a slave a little girl whom the Kodiaks had found in the ashes of a hut where her parents had abandoned her in their flight from the invaders. At Kodiak she had been brought up by her owner like one of his own children. Among the Aleuts whom the Russians brought with them was the father of this girl. Whether he recognized his daughter or whether he had previously heard of her whereabouts is not clear but at any rate he came to Arsenti's father and warned him that the Russians would take the furs offered for trade without making any return. The other Aleuts, however, took the part of the Russians and fell upon the Koniag with weapons which were concealed in their kayaks. Several Koniag were killed and their furs were taken from them (131-34).

The Aleuts said that they did not make war with either the Chugatch or the Kenaitze, for they considered them to be relatives of themselves (Veniaminov 2:98), explaining that they had a story of colonization on the Alaska Peninsula and of Aleuts spreading eastward even beyond Cook Inlet (2:273-75). But they did fight their near neighbors on the mainland. For example, concerning the villages on the west coast of the Alaska Peninsula, Petrof related, "The people of Port Moller and Oogashik are of the Aleutian tribe, which in former years made warlike expeditions along this coast, extending as far to the northward as the Naknek River and Lake Walker" (83).

There was also bitter war within each tribe or rather we should say within each linguistic and cultural unit. In both the Kodiak and Aleutian areas these quarrels became so common that the stay-at-homes of the weaker groups were obliged to shut themselves up during the summer, when the men were scattered to the various hunting and fishing grounds, in secluded and inaccessible fortified places such as steep and naturally fortified islets. Holmberg said that he himself had seen such places (130). Even then the people often were besieged and compelled to surrender (Veniaminov 3:17).

Aleuts on the Peninsula were frequent subjects of raids by Unimak Island natives, who were said to fight all their Aleut neighbors (Coxe:216). Then the Unalaska people and their allies, the Umnak natives, made war on the people of the Atka District. According to Veniaminov, this was the bloodiest warfare in the whole Aleutian group.

In course of time it became impossible for members of the two tribes to meet without a bloody conflict, but the Atkans suffered much more, because they were weaker; and, not daring to attack the villages of their enemies, they were obliged to watch their opportunities when the Oonalashkans were on journeys at distant hunting grounds. These conflicts generally took place on Siguam, Amlia, and Amukhta islands. The Oonalashkans, on the other hand, raided upon the Atkans every year in numbers of from fifty to one hundred bidarkas.

Unable to return the attacks of the Oonalashkans, the Atkans made war upon the Rat and Near islanders as far as Attoo, and were similarly successful (?) (Veniaminov 3:17).

These statements should be accepted only with the understanding that the people undoubtedly magnified all their war stories in order to impress the outsiders. In spite of all these statements, we have good proof of peaceful intercourse between districts and between larger areas, in that trade was carried on throughout an extensive region.

Property and Trade

The most highly prized articles among the ancient Aleuts were: the best bidarkas with ornamented bow and painted paddles; stone knives and daggers; a wooden helmet decorated with sea lion bristles and many colored stones; good spears and lances, etc. Of clothing they had trimmed parkas and finely-stitched kamleikas, and female clothing—and ornaments—sea-otter or fur-seal parkas, finely plaited grass-mats, similar to kercheifs; colored pebbles found in the mountains and various bone ornaments; bone needles for sewing (they were made out of the wing bones of the albatross, and in place of the eye had a narrow slit); and various paints; but the most valuable article of all were the long "tzukley," a bony shell, which were obtained either by trade or bloodshed from the Americans.

In former times "kalgi" or slaves were also accounted as property. The rich and powerful or shrewd in trade possessed from 5 to 20 of them, but since the arrival of the Russians, and especially since the time when the Aleuts became Christians, their slaves were liberated, and at present there is not one to be found. (I have seen one who was enslaved when a small boy as the son of a prisoner of war.) (Veniaminov 2:239-40).

Whereas by Veniaminov's own time, "The property or riches of the Aleuts do not extend much beyond the ordinary necessities of mankind, such as houses, clothing and hunting utensils and equipment, and it is always easy to take in at a glance what there is in the house, while everything is simple and without display of any kind and nearly uniform with all" (2:237); formerly there had been differences indicative of wealth and social distinction. Some parkas were beautifully made, as shown by those in the Lowie Museum, University of California, and the mummies of the "honorables" were wrapped in the finest matting with a pattern of tiny feathers held in the twined weft.

We shall consider here articles that were traded, methods of trade, and groups that participated, only incidentally dealing with the scheme of economic values.

Parts of the earliest statement are rather hard to believe because some of the items were so commonly available and one, masks, was so personal that they need not or could not be traded. Nevertheless, since J.L.S.'s statements from the early journals generally are good, the present one is accepted: "They barter among one another sea-otters, sea-bears [fur seals], clothes made of bird-skins and of dried intestines, skins of sea-lions and sea-calves for the coverings of baidars, wooden masks, darts, thread made of sinews and rein-deer hair, which they get from the country of Alaska" (Coxe:197).

The formalization of Aleut culture is shown by the method of trading.

The Aleuts do not trade in person, but always through reliable agent or clerk who is called *taouianakh*, who is chosen from among the young Aleuts. Having some sort of extra article or an unnecessary one, he sends it with the clerk to another barabara or more often to the newly arrived guests with the instruction to ask tobacco for it or to take anything that they may give. The clerk enters the barabara and says, "This is for sale." But he does not reveal the name of the owner even if the article is known to belong to him. The prospective buyer asks what is demanded for it and the clerk answers. The buyer having examined the article keeps it with himself and sends by the clerk to the seller tobacco or anything else that he too may consider extra or totally unnecessary. The clerk brings this to the seller and if he is satisfied, the affair is closed. If he is dissatisfied, he sends it back and the clerk asks either an increase or some other article. The buyer either increases until the seller is satisfied or refuses to purchase. Then the article for sale is taken to other huts. The Aleuts do not have instances of competitive buying or of increasing prices and hence they are almost always satisfied with the articles traded among themselves. In such an exchange, taking into consideration the value of the articles, one is usually the loser, as very often a valuable article is exchanged for a cheap but necessary one. As long as the trading continues, the owner and the prospective buyer do not see each other. This method of trading is the most ancient one among the Aleuts and has not changed at all even till today (Veniaminov 2:110-11).

There was an even more polite form of barter. Although things often were given merely as gifts to show appreciation, they also were presented with the expectation that a return gift would be made (Veniaminov 2:38-39). An Aleut must have had to know a set of social rules as complicated as those of the Northwest Coast and also how to judge his acquaintances accurately.[12]

There is no indication as to how often people from distant settlements came together for trade. The only clue to the geographic extent of trade carried on by the Aleuts is contained in the following passage:

Around their neck, wrists, and even ankles they wore various kinds of bracelets, which were made from various colored stones and especially amber and also bones [may mean ivory]. All such feminine jewelry and especially necklaces were considered very valuable. Oftentimes the brave and audacious Aleuts with great difficulty and danger would undertake long trips to distant islands (they went as far as the territory of Kenaitze and Chugatsch) so that they could obtain by barter or raids crystals or something of that nature for their sweethearts (Veniaminov 2:112-13).

One would judge from this that such trading journeys were not made very often, the common trade being carried on between contiguous or nearby communities. Even by the method of trading from one village to the next, an article could travel a long way. The more rare it was, the farther it went, and the farther it went, the more valuable it became, as is well illustrated by the trade in dentalium. Speaking primarily of Kodiak Island, Holmberg said,

[12] The context of this passage on reciprocal giving does not suggest the potlatch.

Further, Dentalium formed a very expensive and treasured ornament likewise among the men as among the women. As is known, these little animals do not occur in Russian America but go by trade from the more southerly peoples on the Columbia River the length of the whole coast to Kadjak and even still further to the Aleutian Islands. As late as the year 1802 one counted on Kadjak, according to Davidof's account, one pair of such shells as worth a suit made of Spermophilus fur (81-82).

Langsdorff added his testimony in regard to the Unalaska District. He said that dentalium was so much sought after that "any one would willingly give three or four sea otter skins, that is, the value of a hundred roubles, for a small string of them" (40). And finally, Veniaminov said: "The most valuable article of all were the long 'tzukley,' a bony shell, which were obtained either by trade or bloodshed from the Americans" (2:240).

Among the Aleuts amber was second in value to dentalium whereas, according to Holmberg, to the Koniag it was more valuable than the shell. Amber, found on the south shore of Kodiak and on Ukamok Island, formed an important article of trade between these islands and the Alaska Peninsula, and even farther north around Bristol Bay (82). On the other hand, Sarytchev said that amber was traded from the natives of the mainland to the Unalaskans (9).

In the Aleutian group, the best amber was found at a spot in the northern part of Umnak Island. It was such a valuable article of trade that many who could not afford to buy it tried to steal it from this place (Veniaminov 2:95). (This shows that the Aleuts would steal when they had a big incentive to do it.) Veniaminov said that porphyry also was found on the north side of Umnak and was an important and valuable trade article.

Regarding a carefully made bracelet composed of little rings of birds' claws, which Dall found with Kagamil Island mummies, he exclaimed, "This last is exactly similar to one

seen by me among the Magemut Eskimo of the north end
of Nunivak Island, in 1874." Among other things found by
him at the same place were some pieces of loose red pine
bark and a small carefully preserved roll of birchbark,
which must have come from the mainland. A small birchbark case containing paints also was found by him in a
cave on Amaknak Island. He found four pieces of gypsum
which he thought might have been traded from "near
Nunivak Island," one amber bead, and some hair from
reindeer hoofs (1878:21-24). Dall said he had seen natives
save the tufts of hair from the hoofs when they skinned a
deer, as they were valuable for trade (1878:12). None of
these things could have been obtained in the immediate
region where they were found except possibly the amber
and the bracelet; thus we have a good example of the type
of less valued objects of barter between areas.

END OF AN ERA

The Cultural Break

We do not know exactly how the aboriginal culture broke up, but we know why, and this suggests how it happened. It broke under oppression or, in modern terms, under extreme stress. First, we have seen that there was a great loss of population—probably as much as four-fifths—in the first seventy-five years of Russian domination. Second, the Aleuts learned that they could not by themselves oppose the rapacious fur hunters and traders. It was only after the Russians had brought some order among themselves that the Aleuts were saved from the worst tyrannies. In short, they lost their war. There was no satisfaction of triumph or maintenance of independence to offset the loss of population, the breakup of communities.

Hubert Howe Bancroft published accounts of several Russian atrocities, Aleut reprisals, and Russian counter-reprisals. (We should recall that his *History of Alaska 1730–1885* was published in 1886, when the conquest of Alaska was not so remote as it appears to us.) His story of the conflict begins as follows:

[In September 1745, three years after the Discovery, the *Yevdokia* piloted by a man who had been with Bering arrived at Agatoo (or Agattu, near Attu).] . . . over a hundred armed natives assembled on the beach and beckoned the Russians to land, but it was not deemed safe in view of their number; so they threw into the water a few trifling presents, and in return the natives threw back some birds just killed. [Two days later] Chuprof landed with a few men armed with muskets for water. They met some natives, to whom they gave tobacco and pipes, and received a stick ornamented with the head of a seal carved in bone. Then the savages wanted one of the muskets, and when refused they became angry and attempted to capture the party by seizing their boat. Finally Chuprof ordered his men to fire, and for the first time the thundering echoes of musketry resounded from the hills of Agatoo. One bullet took effect in the hand of a native; the crimson fluid gushed forth over the white sand, and the long era of bloodshed, violence, and rapine for the poor Aleuts was begun. As the natives had no arms except bone-pointed spears, which they vainly endeavored to thrust through the sides of the boat, shedding of blood might easily have been avoided.

[Later, in a scuffle with fifteen Aleuts, men from this ship took a man and an old woman captive and apparently killed two men. Still later,] The old woman, who had been released, returned with thirty-four of her people; they danced and sang to the sound of bladder-drums, and made presents of colored clay, receiving in return handkerchiefs, needles, and thimbles. After the first ceremonial visit both parties separated on the most friendly terms.

[On Attu, however, Beliaief, sent with ten men to explore,] managed to pick a quarrel, in the course of which fifteen of the islanders were killed (Bancroft:102-105).

According to this historian, that series of episodes was the beginning of the conquest of the Islands. From here eastward, island by island, the harsh encounter of two peoples was repeated.

Third, people were transported here and there as hunters, servants, keepers, and mistresses. (In 1762, allegedly twenty-five women were taken to Kamchatka "to pick berries." All died, were killed, or killed themselves—Bancroft:125-26.) No matter what were the motives of the Crown, the dominant motive of the men who lived in and ruled Russian America was accumulation of wealth from the fur trade. They therefore took or sent hunters wherever the fur-bearers still were plentiful, inevitably farther and farther from the old hunting grounds. (Regarding their transport to California, see Bancroft:477-78.) Thus, also inevitably, the old human communities were broken up or deserted and new ones formed on a new model. For example, the priest for the Atka District wrote that in 1830 there were seven houses at Atka village: four for the Russian-American Company and three providing living quarters for Russians, creoles, and Aleuts (Alaska Church Collection, in Documents 2:23-31).

Bancroft figured that the total value of fur shipments by the Shelikov and Golikov Company, later to become the Russian-American Company, "between the years 1788 and 1797 was 1,500,000 roubles—equal then to three times the amount at the present day [1885–1886]" (253). It is difficult for city people to visualize the many hundreds of sea hunting parties composed usually of fleets of two-man kayaks (bidarkas) and hundreds of single trappers ashore in this foggy, frequently gale-ridden region, mountainous on land and reef-broken offshore. Perhaps the following inventory of skins valued at 778,521 rubles brought to Kamchatka on two vessels in 1809 and 1810 by the Russian-American Company, according to its Board of Directors' Report for 1810, will help the reader understand the human effort required. (Henceforth, when one looks at paintings of European royalty in their fur-lined and fur-decorated robes of the period, one may also glimpse an Aleut hunter.)

Fur seal	39,678	Land otter	251
Sea otter	5,414	Bear	139
Young sea otter	377	Mink	29
Sea otter tails	3,976	Wolf	4
Red fox	2,556	Glutton	1
Blue fox	2,527	Sea otter, finished fur	8
Cross fox	936	Walrus tusk (poods)	98
Silver fox	707		

(Yudin Collection, in Documents 3:202)

Fourth, although the men knew that they were essential for the dangerous sea-otter hunt, they lost self-confidence and lost control of their homes when the women lived with "Russians," many of whom actually were Siberians and creoles. The loss of morale, seen in similar but more recent situations, must have been not only personally but socially demoralizing.

Fifth, the old religion, including a society of men withholding sacred secrets from women (Lantis 1947:27-30), could not be maintained against a combination of the above Russian male dominance and Orthodox priestly domination.

In the Yudin Collection, included in the "Documents Relative to the History of Alaska," there is a copy of complaints made by "the natives of the Unalaska District to the Government inspectors in 1789–1790." These inspectors evidently were members of the Billings expedition, which visited the area in 1790 and wintered at Unalaska 1791–1792. Bancroft wrote (294), "The officers doomed to pass a wretched winter in this desolate place [several crew members died of scurvy] were captains Robert Hall and Gavril Sarychef, Lieutenant Christian Bering, Surgeon-major Robeck, Surgeon Allegretti, and Bakof, Bakulin, Erling, Pribylof, and Sauer." (Another member was Merck.) Natives who came from Shelikov's· establishment at Kodiak "made many complaints of ill-treatment at the hands of Russian promyshleniki, which Sauer considered well founded" (Bancroft:295).[1] The dominant fur-trading

[1] As early as 1787, in response to complaints reaching Okhotsk, two documents were issued by the commander of that port in the name of the Empress, one directed to navigators and traders, the other "intended as a reassuring proclamation to the native chiefs as representatives of their people" (Bancroft:310). Evidently the documents alone had no immediate effect for improvement of Russian-Aleut relations. They were, in fact, pathetically useless. The increasing communication between Okhotsk authorities and the Islands, of which these papers were first evidence, must have brought, however, increasing control. The Shelikov-Golikov Company was several thousand versts from the center of royal authority but not completely beyond its reach. An excerpt from the document addressed to the Aleuts follows:

Medals "were sent to you as proof of the motherly care of the Empress. . . . These medals will be distributed at every place where the Russian trading-vessels can land in safety, and thus they will protect you against ill-treatment not only by Russian hunters, but at the hand of our allied

company of that period ("already in virtual possession of their exclusive privileges of trade"—Bancroft:299) was the Shelikov and Golikov partnership, which became in 1799 the Russian-American Company (Bancroft:375-83). This document shows, even when one discounts possible exaggeration, the various types of stress, physical, moral, and social, to which Aleuts were subject.

1. June 7, 1789, the Aleuts of Unalaska Island—Chief Algemalinag, in Russian "Michael"; interpreter "Saguiakh, formerly called by the Russians *monkey*, but after baptism Ivan Chuloshnikov" and the Aleut woman, Anshiges—being questioned about the conduct of the Company's hunters, testified that during the wintering of navigators Ocheredin and Orekhov with their assistants, Izmailov, Gogolev and Lukanin, a quarrel arose over the division of hunting places. Ocheredin and Polutov, as the strongest, took most of the Aleut workers and forced them to hunt even during the worst winter storms, which resulted in the drowning of three Aleuts.

Leaving Unalaska for Alaska [the mainland], Ocheredin and Polutov carried with them over a hundred Aleut men and women;

---

powers who may visit your shores. From the latter you may feel entirely safe, for even if any foreign vessel should attempt to appropriate your islands to its own country, the sight of these medals of the Russian Empire would disperse all such thoughts, and if any disputes should arise they will be settled by friendly negotiations with these powers. As far as the Russian vessels are concerned that visit your islands for the purpose of trade and hunting the fur-bearing animals, I have already received through the hands of my officials at Kamchatka and Okhotsk several complaints, the first through Sergeant Alexeï Buynof, the second from the son of the chief of the Andreianof Islands, Izossim Polutof, and the third from the Aleut of the Lissievski Islands Toukoutan Ayougnin; from which complaints I have learned to my sorrow of the inhumanities inflicted upon you by our Russian trading-ships, of which the government up to this time had received no information; it was thought that no actual violation of the laws had taken place in those distant regions. But now your petitions have been forwarded by me to the highest authorities and I trust that you will before long receive full satisfaction. In the mean time I ask you to be content and not to doubt the kindness and justice of the great Empress of All the Russias who is sure to defend and protect you, knowing your sincere submission to her sceptre. You must show this order to all Russian vessels that visit you and it will protect you in so far that every inhabitant of your islands may remain in his village, and cannot be compelled to go to any other island unknown to him. But if one of you goes abroad with his free from those who were left on the islands they took all bidarkas, arrows, parkas and foodstuffs. Only a few of the hundred remained alive after four years' privation of food and clothing.

Among the worst oppressors at Unalaska was named baidarschik [maker of bidarkas] Pshenichnoy, who "treated the islanders tyrannically, kept several Aleutian girls and women as mistresses, mercilessly whipped the Aleuts with ropes and sticks." Six Aleuts were whipped to death and sixteen were starved to death; more than three hundred Aleuts died of starvation during two winter months because their foodstuffs were taken away by the hunters.

The Aleuts suffered similar treatment from Polutov, Panin and Popov. The last one murdered ["speared"] all the Aleutian girls and two men in the Bobrovoy settlement.

"After that Unalaska was visited by the hunting ships of Greek Delarov, Cherepanov and Nagaev; there were Shishaev and Pilot Potap Zaikov of Orekhov's company; Shelekhov also stopped for a brief time and left the same summer. Delarov spent the winter, took the best Aleutian men from Kigolgan and Unimak and went to Kodiak. Shishaev and Zaikov of Orekhov's company carried away about thirty men and twenty women;

consent, he will be provided with food and clothing until the time of his return, and the food shall be such as he has been accustomed to. If you believe that you have been ill-treated by any people belonging to the Russian Empire, or if you have suffered compulsion or injury at their hands, I advise you to take notice of their name and that of their ship, and what company of merchants they belong to, and in due time you can forward your complaints upon the matter, and upon satisfactory proof such men will be punished according to their offences and you will get satisfaction. Information has also reached me to the effect that the hunters receive from you furs of good quality as tribute, but change them and forward poor skins to the Empress; therefore I advise you to mark such skins with special signs and tokens, making cuts or brands which cannot be easily changed, and if it is done in spite of these precautions the offenders will be punished very severely. Furthermore I assure you of the continued protection and care of all the inhabitants of your islands by her most gracious Imperial Majesty and her supreme government, as well as of the best wishes of the Commander of the Province of Okhotsk and the district and township of Nishnekamtchatsk. Signed the 15th day of June 1787, by Grigor Kozlof-Ugrenin."

Three copies still extant of the original document bear the following signatures: "Have read the original. Master Gavril Pribylof." "Have read the copy. Master Potap Zaikof." "Have read the copy. Foreman Leontiv Nagaief" (Bancroft:311-12).

these people have not returned. Cherepanov and Nagaev remained on the islands.

"Now Cherepanov's and Nagaev's companies do not indulge in such cruel tyranny and murder (as described above), yet they send us to hunt against our will, to provide food and to do domestic work without pay. From Cherepanov's company we get for each sea otter either a kettle or a shirt or a knife or a kerchief or a plane for making arrows or ten strings of corals or five, six to ten leaves of tobacco with the addition of a handful of beads to each of these things paid for a sea otter. . . .

"The difference between these two companies is that . . . the other [Nagaev's] company pays lass for a sea otter and does not supply any clothing, either to domestic servants or to hunters, who are often sent naked to hunt and to fish. From such poor keeping and treatment many run away to Cherepanov's company, seeking protection from these unbearable conditions.

"Not a little do we suffer from the seizure of our girls, wives, daughters and sisters, practised in general by all companies (except Panov's which acted in an orderly manner in comparison with the companies which were here before and after it). [Though] seeing our women kept as mistresses and cruelly treated and knowing the beastly temperament of the hunters, we can not oppose, can not even raise our voices against it. We have to suffer it, being afraid of the recurrence of the event which happened in the time of peredovschik (?) Solovey, who plundered the islands of Unalaska, Sannak, Akun, Akutan, Azutan and Igilga and shot the entire male population on them. Even more so, as a final outrage, he lined up the men and tested his rifles on them to find how many men could be killed with one bullet. The cruel treatment of us by their hunters is known to all the companies. Sergeant Builov, who was here to collect the taxes, said that such treatment is forbidden by the Government and he promised us that upon his return to Russia he would [take steps to] stop the cruelties of the hunters. Yet, even now we do not see any relief.

"We learned that your ship is not a company ship but one sent by the Russian Empress, and that its commanders are higher than the navigators of the company ships, whom we considered the greatest masters because of severity in actions and because they themselves proclaimed that there are no masters over them. Seeing the obedience shown to you by the hunters and their chiefs, we do not hesitate to report to you about the oppression by the hunters and traders and to request your protection from them. Collated with the original draft of the inquest, Acting Secretary and Collegiate Registrar, Gavrilo Ermilov." [No such person was identified by Bancroft, as evidently his assistant, Ivan Petroff, did not see this document.]

5. "July 5, 1790, Kodiak Island, Pilot Gerasim Izmailov, employed by the Golikov and Shelikhov Company, was again questioned by Navy Captain of the Second Rank, Gavrilo Sarytchev . . . , and testified:

"That, according to the information furnished by Delarov's peredovschik [?], Purtov was sent to hunt various animals not in 200 but in 20 bidarkas, and that Delarov used to send up to 600 bidarkas to hunt sea otters in the so-called Gros Fles Bay. . . . The hunter chosen to make settlement with the islanders is supplied by the Company with beads, corals and iron hatchets about four inches long. I was not present at the hunt and do not know about the number [of animals killed]. An order is [usually] issued to have the new bidarkas finished and the old repaired and ready by April 15; on this date they go [to hunt]. Original signed, Pilot Gerasim Izmailov. Collated with the original, Collegiate Registrar, Gavrilo Ermilov" (Documents 3: 237-38, 240).

Acceptance of the New Order

Human durability is sometimes amazing. Some individuals survived and part of the old culture survived. Before digressing to the Russian documents, we mentioned the Russian Orthodox Church. The priests did try to help the people, they did offer a rationale for existence; moreover, in their rich music, graphic art and ritual offered some relief from the labor and hazard of service for the Russians. Unwillingly and unwittingly, the Aleuts began to develop a new culture. This meant the end, however, of most of the old social structure and religion.

Several elements of technology survived, as one would expect. In the social sphere, the only strong survival was chieftainship, essential to the Russians for organization and leadership of work and hunting parties. Bride-service, even polyandry, both showing the strong position of women, survived quietly. Although Russians, particularly in the eighteenth century, took women from their families, there may have developed at times the kind of relationship that existed under American jurisdiction, namely, a modern form of polyandry. An Aleut man would remain head of the family and its principal support while the wife accepted a Caucasian lover in a stable relationship, the white man also providing for the family with supplies of "store goods." Since Aleut males had to spend long periods on other than their domicile islands, hunting and trapping, the arrangement was economically and socially more functional than dysfunctional (Lantis:n.d.).

Although the Aleuts could no longer openly hold slaves and maintain the traditional class system, they may have held the old concepts and values, actually inducing them to accept the Russian treatment. As in their small warfare, conquerors had taken captives and made them work and had made the women concubines, so now the Eurasian conquerors treated them. The despair and resignation of slaves must have been familiar. Yet, as in the old days when the captives would seek ransom or deliverance by their wealthy and chieftainly kinsmen, so now they sought relief from the new authority figures, as we saw in their complaints to the Billings expedition. Although conditions improved and communication obviously improved, the Aleuts twenty years later still were complaining of mistreatment, as shown by "Extracts from the Report of Mr. Minitzky, commander of the Okhotsk Port, and the replies of the Russian American Company to the points of accusation"

(Russian-American Company Archives, in the Documents). The Company answer to charges, which sounds like a self-righteous statement by any privileged company in a colonial situation, reveals something of the acculturation process, well under way by 1810.

I

From the copy of Mr. Minitzky's Report

1 and *2*. Hunters on the Island of Atka and other islands of the Andreianovsky group oppress the aborigines. The naval officers, commanding the Company ships sailing there, oppress them even worse. It is necessary to establish supervision of these islands by the Okhotsk authorities, as the Russians there are not restrained by anybody, being separated from Administrator-General Baranov by the long distance which saves them from prosecution.

Reply [of the Company].

If the Russian hunters on Atka and other islands committed such offenses as reported by the authorities of the Okhotsk Port, those offenses could not have remained unknown to the Company's Office at Okhotsk, which would have had the Board of Directors informed about them. The Board of Directors had not received such information from anybody. . . . The offenses, especially if they recur often, could not remain hidden and unknown even for a brief period of time because the Aleuts of those islands, coming to Okhotsk with every ship leaving Atka, could report about them. Here is an example: When the ship *Finland,* commanded by pilot Vasiliev, left Atka in 1812, the complaint of the Aleuts and the traders against this same pilot did not remain concealed but was brought to the attention of the Board of Directors by the former manager of the Okhotsk Office, Mr. Kolobov.

The offenses of pilots Vasiliev and Dubinin occurred because of their abuse of authority; the Board of Directors never approved and does not approve of such. The Government must agree that the Board of Directors could never consent to grant the commanders of their ships any other authority but to sail their ships. The Board has no means to prevent them from committing offenses similar to those mentioned. This is out of our jurisdiction and can be done only by the Minister of the Navy to whom the naval officers are completely subordinated.

The supervision of Atka and the other colonies on the Aleutian Islands by the Okhotsk authorities is incompatible with the reasons formerly presented to you by the Board of Directors and with the privileges of the Company, approved by His Imperial Majesty, which remaining in force, leave all the Aleutian Islands in direct dependence on the Company. Because of these privileges, they are not included in the Kamchatka or Okhotsk government districts.

[Reference is made to the new Military and Civil Regulation which authorizes the Governor of Kamchatka to send a Government boat to America for surveying but not for governing the colonies.]

3. Chief Gilev and other Aleuts, who arrived at Okhotsk on the *Finland* in 1812, complained about numerous offenses of the Russian hunters at Atka, especially of pilot Vasiliev.

Reply.

We admit that the Russian hunters sometimes cause some grievances to the Aleuts, but we know that the hunters themselves often suffer from the savages' attacks. Rumors can not help you to form correct judgement of the savages who live more than 5,000 versts away. It is but natural that the Aleuts arriving at Okhotsk are meek; they are surrounded by Russians.

To know whether they are the same in their native land it is necessary to remain among them for a long time and to be with them in various circumstances. It has been proved on many occasions and become a recognized fact that they are ready to attack you at the slightest opportunity. When misunderstandings arise between the hunters and Aleuts, the local managers immediately endeavor to settle them by peaceable means; the Board of Directors always reminds the local authorities about this, as you can find from all our instructions and regulations to the

Offices and office managers. In several cases the offenders were deported from the islands.

It is reported that the Aleut women are abducted by the hunters. It usually takes place in this manner: The Aleut women, no matter how young or old they are, have no shame at all and are ready to take a new husband any time they want one; it is only natural that they should leave their husbands or fathers for a more advantageous life with the Russian hunters; jealous Aleut men consider this an offense. If you look upon this from the political point of view, you will find that these bonds of Russians with the Aleut women are almost necessary for the detection of harmful plots as well as for strengthening our ties with the natives; the children resulting from these unions necessarily strengthen the bonds of the Russians with their kindred Aleuts. These children, being baptised, are raised as Russians rather than Aleuts, and such intermarriages promote Russian stability [in America]. The creoles born in America, educated in academic and industrial subjects, compose a class of people admitted to the better ranks. We have many examples of this already. Some are employed as navigators; creole Burtzev, sent from here not long ago, is a ship-carpenter, others work as managers, clerks, and in other capacities" (Documents 4:155-57).

Letter from the [Russian-American Company] Board of Directors to Administrator-General Muraviev.

No. 130
March 4, 1821

From the report of the Unalaska manager, Kriukov, to Mr. Yanovsky, transmitted and explained by the latter in his letter of February 18, 1820, No. 35, we find that the cod-fishing, fox and bird hunting are done by Aleuts for a niggardly wage, mostly in the form of economic goods which makes it even smaller. Yet even this small pay does not make the Aleut hunters more industrious, and they would have been doing nothing at all if they had not had a craving for tobacco, used chiefly for payment of their labor.

The Board of Directors points out that such a free and cheap method of forcing the Aleuts to activity must be kept permanent-

ly as it is not in the least offensive to the Aleuts and not dis-
creditable to the Company. When you visit that Office, you may
introduce improvements so that outsiders visiting those places
would find no cause to reproach the Company for unjust treatment of the Aleut hunters. Therefore, you should instruct that
Office always to have on hand a goodly proportion of tobacco
and other articles needed by the Russians, as well as by the
Aleuts.

[Signed]   Director Venedict Kramer
Director Andrei Severin
Administrator of the Chan-
cellery Zelensky
(Documents 4:224)

The Russian half of the acculturative relationship is difficult
for us to conceive, much less feel. The adventurer hunters
and traders risked annihilation on every voyage. Their
lives were physically miserable, their investments pre-
carious and often lost. At the end of that first encounter
with Aleuts on Attu and Agattu, for example:

The return voyage was not a fortunate one; for six weeks the
heavily laden craft battled with the waves, and at last, on the
30th of October, she was cast upon a rocky coast with the loss
of nearly all her valuable cargo. Ignorant as to their situation
the men made their way into the interior, suffering from cold
and hunger, but finally they succeeded in finding some human
habitations. On questioning the natives they learned to their
consternation that they were not on the mainland, but on the
island of Karaghinski off the coast of Kamchatka. The Koriaks
were already tributary to the Russians, and treated their visitors
kindly until Beliaief made advances to the wife of the *yessaul,*
or chief, whose wrath was with difficulty assuaged (Bancroft:
105-106).

Facilitating the development of a Russian-Aleut society
was the fact that in the eighteenth century the Russians
could not live entirely apart except for those, as on the

Billings expedition, on the larger vessels who could live all winter aboard ship. By the time the Russian-American Company had established its headquarters at Sitka, in Tlingit Indian territory, the Europeans were forming their own society. In the Aleutians, however, increasingly through the second half (1780–1810) of the period in which we are interested, the relationship developed as follows:

There can be no doubt that in their [Russians'] hands alone would the wealth of the coast region be husbanded, for their interests now began to demand an economic management, and their influence by far exceeded that of any other nation with whom the natives had come in contact. Long before the universal sway of the Russian American Company had been introduced we find unmistakable signs of this predilection in favor of those [the Russians] among all their visitors who apparently treated them with the greatest harshness while driving the hardest bargains. The explanation lies in the fact that the Russians were not in reality as cruel as the others, and, above all, that they assimilated more closely with the aborigines than did other traders. At all outlying stations they lived together with and in the manner of the natives, taking quite naturally to filth, privations, and hardships, and on the other hand dividing with their savage friends all the little comforts of rude civilization which by chance fell to their lot.

Cook and Vancouver expressed their astonishment at the miserable circumstances in which they found the Russian promyshleniki, and both navigators agree as to the amicable and even affectionate relations existing between the natives of the far north-west of this continent and their first Caucasian visitors from the eastern north. Captains Portlock and Dixon even complained of this good understanding as an injury to the interests of others with equal rights to the advantages of traffic with the savages. The traffic then carried on throughout that region is scarcely worthy of the name of trade; it was a struggle to seize upon the largest quantity of the most valuable furs in the shortest time and at the least expense, without regard for consequences (Bancroft:250-51).

In the new society, the creoles had constructive functions. Far from being outcast half-breeds, they were given special protection and consideration by the Russians. This better educated bilingual group served as communicators, transmitters of each culture to the bearers of the other culture. Folk belief and practice became a syncretic combination of Aleut and White Russian, with apparently a bit of Koryak or Yakut or other Siberian custom thrown in (Lantis n.d.). Virtually all Aleuts learned the Russian language and learned the liturgy in the old Slavonic of the Orthodox Church. Aleut settlements, all coastal, were so much more accessible than Russian centers of conquest and acculturation in Eskimo territory that the Europeanization could be correspondingly more thorough.

Aleuts now might raise potatoes (as many of them did) and cattle (occasionally), but there evidently was not much pride in the new life, as indicated by the Russian-American Company's statement—naive and recognizing no culpability of its own—that the natives worked only for tobacco. The burning of tobacco was no substitute for the inner fire that had gone out of them.

SUMMARY

Early visitors to the Aleutian Islands gave a fairly good picture of Aleut home life but did not record much on social structure. The following is an outline summary of whatever firm data they did record.

Aleut population at mid-eighteenth century appears to have been between 12,000 and 15,000, distributed in many small settlements. The typical house was large, containing several related nuclear families. In fact, a whole village might be composed basically of kindred. In many settlements, evidently only a few houses were occupied at one time, usually two or three, although a large village would have six or seven. These were the permanent settlements; in addition, there were places of seasonal occupation. Unlike their Eskimo neighbors, Aleuts had no ceremonial house or bathhouse. Instead, bathing in the sea to harden them was enforced especially on the males.

The household comprised a man and his wife or wives, his older married sons and their families, and perhaps a younger brother and family. The household head's adolescent sons were sent to their mother's village to be reared by her elder brother. Similarly, a man would have a nephew working for him, who might marry one of his daughters. The older sons would have already completed their bride-service (whether or not for a cross-cousin), would have fathered a child or two, and then brought their wives to the paternal home. The eldest brother among the siblings was a substitute father, but since it was permissible for a man to remain with his wife's kin, it appears that younger sons did not always return home to live. (Thus there was matrilocal or matripatrilocal residence.) Aleuts probably were like Eskimos in being practical and rational regarding subsistence activities: if a man had capable sons to succeed him, there was no pressure to keep a nephew. If he had daughters and no son, he could keep one or two nephews. We can surmise that training by the maternal uncle may have been necessary to transmit hunting secrets and powers, to maintain ties between villages and even islands, and to maintain an inherited status. If a woman had high status from her family, she could maintain this by sending her son to her brother, head of her family of origin, for training.

Regarding relations among siblings and cousins, a man could marry his older brother's widow—and might be permitted to have intercourse with her in his brother's lifetime—but the elder could not take the younger brother's wife. A man might also marry his wife's sister. In short, there were simultaneous and successive levirate and sororate. Parallel collateral relatives were regarded as lineal, but cross-cousin and other "cross-" relatives were not. The kin terminology clearly expresses the relationships of avunculate, cross-cousin marriage, levirate and sororate. It also distinguishes between older and younger siblings, reminding one of the Yuit (Eskimo) seniority principle.

The rule of descent was, of course, not expressed in modern anthropological terms. It appears to me that what the early visitors to the Islands did say can be interpreted as matrilineal descent. Another reader of these accounts might come to a different conclusion.

At life crises, there was nothing dramatic or unusual except in the death observances for people of high status. For women at first menses, regular periods, and after childbirth there was seclusion, and various tabus were enforced so that she would not contaminate the hunters, their gear, or the food supply. To protect the foetus, there were a few tabus on a man's activities during his wife's pregnancy, but none afterward, at least none recorded. At puberty, there were no operation on the genitals for either boys or girls and no tests of fortitude. We might regard tattooing as a test, but the Aleuts seem not to have done so.

Marriage was supposed to be arranged by the parents—the folktales suggest that here as elsewhere marriage rules were not always followed—with the groom's parents presenting gifts to the bride's family and the latter providing a dowry. Some of the early writers thought that the gifts constituted purchase of a bride, but gift exchange would be a more accurate term. We can guess that a young man might think that he was buying a wife dearly by his two years' work for her father. Actually this was a trial marriage and a test of responsibility and suitability for the young people.

Aleuts were, in general, quite permissive regarding sex relations and marriage. Both polygyny and polyandry were permitted and a high-status man might offer a concubine to a guest—there is conflicting evidence as to how common was wife-lending by others—and transvestism was accepted openly, although it seems not to have been so common as among the Koniag to the east of the Aleuts. At the same time, as among all peoples, incest was defined and was prohibited in accordance with the definition.

Most spectacular were the mummification of the body of a highly honored person, the fine wrappings and grave goods, and the occasional killing of slaves to accompany the master or, more accurately, to show the grief of the principal survivor. Also remarked by several observers was the keeping in the house of a body, especially that of a beloved child. As with Eskimos, suicide was laudable. Although there was power in a corpse, it was not avoided and disposed of as quickly as was done by the Inuit. In death observances as in geography, the Yuit were between the Aleut and Inuit extremes.

Most confusing in the eighteenth century and early nineteenth century accounts are the statements on the composition of the three classes. The position and status of chiefs and slaves (captives and orphans) can be understood, at least in outline, but who and how numerous were the commoners? Members of small families without an "honorable" as a family head? Distant and dependent relatives of the chiefs or honorables, not in their line of inheritance? We do not know.

There was a tendency to inheritance of chieftainship although the higher chief for a group of villages or a whole island was chosen from among the lesser chiefs. Beyond one island there was no authority—only the duties of a kindred, and these might be divisive. Before the Discovery, there were feuds between kindreds: insults, raids, and murders being avenged. The formal accusation, hearing, and pronouncement of sentence that Aleuts were later reported to have had probably came after the Russian invasion.

Wealth was important, not only wealth in the form of dentalium shells and amber that could be counted but also gestures of generosity, such as the freeing of slaves. Yet, although there was a memorial ceremony, there is no evidence that there was anything that we today would call a potlatch.

Even though this survey of the literature gives us more information than has been assembled in one place before, the cultural and historical place of the Aleuts among the peoples of their region is still something of a mystery. If we dare to predict the results of the next step—comparison of Aleut culture and those cultures both east and west— the finding will be that over a generalized Yuit base there is an overlay of Pacific Eskimo and, through it, Tlingit culture in such things as wealth and status and also that there are cultural links with the Itelmen (Kamchadals), Koryak, and possibly other Siberians. We do not pretend to have demonstrated such ties. We are only trying to stimulate and encourage the use of the ethnohistoric record here provided to delineate both North Pacific and Bering Sea culture histories.

REFERENCES

Alaska History Research Project
   Ms   Documents Relative to the History of Alaska. 12 vols.
1936–1938 Division of Documents, Library of Congress, Washington.

Anderson, H. Dewey, and Eells, Walter C.
   1935   Alaska Natives: A Survey of Their Sociological and Educational Status. Stanford, Calif.

Andreev, Aleksandr Ignatevich
   1944   Russkie otkrytiya v Tikhom okeane i Severnoi Amerike v XVIII-XIX vekakh. (Russian discoveries in the Pacific Ocean and North America in the 18th-19th centuries.) Geographical Society, U.S.S.R.

Applegate, Samuel
   1893   The third or Unalaska District. *In* Report on Population and Resources of Alaska at the Eleventh Census: 1890 (Robert P. Porter, Superintendent, Census Office), 81-90. Washington.

Arctic Bibliography (See Tremaine)

Bancroft, Hubert H.
   1886   History of Alaska, 1730–1885. San Francisco.

Barsukov, Ivan P.
   1897   The Life and Work of Innocent, the Archbishop of Kamchatka, the Kuriles and the Aleutian Islands, and Later the Metropolitan of Moscow. (Privately printed in San Francisco.)
1897–1901 Letters of Innokenty, Metropolitan of Moscow and Kolomena, 1828–1878. (3 vols., in Russian.) St. Petersburg.

Bergsland, Knut
   1959   Aleut dialects of Atka and Attu. American Philosophical Society Transactions 49 (3).
   1969   Letter to Margaret Lantis, September 15, 1969. (Unpublished.)

Campbell, Archibald
   1825   A Voyage Round the World, from 1806 to 1812. 4th American edition, Roxbury, Mass.

Caswell, John E.
1956   Arctic Frontiers: United States Explorations in the Far North. Norman, Okla.

Cook, James
1784   A Voyage to the Pacific Ocean, Vol. 2. London.

Coxe, William
1787   Account of the Russian Discoveries between Asia and America. 3d edition, London. (Contains translation of *Neue Nachrichten.*)

Dall, W. H.
1870   Alaska and Its Resources. (1897 edition consulted.) Boston.
1877   Tribes of the extreme Northwest. *In* Contributions to North American Ethnology. Geographical and Geological Survey of the Rocky Mountain Region, Vol. 1, Pt. 1. U. S. Department of the Interior, Washington.
1878   On the remains of later prehistoric man obtained from caves in the Catherina Archipelago, Alaska Territory, and especially from the caves of the Aleutian Islands. Smithsonian Contributions to Knowledge, Vol. 22, Art. 6. Washington.
1884   On masks, labrets, and certain aboriginal customs. Bureau of American Ethnology, Annual Report, 3:67-203.

Davidov, G. I.
1816   Reise der russisch-kaiserlichen Flott-Officiere Chwostow und Dawydow von St. Petersburg durch Sibirien nach Amerika und zurück in den Jahren 1802, 1803 und 1804. Berlin.

d'Orbigny, Alcide
1854   Voyage dans les deux Ameriques. Paris.

Documents Relative to the History of Alaska (See Alaska History Research Project).

Erman, A.
1870–1871   Ethnographische Wahrnehmungen und Erfahrungen an den Küsten des Berings-Meeres. Zeitschrift für Ethnologie 2:295-327, 369-93; 3:149-75 and 205-19.

Golder, Frank A.
1903   Tales from Kodiak Island. Journal of American Folk-Lore 16:16-31, 85-103.
1905   Aleutian stories. Jour. of Amer. Folk-Lore 18:215-22.
1907   The songs and stories of the Aleuts, with translations from Veniaminov. Jour. of Amer. Folk-Lore 20:132-42.

1909   Eskimo and Aleut stories from Alaska. Jour. of Amer. Folk-Lore 22:10-24.

1917   Guide to materials for American history in Russian archives. Carnegie Institution of Washington Publication No. 239.

1922   Bering's voyages, Vol. 1, 1922; Vol. 2, 1925. American
1925   Geographical Society Research Series 1 and 2.

Gruening, Ernest
1954   The State of Alaska. New York.

Hrdlicka, Ales
1945   The Aleutian and Commander Islands and Their Inhabitants. Wistar Institute of Anatomy and Biology, Philadelphia.

Ivanov, S. V.
1928   Aleut hunting headgear and its ornamentation. International Congress of Americanists, Vol. 23. New York.

J.L.S.
1776   Neue Nachrichten von denen Neuendeckten Insuln in der See zwischen Asien und Amerika aus mitgetheilten Urkunden und Aufzugen verfasset von J.L.S. Hamburg and Leipzig; 1787, 3d ed., London.

Jacobi, Arnold
1937   Carl Heinrich Mercks ethnographische Beobachtungen über die Völker des Beringsmeers 1789–1791. Baessler-Archiv 20 (3-4): 113-37. (Old series)

Jochelson, Waldemar
1925   Archaeological investigations in the Aleutian Islands. Carnegie Institute of Washington Publication No. 367.
1928   People of the foggy seas. Natural History 28(4):413-24.
1933   History, ethnology and anthropology of the Aleut. Carnegie Institute of Washington Publication No. 432.

Lantis, Margaret
n.d.   Aleutian Islands Field Notes, 1933-34.
1938   The Alaskan whale cult and its affinities. American Anthropologist 40:438-64.
1940   Note on *The Alaskan Whale Cult and Its Affinities*. American Anthropologist 42 (2):366-68.
1947   Alaskan Eskimo ceremonialism. American Ethnological Society Monograph 11.

Levin, M. G., and Potapov, L. P., eds.
1964   The Peoples of Siberia. Chicago.

Literary Collections
1790   Pt. 5, 147-64. St. Petersburg. Ms. translation by I.
            Petroff, Bancroft Library, University of California.

Litke, Frederic (See Lütke)

Lütke, Frederic
1835–1836   Voyage autour du Monde, . . . pendant les Annees 1826,
            1827, 1828 and 1829; . . . Paris.

Masterson, James R., and Brower, Helen
1948   Bering's successors, 1745–1780. Seattle, Wash.

Nelson, Edward W.
1899   The Eskimo about Bering Strait. Bureau of American
            Ethnology, 18th Annual Report. Washington.

Neue Nachrichten (See J.L.S. and Coxe)

Parmenter, Ross
1966   Explorer, Linguist and Ethnologist. Southwest Museum,
            Los Angeles.

Petrof, Ivan
1900   Population and Resources of Alaska, 1880. Reprinted *in*
            Compilation of Narratives of Explorations in Alaska.
            Washington.

Pierce, Richard A.
1968   New light on Ivan Petroff, historian of Alaska. Pacific
            Northwest Quarterly 59(1):1-10.

Pinart, A.
n.d.   Field Notes from the Kodiak Island Region, 1871–72.
            Ms. in Bancroft Library, University of California.
1873   Eskimaux et Koloches, idees religieuses et traditions des
            Kaniagmioutes. Revue d'Anthropologie 2:673-80.
1875   Le Caverne d'Aknañh, Ile d'Ounga. Paris.

Porter, R. P.
1893   Report on Population and Resources of Alaska. 11th
            Census, 1890, Vol. 8.

Rosse, Irving C.
1883   Medical and anthropological notes on Alaska. *In* Cruise
            of the Revenue-Steamer *Corwin* in Alaska and the N.W.
            Arctic Ocean in 1881, 9-43, Washington.

Sarytchev, G.
1806-1807   Account of a Voyage of Discovery to the North-East of

Siberia, the Frozen Ocean, and the North-East Sea. London.

Sauer, M.
1802   An Account of a Geographical and Astronomical Expe-
           dition to the Northern Parts of Russia, . . . and of the
           Islands in the Eastern Ocean, Stretching to the American
           Coast. . . . etc. London.

Shelekhov, G.
1783–1790 Voyages of G. Shelekhoff. From the Year 1783 to 1790,
           . . . etc. St. Petersburg, 1812. Ms. translation by I.
           Petroff, Bancroft Library, University of California.

Sherwood, Morgan B.
1965   Exploration of Alaska 1865–1900. New Haven, Conn.

Staehlin von Storcksburg, Jacob
1774   An Account of the New Northern Archipelago, Lately
           Discovered by the Russians in the Seas of Kamtschatka
           and Anadir. (Translated from German by C. Hey-
           dinger.) London.

Tremaine, Marie, ed.
1953–1967 Arctic Bibliography, Vols. 1-13. Vols. 1-12, Washing-
           ton; Vol. 13, Montreal.

Veniaminov, I.
1840   Notes on the Unalaska District. (In Russian.)   St.
           Petersburg.

von Baer, K. E.
1839   Statistiche und ethnographische Nachrichten über die
           Russischen Besitzungen an der Norwestküste von
           Amerika. Gesammelt von dem ehemaligen Oberverwalter
           dieser Besitzungen, contre-admiral v. Wrangell. Beiträge
           zur Kenntniss des Russischen Reiches. Bd. 1, St. Peters-
           burg Academy of Sciences.

von Chamisso, Adalbert
1819   Bemerkungen und Ansichten von dem Naturforscher der
(1825)   Expedition, Adalbert von Chamisso. Berlin. Published
           as Volume 3 of: Otto von Kotzebue. Entdeckungsreise
           in die Sudsee und nach der Berings-Strasse zur
           Erforschung einer nordöstlichen Durchfahrt. Kaulfuss &
           Drammer, Wien, 1825.

von Kotzebue, Otto
1821   A Voyage of Discovery into the South Sea and Beering's
           Straits. . . . etc. 3 Vols. London.

von Langsdorff, G. H.
1814   Voyages and Travels in Various Parts of the World, during the Years 1803, 1804, 1805, 1806, and 1807, Pt. 2. London.

von Wrangell, F. (See von Baer)

Weyer, E. M., Jr.
1929   An Aleutian burial. American Museum of Natural History, Anthropological Papers 31 (3).
1930   Archaeological material from the village site at Hot Springs, Port Möller, Alaska. American Museum of Natural History, Anthropological Papers 31:239-79.
1932   The Eskimos. Their Environment and Folkways. New Haven, Conn.

Woldt, A.
1884   Capitain Jacobsen's Reise an der Nordwestküste Amerikas 1881–1883. Leipzig.

INDEX

Abercrombie, W. R., 89
Ackerman, Lillian, 19
Ackerman, Robert E., 5-6, 50, 135-36, 174 n
Afognak Island, 81
Agadak Island, 174
Agatoo Island. *See* Agattu Island
Agattu Island, 277-78, 289
Aglagax 1 and 2 (sites), 176
Aglegmiut. *See* Aglemute Eskimo
Aglegmute Eskimo, 78, 80, 268-70
Ainu, 169
Akouna Island. *See* Akun Island
Akoutan Island. *See* Akutan Island
Akulivikchuk (excavation), 60-61
Akun Island, 174 n, 178, 283
Akutan Island, 174 n, 178, 182, 264-65, 283
Alaska Church Collection, 207, 250, 279
Alaska Commercial Company, 56, 63, 88, 93
Alaska History Research Project. *See* "Documents Relative to the History of Alaska"
Alaskan Eskimo, 65, 159, 240
Alaska Peninsula, 53, 80, 150, 157, 164, 171, 174, 178, 270-71, 275
Alaska Russian Church Archives, 53-54, 58, 76, 83
Aleksandrovski Redoubt (excavation), 53, 55, 58, 60, 62
Aleut-Kamchatka Expedition, 1909-1910, 166
Alexander I, 152-53
Algemalinag, Chief, 281
Allegretti, Peter, 280
Allen, H. T., 106
Alsek River, 106
Amaganak, Chief, 182
Amaknak Island, 176, 276
Amaknax (excavation), 176
Amchitkha Island, 174 n
American Geographical Society, 165

American Society for Ethnohistory, 3
Aminak, Arsenti, 269
Amlakh Island. *See* Amlia Island
Amlia Island, 174, 254, 271
Amlyn Island. *See* Amlia Island
Amukhta Island, 271
Anderson, H. Dewey, 167
Andreev, Aleksandr, 147, 154-55
Andreianof Islands, 281 n, 286
Andreianovsky Islands. *See* Andreianof Islands
Andreyev, A. I., 80, 82
Angoon, village, 104 n
Anshiges, 281
Arctic Health Research Center, 77
Ascher, R., 11, 35
Athabascan (term), 30, 164
Athabascans, 72, 115-16, 126
Atka, village, 212, 279
Atka District, 177-78, 250, 257, 261, 271, 279
Atka Island, 165, 167, 174 n, 176, 217, 224, 238 n, 239, 254, 261, 286-87
Atkans, 206, 226, 228, 233, 243, 250, 257, 264, 266-67
Atkha Island. *See* Atka Island
Atna Indians, 104 n, 105-6, 115 n, 116
Attoo Island. *See* Attu Island
Attu, village, 230
Attu Island, 174, 176, 217, 237 n, 238 n, 271, 278, 289
Atxalax (site), 176
Avacha Bay, 148
Avatanak Island, 174 n, 178
Ayougnin, Toukoutan, 281 n
Azutan Island. *See* Akutan Island

Baerreis, D. A., 11
Baird, S. F., 164
Bakof, Afanassi, 280
Bakulin, 280